T0392483

# MULTIVOCAL ARCHAEOLOGIES OF THE PACIFIC WAR, 1941–45

This volume draws together the ground-breaking work of researchers and archaeological practitioners, working in multiple countries, to explore and understand the material and cultural impacts of the Pacific War.

The combat taking place in the Pacific region during the years 1941–45 was characterized by a brutality and violence unmatched in any other theatre of the Second World War. Described by indigenous Micronesians as a 'typhoon,' the war was an unstoppable force that rolled across the islanders' homes, leaving only a trail of destruction in its wake, with physical, psychological, and cultural impacts that continue to resonate today. This difficult period is examined in a variety of ways through chapters that include targeted studies of archaeological sites, wider surveys of battlefield landscapes, and the ways in which we commemorate the experiences and legacies of both combatants and civilian populations. The translation of important research by Okinawan, Japanese, and Russian archaeologists brings into focus regions that have previously been neglected in Anglophone literature, and enriches this comprehensive exploration of the archaeology of the Pacific War.

This book will be of interest to archaeological practitioners, students, and members of the general public working in conflict studies or with an interest in the material culture, history, and legacies of the Pacific War.

**Ben Raffield** is an Associate Professor of Archaeology at the University of Uppsala, Sweden.

**Yu Hirasawa** is an Associate Professor in the Faculty of Human Sciences at University of East Asia, Japan.

**Neil Price** is Distinguished Professor of Archaeology at the University of Uppsala, Sweden.

# MULTIVOCAL ARCHAEOLOGIES OF THE PACIFIC WAR, 1941–45

## Collaboration, Reconciliation, and Renewal

*Edited by*
*Ben Raffield, Yu Hirasawa, and*
*Neil Price*

 Routledge
Taylor & Francis Group

LONDON AND NEW YORK

Cover image: A demined pathway cleared and marked through the jungle on Peleliu island, Republic of Palau. Photo by Neil Price

First published 2024
by Routledge
4 Park Square, Milton Park, Abingdon, Oxon OX14 4RN

and by Routledge
605 Third Avenue, New York, NY 10158

*Routledge is an imprint of the Taylor & Francis Group, an informa business*

*British Library Cataloguing-in-Publication Data*
A catalogue record for this book is available from the British Library

ISBN: 978-0-367-22041-9 (hbk)
ISBN: 978-0-367-22043-3 (pbk)
ISBN: 978-0-429-27046-8 (ebk)

DOI: 10.4324/9780429270468

Typeset in Bembo
by codeMantra

# CONTENTS

# FIGURES

# CONTRIBUTORS

**Brad Duncan** is Senior Maritime Archaeologist for Heritage New South Wales (Department of Planning and Environment) and adjunct senior lecturer at the University of New England (Armidale, Australia). Brad's PhD thesis and continuing research interests are in maritime cultural landscapes, and he has been lead investigator in a range of World War II-related maritime archaeological investigations. He is the co-author with Martin Gibbs of *Please God Send Me a Wreck: Responses to Shipwreck in a 19th Century Australian Community* (Springer).

**Martin Gibbs** is Professor of Australian Archaeology at the University of New England (Armidale, Australia). His main fields of research are in Australasian-Pacific historical and maritime archaeology, and he has been a long-time collaborator with the Solomon Islands National Museum, including the *Beyond the New World* project which investigated the failed 16th-century Spanish colonies of the Solomon Islands.

**Yu Hirasawa** is an Associate Professor in the Faculty of Human Sciences at University of East Asia. His primary research focus is human migration history in Beringia. He has been working in Alaska and Hokkaido to explore technological relationships through multi-regional comparisons of microblade production technology. His other main research interest is Indigenous archaeology. To practice and establish better archaeological methods, he has worked with Ainu people on Rebun Island, Japan, since 2011. From 2019, he joined the "Food Life History" project team, which studies the environmental change impacts on food storage practices in Siberia, Alaska, and Japan. His role in the project is studying the history of ice cellars and other underground freezing and cold storage practices from an archaeological perspective. He has published both English and Japanese articles in peer-reviewed journals.

**Akira Hokumori** graduated with a BA at the Department of Geological and Historical Anthropology, University of Ryukyus. He has worked for the Haebaru Cultural Museum since 2016. He has been engaged in the research, preservation, and utilization of various archaeological sites in the town, including battlefield sites designated by the town, as well as the efforts to preserve and open the *Okinawa Army Hospital Haebaru Cave* to the public.

**Bill Jeffery** is an Associate Professor, Anthropology, University of Guam and holds a PhD from James Cook University, Townsville, Australia. His primary interest is maritime archaeology, which he commenced in Australia in 1981, before going on to work with the Federated States of Micronesia National Historic Preservation Office, Sri Lanka, Hong Kong, and in East Africa. His interests are in researching traditional indigenous material culture and living heritage particularly in Oceania, revealing multi-vocality perspectives of underwater cultural heritage, developing community maritime archaeology, and highlighting how maritime cultural landscapes and seascapes can reflect maritime cultural identities.

**Matthew Kelly** has been a historical archaeologist working as a consultant in Australia for nearly 40 years. He has worked on a variety of colonial sites across the country. From 2010, he has also been involved with conflict sites in Papua New Guinea (PNG). These sites include Jacquinot Bay, East New Britain, Blamey's Garden (Namanatabu), and most notably the battlefield of Etoa (Eora Creek) on PNG's mainland. The work at Etoa is in conjunction with the PNG National Museum and Art Gallery and the Japan Association for Recovery and Repatriation of War Casualties.

**Lawrence Kiko** is Deputy Director of the Solomon Islands National Museum and has a BA in Archaeology from the University of Papua New Guinea. Lawrence has been at the forefront of World War II archaeology in the region, working with Japanese, American and Australian military recovery and archaeological research teams on a range of projects over the last 30 years.

**Noriko Koga** was born in Fukuoka, Japan in 1971. She finished her MA in Area Studies at Okinawa International University. She contributed to academic literature relating to the Himeyuri student corps, such as *Okinawa Army Hospital Haebaru Cave* (2010, Koubunken) and *Encyclopedia of the Battle of Okinawa: Non-experienced Generation Tells Their Stories* (2019, Yoshikawa Kobunkan). She also wrote articles for the History of Haebaru Town and the History of Okinawa Prefecture.

**Sergey Ilyich Kuznetsov** is Doctor of Historical Sciences, Professor, and Head of the Department of World History and International Relations, Irkutsk State University. He also holds a position as Professor at the Global Station for

Indigenous Studies and Cultural Diversity at Hokkaido University in Japan. He is the author of more than 150 articles, reports, and a monograph on the problems of internment of Japanese prisoners of war in the USSR (1945–56), published in Russia, Japan, Mongolia, UK, Czech Republic, Poland, the Republic of Korea, and France.

**Gavin Lindsay** is a specialist in community-based research approaches and the archaeology of recent conflict with over fifteen years of professional, academic, and voluntary expertise in the archaeology, museums, and cultural heritage sector. He studied undergraduate archaeology at the University of Durham before moving to Orkney where he graduated with a Master's in Archaeological Practice from the University of the Highlands and Islands. After five years of archaeology and museums employment in Orkney, he moved to Aberdeen where he completed his PhD in Archaeology at the University of Aberdeen in 2017. As a self-employed consultant, he delivers a broad range of small-scale archaeological interpretation, education, and research projects to an international clientele from his base in central Scotland. In recent years, this has included provision of on-screen and research expertise for National Geographic documentaries on various World War II conflict zones including Peleliu.

**Stephen Manebosa** is Senior Field Officer (World War II) for the Solomon Islands National Museum and has a BA in Archaeology from the University of Papua New Guinea. He is responsible for listing and assessment of World War II sites and has also been assisting with research across the Solomons.

**Rachel Mason** is a Cultural Anthropologist who has worked for many years in Alaska, most extensively in the Aleutian Islands and the Kodiak area. She currently serves as the Senior Cultural Anthropologist for the National Park Service, Alaska Region, and also as the Program Manager for the Aleutian World War II National Historic Area.

**Jennifer McKinnon** has a background in historical and maritime archaeology and cultural heritage management. She has worked in the US, Australia, the Pacific, and Europe on sites ranging from the colonial period to World War II. Jennifer has published a number of book chapters and journal articles and co-edited (with Dr. Toni L. Carrell) a book with Springer Press entitled, *Underwater Archaeology of a Pacific Battlefield: The WWII Battle of Saipan*. McKinnon is a Research Associate of Ships of Exploration and Discovery Research, Inc., a nonprofit organization with which she has partnered to conduct World War II-related research in the Pacific. Prior to teaching at ECU, she was a Senior Lecturer in Flinders University's Program in Maritime Archaeology in South Australia and a Senior Underwater Archaeologist with Florida's Bureau of Archaeological Research, Department of State.

**Julie Mushynsky** is an SSHRC Postdoctoral Research Fellow in the Department of Anthropology at the University of Regina and a Marie Skłodowska-Curie Fellow in the Humanities Department at Pompeu Fabra University. Her research interests include conflict archaeology, the archaeology of colonialism, maritime archaeology, museum studies, and heritage studies. Her dissertation on karst defences won the Flinders University Vice Chancellor's Award for Doctoral Thesis Excellence in 2018.

**Katsuya Nakahodo** is a curator at the Okinawa Prefectural Peace Memorial Museum. He earned his undergraduate degree from the Department of Society and Regional Culture at Okinawa International University. His study focuses on the battery and trench remains at battlefield sites in Okinawa prefecture. He is in charge of revising the inventory of the museum's collection of approximately 30,000 items and checking their state of preservation. He is also examining ways to preserve fragments of rusted shells that were donated to the museum.

**Neil Price** is Distinguished Professor of Archaeology at the University of Uppsala, Sweden. He is primarily a specialist in the Viking Age and the pre-Christian religions of the North, with research interests focusing on explorations of identity, world view, and interaction across the Viking diaspora. In addition to the early medieval period, Neil also works on the historical archaeology of the Asia-Pacific, with a particular emphasis on World War II. Together with Rick Knecht, he has been co-director of the Peleliu survey since its inception in 2010. His publications have appeared in twenty languages, and he is a frequent consultant and contributor to television and film. Neil's most recent books are *The Viking Way: Magic and Mind in Late Iron Age Scandinavia* (2019) and *Children of Ash and Elm: a History of the Vikings* (2020).

**Ben Raffield** is an Associate Professor in the Department of Archaeology and Ancient History at Uppsala University. He obtained his PhD from the University of Aberdeen in 2014, and since then he has held positions at Simon Fraser University, the University of Pittsburgh, and Uppsala University. Raffield specializes primarily in the archaeology of the Viking Age, with his research revolving around the themes of conflict and violence; captivity, slavery, and social inequality; and cross-cultural interaction within transnational settings. Raffield's research interests in conflict archaeology have also led him to engage more broadly with studies of conflict and its impacts on human societies. He has been a member of the joint Aberdeen-Uppsala field team working on Peleliu, the Republic of Palau, since 2014. He has published his work in a range of peer-reviewed journals, edited volumes, and books.

**Tetsuya Seto** acquired his PhD at the Faculty of Letters at the University of the Ryukyus. His primary research fields are the material culture of porcelains and battlefield archaeology. He has worked for Okinawa Prefecture Archaeological Center since 2021.

# ACKNOWLEDGEMENTS

This volume is in part the product of two academic meetings – a session on the wartime heritage of the Pacific, held at the 8th World Archaeological Congress in Kyoto, in 2016, and a workshop on *Island Archaeologies of the Pacific War* held the following year in Naha, Okinawa. However, it is even more an outcome of multi-layered, long-term collaborations, not only between the editors and the authors, but also between the authors and the communities within which their research has been situated. When studying the recent past, and, in particular, the legacies of a conflict that remains in living memory, it is essential that archaeologists engage with and work with the explicit permission of the communities who bore witness to those events, and for whom the impacts of the Pacific War continue to resonate as part of their daily lives today. As such, the editors would like to acknowledge the hospitality and support that they and the contributors have received, as well as the numerous working partnerships with local groups, government institutions, non-profit organizations, and individual collaborators that underpinned the creation of this volume. Suffice to say, this work would not have been possible otherwise.

The editors would also like to thank several individuals whose hard work and guidance made the production of this volume possible. The first is Dr. Rick Knecht, who co-directed the work of the Aberdeen-Uppsala research team on Peleliu, and who has always provided enthusiastic guidance and contributions to subsequent conference sessions and publication efforts. The second is Professor Hirofumi Kato, who – together with our Okinawan colleagues – played a key role in arranging and organizing the 2017 workshop in Naha; Kato-san has also been a consistently strong supporter of the wider project. Lastly, Ben and Neil wish to thank Yu, whose editorial endeavours have made our Japanese and Okinawan collaborations possible.

# 1

# INTRODUCTION

## A War of the Worlds

*Ben Raffield, Yu Hirasawa and Neil Price*

### When Worlds Collide

The 1941–45 Pacific War was a conflict in which multiple disparate worlds collided. Unfolding across an arena comprising thousands of miles of ocean and dozens of atolls and island nations, the war created a crucible of violence within which combatants from all nations would encounter both enemies, allies, and bystanders whose culture and ideology contrasted greatly to their own. The resulting dehumanization of opposing forces played a major role in escalating the intensity and ferocity of combat to levels exceeding those encountered in any other theatre of the Second World War. The inhabitants of the Pacific, whose island homes held the key to external actors' achievement of naval and air superiority in the region, found themselves embroiled in the conflict. Described by present-day Micronesians as a 'typhoon,' the war was indiscriminate in its capacity to wreak havoc on communities who themselves possessed little stake in the outcome of any individual battle (see Poyer et al. 2001). Many thousands of people were killed and displaced, their natal land- and seascapes forever transformed by fortification construction programmes, intensive shelling, and seizure by occupying military forces.

Today, the island battlefields of the Pacific represent an arena of interaction that is occupied by numerous parties. At the centre of this discourse are the Pacific Islanders themselves – the inhabitants of ancient cultural landscapes that, in the course of just a few decades, were brutally reshaped by militarization, conflict, and post-war development. However, until recently, both archaeological and popular perspectives of the Pacific War have been dominated almost wholly by Western (and in particular American) narratives. The most famous first-hand accounts of the war were penned in the decades following the conflict by former Marines – authors such as Eugene Sledge and Robert Leckie, whose eloquent

DOI: 10.4324/9780429270468-1

memoirs *With the Old Breed* and *Helmet for my Pillow* were reproduced in graphic detail as part of HBO's high-profile television mini-series, *The Pacific* (2010). These works are complemented by a raft of other publications, including both first-hand accounts and later synthetic histories based on interviews and archival research, which add further details to the American experience of frontline combat.

It goes without saying, however, that the perspectives gleaned from these accounts offer a largely one-sided view of the conflict. The experience of war as told by Marines such as Sledge and Leckie is that of well-educated white men – a fact of which the authors themselves are acutely aware in their writings. When we are drawn into their world, it becomes easy to forget that the Marine Corps, and indeed the US military itself, was a microcosm of 20th-century American society (Price et al. 2013: 200). The perspectives of Native American, Hispanic American, and African American troops, however, still have not been afforded the attention they deserve (Price et al. 2013: 200–05; though see McLaurin 2009). The focus on gruelling narratives of frontline combat, furthermore, also makes it easy to forget the roles of women, over 350,000 of whom served in the US military alone (Dawson 2019). Although women did not take combat roles, many worked close to or on the frontlines as support and medical staff, something which brought with it exposure to danger and visions of the horrific injuries suffered by combat troops. In other contexts, and, in particular, during the early months of the Pacific War, women serving in regions such as the Philippines and Guam were captured and held as Prisoners of War (POWs) alongside their male counterparts. While their experiences are now coming to light through historical research (see, e.g. Norman 1999; Monahan & Neidel-Greenlee 2003), they have yet to receive sufficient attention from archaeologists. Further disparate experiences of the war, such as those of gay men and women and those of non-binary gender, are equally demanding of consideration (for a historical perspective, see, e.g. Bérubé 1990).

Similar issues abound when we turn to non-Western perspectives on the Pacific War. The soldiers, sailors, and airmen of the Imperial Japanese military, for example, remain largely anonymous to audiences beyond their homeland. They are of course present in both official Western histories and first-hand accounts of the war, but almost always in a dehumanized form – an embodiment of the fascist regimes that the Allies strove to overcome. Today, they are remembered in many Western minds for their brutal treatment of both civilians and captured military personnel. The stereotype of the fanatical Japanese soldier, however, deserves some kind of deconstruction, as now seen both in academic studies (e.g. Eaves-Young 2019) and popular publications (see Price, this volume) that have sought to disentangle individual stories of conflict from wider historical narratives. In addition, we must remember that Imperial forces were, like those of the Allied powers, diverse in their composition. On many battlefields across the Pacific, large numbers of Korean, Taiwanese, and Okinawan labourers from Japan's overseas dominions were conscripted to serve in the armed forces, suffering innumerable casualties in combat. The failure to account for the experiences of these communities not only colours our understanding of the conflict as perceived by non-Japanese troops, but it also has obvious cultural and political implications for the recovery and repatriation of war dead.

A final group who have been almost wholly neglected in discussions of the Pacific War are civilians (for notable exceptions, see Murray 2005, 2006, 2016), many hundreds of thousands of whom were killed or displaced from their homes (Peattie 1988). On several island battlefields such as Saipan and Okinawa, civilians were not only exposed to shelling, but also to acts of brutality that were committed by combatants on all sides. Others committed suicide rather than be subjected to the abuse and violence that they were told they would receive at the hands of advancing American forces (Mushynsky, Koga, this volume). The conflict itself generated huge psychological and cultural shocks that continue to resonate among communities today, as seen, for example, on Okinawa where large parts of the island continue to be occupied by the American military (see Seto, this volume). The presentation of civilian populations purely as the victims of war, however, overlooks the resilience that many showed in adapting to life within a combat zone, as well as the crucial roles in which many members of indigenous communities served – both voluntarily and by coercion, but nevertheless at great personal risk – as non-combatant personnel and members of irregular forces (see, e.g. Feuer 1992; Kwai 2017: 15–50; Koga, Kelly, Gibbs et al., this volume). Just as there is a need to develop a more holistic understanding of the Pacific War as experienced by Allied and Japanese troops, we must also endeavour to integrate this with the perspectives of local populations (Murray 2016: 3–4).

The move towards the study of conflict as a multi-cultural phenomenon has the potential to influence contemporary discourse on heritage, commemoration, and remembrance. Today, much of this discussion takes place very much in the public sphere (see, e.g. Gibbs et al., Jeffrey, Mason, Price, this volume). While for non-locals the battlefields and monuments to the Pacific War are considered as sites of remembrance and places of historic interest, these views often do not align with those of landowners and communities who now find themselves the custodians of a heritage to which they, in some cases, possess little to no cultural or ideological connection (White 2015). The obvious need to honour and balance the interests of landowners and communities with government-mandated heritage legislation means that archaeologists have generally worked hard, at the very least, to operate within the boundaries set by local populations, and ideally in direct cooperation with them. These collaborations are now allowing researchers and practitioners to situate the events of the Pacific War within an extended historical trajectory, accounting not only for the long-term cultural history of island nations, but also post-war developments taking place over the last eight decades. Increased dialogue of this kind has the potential to facilitate the emergence of a more inclusive understanding of the conflict, and with that to pave the way for the development of sustainable heritage practices in future decades.

The contributions in this volume outline the ways in which recent and ongoing work by archaeologists and heritage practitioners has sought address elements of these issues. The work presented here intersects with and draws on previous scholarship within the field (among several important works published over the last twenty years, see, for example, Poyer et al. 2001; Falgout et al. 2008; Carr & Reeves 2015; McKinnon & Carrell 2015; Murray 2016). There is also a sense in which the volume offers a regionally specific take on developments in the larger discipline of conflict archaeology. The last forty years have seen a dramatic expansion of the field from a relatively small, specialist interest group to a distinctive arena of historical research. From initial studies of early modern conflicts (perhaps most obviously epitomized by the hugely successful and influential work on the battlefield of the Little Bighorn in Montana), with emphases on ballistic analysis and tactical revisionism, the discipline has also now broadened to embrace the social study of conflict in all its disparate forms. It extends not only to the Modern period, but also far back into prehistory, and the reach of conflict archaeology has also become truly global – progress represented not least in the dedicated *Journal of Conflict Archaeology*, founded in 2005.

## An Outline of the Current Volume

The origins of this book lie in the wider ramifications of archaeological field surveys that began in 2010 on the island of Peleliu in the Republic of Palau, western Micronesia (see Lindsay, Price, this volume, with references). The project was directed by archaeologists from the universities of Aberdeen and Uppsala, with an international team of participants and funding from the US National Park Service and non-profit commemorative organizations. Crucially, however, the study was conducted at the behest and in the employ of the Palauan national heritage services, whose staff acted as co-directors and participated throughout in equal partnership with the visiting field crew. The fieldwork, which continued over several seasons, marked a new stage in the collaborative, multi-vocal, and multi-cultural exploration of the war through its material remains and less tangible legacies. It quickly became apparent that this was part of a larger movement unfolding across the Asia-Pacific region, a transformation in practice that sees non-local academics and field archaeologists working alongside and on behalf of Islanders, their governments, and communities. In effect, these activities promote a new and inclusive perspective on the conflict itself, reflecting its true diversity and range of cultural contexts – hence, the shift embodied in our title, from a World War to a War of the Worlds.

The specific contents of the volume reflect this movement and those engaged in it, building in part on papers presented at two different events. The first was a session coordinated by the directors of the Peleliu project and held in 2016 at the 8th World Archaeological Congress in Kyoto, Japan, where a number of the volume contributors presented their current research on aspects of the Pacific

War. The second was a workshop held the following year at the University of the Ryukyus on Okinawa, organized by Prof. Hirofumi Kato of the University of Hokkaido, in collaboration with Prof. Hajime Ishida, and again involving the Peleliu team. Additional contributions were sought from researchers and practitioners working across the Pacific region.

The contributions in this volume are arranged chronologically. Part 1 of the book covers the years 1942–43, a period when the Allied powers fought to contain the rapidly expanding Japanese Empire. We begin in the Aleutian Islands, where **Rachel Mason** highlights the ongoing efforts of local communities, working in partnership with heritage practitioners, to acknowledge and honour the wartime experiences not only of American and Japanese combatants, but also those of indigenous Unangax̂ communities. Mason provides not only a detailed and candid overview of the challenges that communities today continue to face in reconciling these perspectives, but also the necessity of communicating knowledge that can facilitate the education of future generations.

Moving to the southwestern fringe of the Pacific, the next two chapters deal with indigenous experiences of and perspectives on conflict in Papua New Guinea and the Solomon Islands. As part of his work in PNG, **Matthew Kelly** has spent years conducting research on the famous Kokoda Track and the decisive battle that took place along its extent in 1942. Collective memories of the Kokoda campaign, which occupies a central place in the identity of both the Australian armed forces and the country, often marginalize the fundamental roles played by, and experiences of, local populations. In developing his work at Eora Creek as part of the Etoa Battlefield Project, Kelly explores the resilience of communities who, caught between two colonial powers, were forced to adapt to the challenges of living in a conflict zone.

In the next contribution, **Martin Gibbs, Brad Duncan, Lawrence Kiko,** and **Stephen Manebosa** examine the materiality of conflict and issues associated with conservation and the commemoration of the Pacific War in the Solomon Islands. The authors offer a detailed view into the ongoing dialogue between archaeologists and local communities that, over the last few decades, has revealed conflicting viewpoints on the need to balance issues concerning preservation and conservation with those relating to daily life and subsistence.

Part 2 of the volume deals with the crucial year of 1944, when the reconsolidated forces of the Allied powers began – for the first time – to make progress towards the Japanese home islands. In the Central Pacific, the US forces embarked on an island-hopping campaign that would involve the capture of strategically located atolls and islands that could be used as airbases, supply centres, and staging posts for future operations. In the opening discussion of this part of the volume, **Bill Jeffrey** provides a detailed overview of the management of cultural heritage in Chuuk Lagoon, with a focus on maritime archaeology. His contribution highlights how long-term histories of colonization, conflict, and occupation have shaped the lives of present-day Chuukese and other Pacific Islander populations.

These themes are further elaborated on in the discussion by **Jennifer McKinnon**, who offers a thoughtful reflection on community archaeology in Micronesia, with a particular focus on the underwater archaeology of Saipan. Drawing on years of work with local populations and veterans of contemporary wars in collaboration with the non-profit organization, Task Force Dagger Foundation, McKinnon succinctly outlines the various challenges and possibilities associated with building an inclusive, community-oriented framework for archaeological research and cultural resource management.

In the next contribution, we remain on Saipan, where **Julie Mushynsky** discusses the theoretical, methodological, and ethical issues associated with conducting research on the Second World War. In tackling this complex arena of contemporary archaeological discourse, Mushynsky provides an overview of her own research focusing on Imperial Japanese karst defences – the countless caves and tunnels occupied by both military forces and civilians during the fierce battle for the island.

The final contribution in this part of the volume moves to the Republic of Palau, where **Gavin Lindsay** explores disparate experiences of conflict on the island of Peleliu. Drawing on two seasons of fieldwork conducted in 2010 and 2014, Lindsay demonstrates how the archaeological record of this well-preserved battlefield landscape has the potential to offer uniquely personal insights into the experiences of individual combatants – including those of Imperial Japanese forces whose stories remain for the greatest-part untold.

In Part 3 of the volume, we cover the events of 1945, and, in particular, the Battle of Okinawa fought from April to June of that year. The contributions here deal with the recording and preservation of archaeological materials, as well as complex issues surrounding memory, commemoration, and the long-term legacies of conflict. The Ryukyu Islands are the only region of modern Japan in which remains from the war are formerly designated as protected ancient monuments, an attitude that reflects crucial differences between the Okinawan and mainland Japanese experiences of the conflict.

The first chapter in this section is authored by **Tetsuya Seto**, who provides a detailed overview of the current condition of the archaeological record relating to the battle. The author reveals the challenges associated with the documentation and preservation of archaeological materials and sites that, until recently, were not characterized as heritage assets. Seto also highlights, however, the potential for archaeological research to shed new light on the ways in which the present landscape of Okinawa has been shaped by the battle and subsequent developments taking place in the post-war years.

The next chapter builds on and complements this work. In his own contribution, **Akira Hokumori** offers an insightful account of archaeological research and preservation work in Haebaru Town, central Okinawa. Focusing on the '20th shelter' site – an underground field hospital constructed in anticipation of and used during the Battle of Okinawa – Hokumori explores in detail the various challenges that have been encountered as part of work to preserve and open the site as an historic visitor attraction. In communicating the lessons learned from this process, the author offers a pragmatic reflection on the use of battlefield sites for public education.

In the final contribution to Part 3, **Katsuya Nakahodo** summarizes recent research on battery positions on Okinawa. Through careful archaeological and archival research, Nakahodo traces the pre-war and wartime development of the Okinawan defensive landscape. This work, like that of Nakahodo's colleagues, highlights the long-term impacts of the Imperial Japanese military presence in the Ryukyu Islands. The focus of this particular work on the evolution of battery positions also offers a valuable insight into the ways in which the militarized landscape of Okinawa was shaped by shifting strategic and tactical concerns in the years preceding 1945.

The final part of this book deals with memory, commemoration, and the cultural legacies of the Pacific War from 1945 to the present. Entitled 'Aftermath,' Part 4 comprises three contributions that explore the long-term impacts of the Pacific War in different regions. In the first contribution, **Sergey Kuznetsov** addresses issues associated with the identification, recovery, and repatriation of Japanese POWs from the territories of the former Soviet Union. Of the c. 540,000 Imperial Japanese military personnel held in Soviet territory following the end of the war, some 60,000 died and were buried there. The work being undertaken to identify their grave sites emphasizes the ways in which archaeological research intersects with public discourse, as well as the roles that heritage practitioners play in addressing prominent social, cultural, and political issues.

Next we return to Okinawa, where **Noriko Koga** discusses ongoing work at the Himeyuri Peace Museum; a facility dedicated to public engagement and education on conflict. The museum itself focuses on the experiences of 240 schoolgirls and their teachers – now known as the Himeyuri Student Corps – who were pressed into front-line service by the Japanese military, in order to serve as medical staff during the Battle of Okinawa. In providing an overview of the museum's mission and a detailed 'walkthrough' of the current exhibits, Koga elaborates on the ongoing work of museum staff and surviving members of the Himeyuri Student Corps to communicate vital messages of peace and dialogue between nations.

In the final contribution to the volume, **Neil Price** reflects on and attempts to disentangle disparate perspectives of the Pacific War on the island of Peleliu. In examining contemporary memories of the conflict, with a focus on local communities and the descendants of wartime combatants in Japan, Price situates recent discourse on the battle within the context of contemporary geopolitics and commemorative activity, highlighting the multi-vocality of this process.

## Looking to the Future: Dialogue, Collaboration, and Reconciliation

The chapters in this book combine to stress a need for further dialogue and collaboration both within and across international boundaries. In many parts of the

Pacific, memories of the war remain very much ingrained in the landscapes, culture, and mindset of present-day populations. Elsewhere, these memories have been concealed by post-war reconstruction efforts, and in some cases they are now obscured by tacit efforts to forget or even reshape narratives of the past. While it is important to recognize disparate perspectives on the Pacific War, the need to manage and responsibly negotiate the legacies of conflict will only become more vital once the wartime generation has left us. The contributions to this volume demonstrate that researchers and heritage practitioners can and do play a genuine role not only in carrying their stories forward, but also in facilitating open and honest discussion between different groups. By exploring the human experience of conflict, and in acknowledging the ongoing influence of the 'present-past,' it is our hope that future work will continue to generate further opportunities for collaboration, reflection, and – we hope and believe – to make a modest contribution to processes of reconciliation.

## A Note on Language

Before continuing, we wish to clarify a few points regarding language revision. In the contributions from authors with English as a second language, the editors made a conscious decision *not* to heavily modify texts. While changes were made to ensure that all authors were able to effectively communicate their arguments, we generally avoided making cosmetic revisions in order to preserve the authors' individual writing style. The Okinawan texts were translated by Yu Hirasawa and edited in collaboration with Raffield and Price, in consultation with the authors.

## Bibliography

Bérubé, A. 1990. *Coming Out Under Fire: The History of Gay Men and Women in World War II.* Chapel Hill: University of North Carolina Press.

Carr, G. & Reeves, K., eds. 2015. *Heritage and Memory of War: Responses from Small Islands.* New York: Routledge.

Dawson, S.T. 2019. 'Women and the Second World War', *International Journal of Military History and Historiography*, 39, 171–80.

Eaves-Young, V. 2019. *Writing Japan's War in New Guinea. The Diary of Tamura Yoshikazu.* Amsterdam: Amsterdam University Press.

Falgout, S., Poyer, L. & Carucci, L.M. 2008. *Memories of War. Micronesians in the Pacific War.* Honolulu: University of Hawai'i Press.

Feuer, A.B., ed. 1992. *Coast Watching in World War II: Operations Against the Japanese on the Solomon Islands, 1941–43.* Westport, CT: Stackpole Books.

Kwai, A.A. 2017. *Solomon Islanders in World War II: An Indigenous Perspective.* Acton: Australian National University Press.

McKinnon, J.F. & Carrell, T.L., eds. 2015. *Underwater Archaeology of a Pacific Battlefield: The WWII Battle of Saipan.* Cham: Springer.

McLaurin, M.A. 2009. *The Marines of Montford Point: America's First Black Marines.* Chapel Hill: University of North Carolina Press.

Monahan, E.M. & Neidel-Greenlee, R. 2003. *All This Hell: U.S. Nurses Imprisoned by the Japanese.* Lexington, KY: University Press of Kentucky.

Murray, S.C. 2005. 'Catastrophe on Peleliu: Islander's Memories of the Pacific War', *International Institute for Asian Studies Newsletter*, 38, 17. [WWW] https://www.iias.nl/nl/38/IIAS_NL38_17.pdf (accessed 21/11/2021).

Murray, S.C. 2006. *War and Remembrance on Peleliu: Islander, Japanese, and American Memories of a Battle in the Pacific War.* PhD Dissertation, University of California at Santa Barbara.

Murray, S.C. 2016. *The Battle over Peleliu: Islander, Japanese, and American Memories of War.* Tuscaloosa: The University of Alabama Press.

Norman, E. 1999. *We Band of Angels: The Untold Story of the American Women Trapped on Bataan.* New York: Random House.

Peattie, M.R. 1988. *Nan'yō: The Rise and Fall of the Japanese in Micronesia, 1885–1945.* Honolulu: University of Hawai'i Press.

Poyer, L., Falgout, S. & Carucci, L.M. 2001. *The Typhoon of War: Micronesian Experiences of the Pacific War.* Honolulu: University of Hawaii Press.

Price, N., Knecht, R., Ballinger, S., Cypra, S., Emesiochel, C., Hesus, T., Kloulechad, E., Lindsay, G., McQuillen, D., & Ngirmang, S. O. 2013. 'After the typhoon: Multicultural archaeologies of World War II on Peleliu, Palau, Micronesia.' *Journal of Conflict Archaeology*, 8 (3), 193–248.

White, G. 2015. 'The Coastwatcher Mythos: The Politics and Poetics of Solomon Islands War Memory.' In: G. Carr and K. Reeves, eds. *Heritage and Memory of War: Responses from Small Islands.* New York: Routledge, 194–216.

# PART 1
# 1941–43

# 2

# BRINGING TOGETHER DIVERGENT EXPERIENCES OF WORLD WAR II IN THE ALEUTIANS

*Rachel Mason*

## The Aleutian Campaign of World War II

The Japanese invasion of the Aleutian Islands in 1942 was preceded by years of apprehension. The Unangax̂, indigenous residents of the Aleutians, noticed an almost ghostly presence of Japanese in the Aleutian Islands. Nick Golodoff wrote in his memoir *Attu Boy* that the Attuans found footprints and other evidence of humans in the years before the war. Sometimes '[a man] would see somebody and when he hollered to that person, it would disappear.' Local people called these apparitions 'tuginagus,' or boogiemen (Golodoff 2012: 31). In retrospect, Nick and others interpreted these as signs that the Japanese were surveying the Aleutian Islands for future attack.

This chapter looks at the difficulties involved in recognizing and commemorating disparate experiences of the World War II Aleutian Campaign. Although most of those who lived through that time are now gone, wartime nationalistic sentiments are still present, as well as unresolved trauma and anger from the injustices. In the 21st century, the National Park Service (NPS) and US Fish and Wildlife Service (USFWS) have commemorated two major events of the Aleutian Campaign: the bombing of Dutch Harbor in 1942 and the Battle of Attu in 1943. For each, the assembled participants included American veterans of the campaign, descendants of Japanese military, and Unangax̂ survivors of evacuation or imprisonment in Japan.

## The Challenge of Interpreting the Aleutian Campaign of World War II

War memorials and battlefields frequently evoke divergent memories and different associations for different audiences. In recent years, US Civil War battlefields

DOI: 10.4324/9780429270468-3

and monuments have provided ample illustration of complex emotions this history evokes (Blight 2001). While some visitors and interpretations remember the bravery and sacrifice of Confederate soldiers, others recall that they were fighting to defend slavery. To take an example from World War II, the 1941 attack on Pearl Harbor is still remembered by many Americans as a symbol of Japanese aggression. Today, interpretative staff lead Japanese language tours for the site's many Japanese visitors and answer questions about the Japanese perspective.

A recurring dilemma for the Aleutian World War II National Historic Area, an Affiliated Area of the NPS, is how to portray the history of World War II in the Aleutians in a way that honors and respects the point of view of all the participants. The National Historic Area's publications and programs must balance the experiences of the indigenous Aleuts (now called Unangax̂), who were forced to evacuate their homes in the Aleutian Islands during the war with those of the military personnel – mainly young soldiers from outside Alaska who were part of the buildup, battles, and aftermath of the Aleutian Campaign. Each year the program produces a World War II calendar with monthly stories that rotate the two main themes of military campaign and Aleut relocation with other topics relating to the Aleutian Islands.

After the Japanese attacked Dutch Harbor and occupied Attu and Kiska Islands in June 1942, the American government evacuated and relocated 881 Unangax̂ residents of the Aleutian Islands to Southeast Alaska, ostensibly to protect them from the Japanese.[1] They were housed in dilapidated camps and former canneries until the Aleutian Campaign was over.

The Japanese invaded Attu on June 7th, 1942. That September, after several months of occupation, the Japanese took the Unangax̂ residents of Attu village prisoner and ordered them to board a boat. They brought them to Japan, where they were housed first in a former railroad dormitory and then in a Shinto monastery. Nineteen of the forty Attuans, including four of the five babies born in Japan, died of starvation and disease before the survivors were released at the end of the war.

For Unangax̂, the primary memories of the war are those of forced evacuation and relocation, separation from home, and the loss of family members. Those who returned to their homes after the war found them greatly damaged by the American military. Americans bombed two Unangax̂ villages, Atka and Attu, and burned them to the ground to prevent the Japanese from using the structures. In other villages, soldiers stayed in people's homes or used them as recreation centers, taking tools and furniture. They looted churches and damaged precious artifacts and icons (Kohlhoff 2008).

The American veterans who remember fighting in the Aleutians as young men have quite different perspectives and memories from the indigenous residents. They remember the trauma of battle and still mourn the loss of fallen comrades.

Although their experiences were quite different, both Unangax̂ evacuees and soldiers felt the pain of isolation in an alien landscape. The soldiers, far away from home, saw the windswept Aleutians as inhospitable and stressful. In contrast, the Unangax̂ who were taken to Southeast Alaska saw the trees there as sinister and claustrophobic.[2] However, while almost all the American soldiers were eventually able to return home after the war, some Unangax̂ were never allowed to return home, while others had to repair and rebuild their houses and churches, with little assistance from the government.

Honoring the Japanese perspective on the Aleutian Campaign has presented other difficulties. Some American veterans still harbor enmity against the Japanese as they remember comrades who fell in battle. Because many of the Japanese troops in the Battle of Attu committed suicide rather than surrender, there were few Japanese survivors of the war in the Aleutians to tell the story. Americans also have differing accounts of the behavior of Japanese soldiers. The Attuans who survived imprisonment in Japan remembered harsh treatment at the hands of some of their captors, but there are also some memories of friendly relations between soldiers and guards and some of the Attuans, particularly the children.

The children of American and Japanese veterans who crave to know more about their fathers' service have even less knowledge of the evacuees' experience. Similarly, while children of Aleut evacuees may continue to feel the trauma of their parents' wartime experience, they have little knowledge of the military campaign. Many know very little about their own parents' experience. It is common for children of both veterans and evacuees to say their parents never talked at all about the war.

Among amateur historians of World War II, there are passionate devotees of the Aleutian Campaign, who are interested in aircraft, weapons, and battles. The Commemorative Air Force (CAF), a group in Anchorage, has restored World War II-era planes and offers tours and plane rides. Some enthusiastic members don 1940s-era uniforms and clothing for the Commemorative Air Force's (CAF) World War II events.

While some of the public narrative of the veterans focuses on patriotism and camaraderie, former soldiers also tell of the boredom of service in the Aleutians. Many of the Americans who served in the Aleutians never saw combat. The oppressive weather, which caused more casualties than enemy fire, shaped their wartime experience. Accounts of visits of well-known entertainers such as Olivia de Havilland, Errol Flynn or Howdy Doody, who all visited the Aleutian Campaign, tell of efforts to provide some diversion to the isolated servicemen.

Less known, or spoken about, is the story of segregation of black troops and their assignment to supporting, non-combat roles (Roe 2012). Even less is known about the forced labor of Chinese prisoners to support the Japanese Imperial Army.

The Aleutian World War II National Historic Area was established as an Affiliated Area in 1996. In a unique partnership, the Ounalashka Corporation (OC) – the profit-making village Native Corporation of Unalaska – owns and manages the land and the NPS provides technical and financial assistance.

Initially, the OC leadership did not want the Affiliated Area to interpret military history; rather, they only wanted to tell the story of Unangax̂ evacuation. The enabling legislation attempted to include both stories.[3]

The World War II Visitor Center, owned and staffed by the OC, was created by renovating a World War II-era weather station, the Aerology Building (Figure 2.1). The exhibits in the building tell both the military story and the Unangax̂ story. The NPS has conducted many oral history interviews with veterans and civilians who experienced the Aleutian Campaign and has put them on a website that features these interviews along with photographs and other materials. The tension between themes has continued, waxing and waning with changes in OC leadership.

Forty-three American enlisted men died in the Japanese attack on Dutch Harbor on June 3rd and 4th, 1942 (Ephriam Dickson, personal communication, 10/18/20). The bombs demolished the hospital in Unalaska, the adjoining Native village. The bombing changed the course of the war; the American military saw the attack as a sign that the Japanese were preparing for further invasions of the Aleutian Islands.

The bombing's effect on the community, however, was only part of a greater disruption caused by the Aleutian Campaign. Even before the bombing, the military buildup in Dutch Harbor created major changes for the village of Unalaska. The formerly isolated Unangax̂ residents had to deal with the mass arrival of

FIGURE 2.1   The Aerology Building, built in Dutch Harbor for the Aleutian Campaign, is now in use as the Visitor Center for the Aleutian World War II National Historic Area. Photo courtesy NPS.

civilian and military personnel in the community, and even with fired construction workers who had no means of leaving the Aleutians (Kohlhoff 1995: 50).

As a result of the Japanese attack, the Unangax̂ residents of the Aleutian Islands, including Atka, the Pribilof Islands, and the villages around Unalaska Island, were removed from their homes and taken to shabby former canneries and camps in Southeast Alaska where they stayed for the rest of the war. Some have unfavorably compared the Unalaskans' dilapidated relocation camp at Burnett Inlet to a nearby facility for German prisoners that was much more comfortable. The evacuation and relocation have profoundly influenced the history, culture, and identity of the Unangax̂ people, not only of the evacuees, but also those of subsequent generations.

The NPS Lost Villages of the Aleutians project, which began in 2004, documented the history of four Aleutian villages that were never resettled after the war (Figure 2.2). After the war, when they returned to the Aleutians, residents of Makushin, Kashega, Biorka, and Attu were told that there were too few of them left to resettle their villages, and they were dropped off instead at Akutan

**FIGURE 2.2** Descendants of the village of Makushin, with former resident Nicholai S. Lekanoff, Sr., stand with the cross planted during a return visit to the village in 2009. L–R: Okalena Patricia Lekanoff-Gregory, Nicholai S. Lekanoff, Sr., Josephine Shangin, and Frederick Lekanoff. Photo by Frederick Lekanoff, courtesy NPS.

or Unalaska. Starting as a modest oral history project, the Lost Villages project expanded to include boat trips to three of the villages in 2009 and 2010 on the USFWS vessel Tiĝlax̂ with former residents and descendants. In 2017, the FWS provided a return trip to Attu with some of the descendants of the village. In 2019, the Museum of the Aleutians in Unalaska opened an exhibit about the Lost Villages project, entitled Chiilulix: The Long Journey Home. Unalaska's radio/TV station, KUCB, created a documentary film based on footage of the boat trips to the villages and interviews with participants.

## The Power of Commemorative Events

The problem of divergent perspectives is especially pronounced in the planning of commemorative events. The NPS collaborated with the OC, the City of Unalaska, and several other organizations to prepare for the 2017 event marking the 75th anniversary of the bombing of Dutch Harbor. It was a bumpy ride.

Invitees to the event included all the surviving veterans who could be identified, all over ninety years old, and all the surviving Unangax̂ evacuees, all of whom were aged over seventy-five. The planning committee debated over whether to mention the military or the Aleuts first in the title of the event, whether to refer to Aleuts or Unangax̂, and whether to hold separate events for veterans and evacuees. We decided that despite the need to honor diverse histories, it was better to keep everyone together for most of the events than to have separate activities for evacuees and veterans.

Eight American World War II veterans, all in their nineties except one who was 101, and forty-two Aleut evacuees, who were taken to Southeast Alaska during World War II, came together in Unalaska in 2018 to commemorate the 75th anniversary of the bombing of Dutch Harbor and the resulting evacuation of Aleut residents (Figure 2.3). Everyone who arrived was greeted with a hug at the airport – even, by mistake, a few tourists who had come to Unalaska for other reasons.

At the storytelling night during the commemoration, veterans and evacuees both had an opportunity to share their memories of the war years. The veterans told of their experiences of the bombing or of battle, or of long weeks of isolation and boredom, grounded by weather. The evacuees told of the sudden orders to leave home, the uncertainty of not knowing where they were going, and the poor conditions in relocation camps. Some wept as they recalled relatives who had died in Southeast Alaska, or the damage that they found had been caused to their houses and churches when they returned to the Aleutians. A few who had been relocated as children remembered how excited they were to go to a new place. Toward the end, Robert Brocklehurst, Sr., one of the veterans, said that when he was in the Aleutians, he never knew why there were no Native people there. Until the commemoration, he never knew about the Aleut evacuation. His comments made a strong impression on the evacuees, who had never considered

**FIGURE 2.3** Veterans of the Aleutian Campaign at the commemoration of the 75th anniversary of the bombing of Dutch Harbor/Unalaska and Aleut Evacuation in 2017. Back row L-R: Joe Sasser, Bob Brocklehurst, and Robert Hinsdale. Front L-R: Clint Goodwin, Bill Greene, Allan Seroll, Paul Schaugnency, and Frank Vaughn. As of May 2022, only Paul Schaugnency was still living. Photo by Nicolette Dent, courtesy NPS.

the point of view of individual soldiers. The event served as a unique opportunity to learn the perspectives of others who experienced the war.

Following the custom in many contemporary Unangax̂ gatherings, the Russian Orthodox bishop was invited to bless the commemoration. On Sunday, he led a Memory Walk to the Unalaska school auditorium (Figure 2.4). At the memorial ceremony, names of those who died in the attack on Dutch Harbor on June 3rd-4th, 1942 were read. Then the names were read of all the Unangax̂ who died while interned in Southeast Alaska. Wreaths were laid for Unangax̂ evacuees; US Army, Navy, and Marines; the Canadian military; the US Coast Guard; and the Japanese military.[4]

The commemoration was a great success. By juxtaposing the stories of veterans and evacuees, and honoring all those who died in the war years, the event brought peace and healing not only to the survivors, but also for following generations. It facilitated mutual learning and increased understanding between those with different experiences of the war years, including the Canadian and Japanese perspectives as well as that of the American military and Native people of the Aleutians.

**FIGURE 2.4**  Archbishop David of Alaska of the Orthodox Church of America (front right) and Father Evon Bereskin (front left), himself a descendant of evacuees, leads a walk in memory of the Unangax̂ relocated to Southeast Alaska during World War II. Photo by Nicolette Dent, courtesy NPS.

## Divergent Accounts of the Invasion and Battle of Attu

The other focus area for the Aleutian World War II National Historic Area is the island of Attu, including the Japanese invasion and occupation of Attu in 1942, the imprisonment of Attu villagers in Japan, and the Battle of Attu in 1943. Attuans, Japanese, and Etta Jones, the island's white American teacher, had different accounts of what happened on June 7th, 1942 – the chaotic day that the Japanese invaded the island. Etta's husband Foster Jones was the radio operator on Attu reporting to the US military, and the Japanese soldiers began to interrogate him. Sources agree that the next morning Foster Jones was dead. Japanese soldiers' accounts, and those of some Attuans, say Foster Jones slit his wrists, and that Foster Jones died from the wounds. Later exhumation of Jones's body showed that he had been shot through the head. Etta was taken prisoner and transported to Japan separately from the Attuans.

After the Japanese invaded Attu village on June 7th, 1942, they raised the Japanese flag, telling the Attuans that they were now liberated from the Americans. Japanese troops stayed on the island throughout the summer. They befriended some of the children. One of the Attuans, Nick Golodoff, was six years old at the time of the Japanese invasion. He retained fond memories of one of the soldiers. When Nick visited Japan in 1995, he met that soldier again (Sugiyama 1984; Golodoff 2012).

In September 1942, the soldiers told the forty-one Attu residents to board a ship, bringing with them all the salmon and other food they had. Apparently, the Japanese thought the Attuans would live permanently in Japan. A Japanese Army-Navy agreement of May 5th, 1942, prior to the invasion of Attu, said 'in the event that native residents are to be removed to the homeland, careful consideration must be made for providing them with a suitable occupation (livelihood) and proper care' (Stewart 1978: 13).

One of the Attu women died on the way to Japan and was buried at sea. The forty remaining Attuans arrived in Otaru on September 27th, 1942. They were held prisoner there until the end of the war. After they landed, adults and children were photographed with numbers pinned on their clothes.

While the Attuans were held prisoner in Japan, their island home became a battleground. After the Attuans were removed from their village in September 1942, the Japanese military temporarily left the island, returning with an advance force of 500 the next month and preparing for a much larger force (Cloe 2017: 33). The Americans were determined to retake Attu, and what the military thought would be a quick battle became a prolonged and grueling ordeal that lasted from the 11th to the 29th of May. At the end of the Battle of Attu, almost all the surviving Japanese either made a suicidal charge or committed suicide in other ways. Only twenty-seven Japanese soldiers were taken prisoner by the Americans. When these men returned to Japan after the war, they and their families were deeply ashamed that they had chosen surrender over suicide (Ephriam Dickson, personal communication, 9-27-20).

The five descendants of Japanese soldiers who attended the commemoration in Anchorage in 2018 had an urgent request: to repatriate the remains of the more than 2000 Japanese soldiers left behind on Attu. One member of the Japanese delegation of descendants was the grandson of Col. Yamizaki, who commanded the Japanese military in the Battle of Attu. Repatriation would be an enormous and expensive undertaking, due to the difficulties in bringing equipment to the remote location.

At the closing ceremony of the Battle of Attu commemoration, four wreaths were laid: one for the Unangax̂ people, one for the American military, one for the Japanese military, and one, at the request of the FWS, for the natural resources of the island that were all victims of the battle.[5]

Although some of the American veterans continued to refer to 'Japs' in their war stories, they no longer saw the Japanese people as enemies. It was still difficult for the American veterans to understand the imperial Japanese principle of death before dishonor – especially given their own pride in surviving seventy-five years beyond the battle. The Attu descendants could not forget their parents' suffering as prisoners in Japan, but they could sympathize with the Japanese descendants' desire to return their fathers' remains to Japan.

Compelling stories have emerged about soldiers fighting on the Japanese side who also had ties to America. Karl Kasukabe grew up in the US, in Pocatello, Idaho, but when he was a teenager, his mother took him back to Japan, concerned about the 'democratic education' he was getting in the US. They wanted him to learn to be loyal to the Emperor. When war broke out, Karl qualified as a first-class military interpreter in English. He was part of the Japanese invasion of Attu on June 7th, 1942 and translated a proclamation to them in English before the Japanese flag was raised. He assisted in the interrogation of radio operator Foster Jones and knocked both Etta and Foster around with his fists. Before Etta left on a Japanese ship a few days later, Karl apologized for hitting her. He said he was just following his commander's orders (Seiple 2011).

Karl went to Kiska with the Japanese troops when they were transferred there from Attu and continued to work as a translator and decoder of American radio transmissions and telegraphs. One day, he heard over the radio that the Americans were coming to reclaim Kiska by force, lining up a large fleet in the waters west of the island. When a US-Canadian force landed on Kiska on August 15, the Japanese had slipped out under cover of fog, almost three weeks before (Kasukabe 2008). At first, confused, the Allies shot at each other, resulting in casualties from friendly fire. Seventeen US soldiers and four Canadians died, and fifty were wounded from either friendly fire or Japanese booby traps.

The story of Paul Tatsuguchi is better known. Tatsuguchi, whose father was a Seventh-day Adventist minister in Japan, was educated in America. When he returned to Japan after medical school, Paul first worked in a tuberculosis sanitarium. He was drafted into the Japanese army and served as a medic during the Battle of Attu. He kept a diary that was found and translated after the battle. The diary ends on the last day of the battle, when Tatsuguchi killed his remaining patients and himself (Obmascik 2019).

The places where the Attuans stayed in Japan were not internment camps or concentration camps, as they have sometimes been called. They stayed first in a former railroad dormitory and later, when their numbers were greatly reduced, at a former Shinto shrine. The Attuans have often been mistakenly referred to as 'Prisoners of War,' and although they were certainly held captive this term is generally used to refer to military personnel who are imprisoned. They recalled mistreatment by some of the guards, although several had fond memories of some of the Japanese who guarded them. Some of the descendants believe that medical experiments were conducted on their parents in Japan. One of the prisoners, Angelina Hodikoff, told her children and others after the war that the Japanese used the prisoners from Attu as guinea pigs for medical experiments (Butts 1948: 37).

Most of the Attuans who died in Japan died of hunger, or of malnutrition exacerbating illness. Some of them suffered from tuberculosis. The Japanese who guarded them were also hungry. The Attuans who survived remembered the kindness of some Japanese who shared food with them, when it was available. When the war was over, the surviving Attuans and the policeman who guarded them painted the letters 'POW' on the roof of their house. Americans dropped food, candy, and cigarettes from planes (Golodoff 2012).

## Commemoration of the 75th Anniversary of the Battle of Attu

Another three-day commemoration took place on May 17th–19th, 2018, in Anchorage to mark the 75th anniversary of the Battle of Attu. The battle was waged over nineteen days on the rough, mountainous terrain of Attu Island. About four hundred Americans lost their lives, compared to more than 2000 Japanese soldiers. Many of the Japanese deaths were suicides on the last gruesome day of the battle.

Nine veterans of the Aleutian Campaign of World War II, five descendants of Japanese fallen soldiers, two surviving residents of Attu village, and some twenty descendants of the village gathered for the events in Anchorage in May 2018. The USFWS, the land manager for Attu Island, was the lead agency in organizing the event with assistance from the NPS and an assortment of other agencies: the Alaska Veterans Museum, University of Alaska Anchorage's Montgomery Dickson Center for Japanese Studies, US Army Center for Military History, Japanese American Citizens League, Aleutian Pribilof Island Association, and the Alaska Aviation Museum.

The events were held in several locations around Anchorage, and we hired two school buses to transport the participants, making sure they had wheelchair access. One of the volunteers decided that it was disrespectful to ask veterans aged over ninety to ride a school bus and organized other volunteers to chauffeur them and their escorts from place to place. Concern followed that the Attu survivors and descendants and the Japanese participants would have to wait for the bus while the veterans were chauffeured from one place to another. The Aleutian Pribilof Island Association responded by hiring limousines to transport the two Attu survivors and their spouses. As it turned out, many of the Attu descendants got rides from relatives in Anchorage, and volunteers attached to the Japanese consulate served as drivers for the Japanese delegation. The only people riding the bus were the USFWS artists in residence and a couple of out-of-town World War II buffs. The school bus was finally cancelled.

Elizabeth Kudrin and Gregory Golodoff were the only remaining survivors of Attu village. Neither had any memories of the years they spent in Japan. Elizabeth was a baby and Gregory a toddler when the Japanese invaded the quiet village. The Attuans were taken to Japan by ship and held prisoner until the war was over. Among those who died were Elizabeth's father, brother, and sister. After the war, Elizabeth, her mother, and two brothers were resettled in Atka. Gregory and Elizabeth were heaped with honors at the event of the 75th anniversary of Battle of Attu. At a luncheon at the Aleutian Pribilof Island Association, the Russian Orthodox choir sang 'God Grant You Many Years' to the two survivors and to the many Attu descendants present. There was a reading of the names of the twenty-two Attuans who died as prisoners in Japan, a number that included four of the five babies born during those years.[6]

The 2018 Battle of Attu commemoration brought together more groups than the 2017 commemoration of the bombing of Dutch Harbor. The biggest

**FIGURE 2.5** Participants in the Battle of Attu 75th Anniversary Commemoration in Anchorage, including survivors and descendants of the village of Attu, American veterans, and descendants of Japanese soldiers. Photo by Lisa Rupp, courtesy USFWS.

difference between this event and those previous was the participation of the children of Japanese soldiers who had fought in the Battle of Attu, but it was just as successful in bringing forward disparate perspectives, along with a message of peace and healing. There were many opportunities for the American veterans, descendants of Japanese soldiers, and Attu survivors and descendants to interact, both informally and in commemoration events (Figure 2.5).

## Ongoing Commemoration: Ruins and Monuments in the Aleutians

Today the ruins of bunkers and other structures remain in Unalaska as evidence of the World War II military presence. Perhaps ironically, given the soldiers' damage to houses and churches in Aleutian villages during the war, the OC struggles to keep local youth and others from defacing the military ruins with graffiti.

In 1987, the government of Japan placed a large titanium Peace Memorial on Attu in memory of all those who died on both sides of the battle (Figure 2.6). American veteran Bill Jones, now deceased, strongly opposed the memorial and campaigned to get it removed. Jack Jonas, a veteran of more recent years, aided Jones by continuing the struggle to remove the memorial before his own death

**FIGURE 2.6**   Peace memorial on Attu, erected by the Japanese government in 1987. The memorial is on Engineer Hill, where the gruesome final battle took place. Photo by John Cloe, courtesy NPS.

in 2015. Jonas contacted some of the Attu descendants to seek their support for getting rid of the memorial. Over the years, several Japanese delegations and family groups have come to Attu to pay respect to fallen soldiers.

Despite the divergent memories of the war, while organizing commemorative events, we learned that it was better to bring everyone together than to have separate tracks. The 75th anniversary of the Battle of Attu is probably the last milestone commemoration that includes anyone who remembers World War II. Only a few veterans are left, and most of the remaining evacuees were children or babies at the time of evacuation. In 2019, we lost Bob Brocklehurst, a veteran who made a special point to reach over the divide between American and Japanese soldiers, and between soldiers and Unangax̂. We are at the end of the time when we could hear about World War II in the Aleutians from those who remember living in that era. At this point, archeological investigations can add considerably to the historical record.[7]

As debates continue throughout the US over war monuments and the portrayal of battlegrounds, some would like to destroy all the evidence of this painful history. Others ask for the placement of other monuments and the providing of contextual information, to show that there were multiple experiences of the same events. The success of the Aleutian World War II National Historic Area's commemorative events shows that bringing together those with widely different experiences of war may be challenging, but that there is potential for mutual education and compassion. Instead of destroying evidence of a painful history, we want to honor all experiences of the war.

## Notes

1 Earlier in 1942, the US government confined Japanese Americans living on the West Coast to camps in California, Idaho, and other locations. The experience of Japanese in confinement camps is much better known than Unangax̂ relocation. Although both groups eventually received restitution payments, a formal apology (under President Ronald Reagan) was extended only to the Japanese Americans.
2 The elders were especially bothered by the trees. Some of the children enjoyed the adventure of playing among the trees (Kohlhoff 1995: 88).
3 The enabling legislation of the Aleutian World War II National Historic Area very generally presents both themes of the program:

> ...to provide for the interpretation, for the educational and inspirational benefit of present and future generations, of the unique and significant circumstances involving the history of the Aleut people, and the role of the Aleut people, and the Aleutian Islands in the defense of the United States in World War II.
>
> (H.R. 4236 SEC. 513. UNALASKA)

4 Canadian forces fought alongside US forces to retake the islands of Attu and Kiska from the Japanese. The Canadians provided anti-submarine support during the Battle of Attu. US and Canadian planes sought to take Kiska from the Japanese in August 1943, only to find that the Japanese had slipped away under cover of fog. The only casualties were from friendly fire.
5 While the Unangax̂ are deeply attached to the natural resources of Attu as well, their cultural attachment to the life-sustaining subsistence resources of their homeland is different from the FWS mission to conserve natural resources for the benefit of all Americans.
6 When the Attuans began their journey back to the United States from Japan, their captors gave them a large box with the cremated remains of those who had died during their years of captivity. The box was lost en route, but was eventually recovered and sent to the survivors who had been resettled in Atka. The remains are buried in Atka.
7 Archeological investigation can resolve some of the remaining questions about the Aleutian Campaign. Archeological studies of the physical remains of battlefields, military occupation sites, civilian communities and relocation camps are needed to supplement the historical records and personal accounts of those who experienced war in the Aleutian Islands. The material culture of World War II in the Aleutians can provide answers to some of the questions that emerge from diverging memories of participants. Just as the question of how radio operator Foster Jones died when the Japanese invaded Attu was resolved by exhuming his body in 1948 to find that he had been shot in the forehead (Cloe 2017), other studies of human and material remains can resolve more puzzles of the Aleutian Campaign.
   To date, the US Army Corps of Engineers has headed most of the archeological work on World War II in the Aleutians (e.g., Mobley 1996, Reynolds, 1998, Pierce 2015, Eldridge 2019). Christopher Roe's MA thesis showed that the construction of buildings at Fort Glenn, an airbase on Umnak Island, followed a hierarchical

pattern with African American soldiers being given inferior quarters (Roe 2012). Further study of the structures and weapons left behind on Kiska can provide valuable information on the everyday lives of soldiers in the Japanese Imperial Army. Mobley's study of Aleut relocation camps in Southeast Alaska (2012) reveals some details of how Unangax̂ communities survived through the war years.

## Bibliography

Blight, D.W. 2001. *Healing and History: Battlefields and the Problem of Civil War Memory.* [WWW] https://www.nps.gov/parkhistory/online_books/rthg/chap3a.htm (accessed 28/11/2020).

Butts, R.C. 1948. 'Prisoners from Alaska', *Alaska Sportsman*, May 1948, 14–15, 36–39.

Cloe, J.H. 2017. *Attu: The Forgotten Battle.* Anchorage, AK: National Park Service.

Eldridge, K. (US Army Corps of Engineers). 2019. *Cultural Resources Survey of Fort Mears East Broadway Avenue World War II housing area (UNL-0606), Unalaska Island, AK.* Alaska: NALEMP Site Investigation and Survey Results.

Golodoff, N. 2012. *Attu Boy.* R. Mason, ed. Anchorage, AK: National Park Service.

Kasukabe, K.K. 2008. 'The Escape of the Japanese Garrison from Kiska.' In: F. Chandonnet, ed. *Alaska at War 1941–1945: The Forgotten War Remembered.* Fairbanks, AK: University of Alaska Press, 121–23.

Kohlhoff, D. 1995. *When the Wind was a River: Aleut Evacuation in World War II.* Seattle: University of Washington Press.

Kohlhoff, D. 2008. 'A Matter Very Close to the Aleut Heart: The Politics of Restitution.' In: F. Chandonnet, ed. *Alaska at War 1941–1945: The Forgotten War Remembered.* Fairbanks: University of Alaska Press, 297–99.

Mobley, C.M. 1996. *Cultural Resource Investigations at Kiska, Little Kiska, and Semisopochnoi, Aleutian Islands, Alaska.* Prepared for the USACE, Alaska District under Contract to Dames & Moore, Inc.

Mobley, C.M. 2012. *World War II Aleut Relocation Camps in Southeast Alaska.* Anchorage: National Park Service, Alaska Region.

Obmascik, M. 2019. *The Storm on our Shores: One Island, Two Soldiers, and the Forgotten Battle of World War II.* New York: Atria.

Pierce, S. 2015. *Archaeological Survey Report: Dutch Harbor Vicinity Formerly Used Defense Sites, Unalaska and Amaknak Islands, Alaska.* Formerly Used Defense Site Program Site Investigation and Survey Results, Alaska District.

Reynolds, G. 1998. *Archaeological Site Investigation of Chernofski Harbor.* Document on file, USACE, Alaska District.

Roe, C.H. 2012. *The Subculture of the U.S. Army during World War II and Its Impact on the Construction of an Airbase on Umnak Island, Alaska.* Master's Thesis, University of Alaska Anchorage.

Seiple, S. 2011. *Ghosts in the Fog: The Untold Story of Alaska's WWII Invasion.* New York: Scholastic Press.

Stewart, H. 1978. *Preliminary Report Concerning the 1942 Japanese Invasion and Occupation of Attu and the Subsequent Removal of Attuans to Japan, 1942–1945.* Report Prepared for the Aleut/Pribilof Islands Association, Inc.

Sugiyama, M. 2010 (1984). *Meetings between Aleutian and Japanese People.* Tokyo: Sugiyama Publishing.

# 3

# CONFLICT LANDSCAPES, INDIGENOUS LANDSCAPES AND COMMEMORATIVE LANDSCAPES

## A Perspective from Papua New Guinea

*Matthew Kelly*

## Introduction

On the 40th anniversary of the 1975 independence of Papua New Guinea (PNG), the director of the PNG National Museum and Art Gallery in Port Moresby, Dr. Andrew Moutu, had no illusions about what he felt was possibly the most significant factor in the formation of the nation of PNG – the Second World War. He declared that the coming of the conflict had broadened the perspectives of people who had hitherto been separated into numerous small groups by topography and language. The integration of people from all over Papua and New Guinea in the Second World War for a single purpose – to oppose the Japanese – opened many eyes, at the time and in subsequent years, to the prospect of a unified nation based on an identity larger than a that of a single valley or an isolated mountain, a language or particular cultural grouping.[1]

Papua and New Guinea – the eastern half of the island of New Guinea, at the commencement of the Second World War, were administered as separate entities by Australia. This was the result of the colonial occupation of the island, Papua having been a British colonial possession from 1884, and New Guinea a German colonial possession from the same time. The separation of Papua and New Guinea was to technically remain the case until 1949. In that year, an administrative union created the Territory of Papua and New Guinea which was to eventually become the nation of PNG in 1975 (Biskup et al. 1970; Waiko 2007). For ease of use, this chapter will use PNG hereafter to refer to both Papua and New Guinea.

For Moutu, the war provided both the proximate cause and a critical ideology of potential national homogeneity that, in hindsight, resulted in the successful declaration of nationhood in 1975. The physical remains from the war are today also an important earner of tourism dollars for the country, and commemoration

DOI: 10.4324/9780429270468-4

of that conflict, including the PNG involvement and that of Australia, Japan and the US, forms an important part of modern PNG's identity. Visitors predominantly from Australia, but also Japan and the US, come to the country for 'culture and history,' which are the most-often cited reason for travel.[2] So, it would not be an exaggeration to say that the Second World War has a critical legacy in the nation's identity and that this continues to play a significant current role in the operation of the economy.

## Local Perspectives

From a First-World perspective, the sentiment that recognizes the critical importance of the Second World War as a seminal event in history is entirely understandable. The conflict, in which sixty million people died, established the political context for the latter 20th Century, the Cold War, the Berlin Wall, the dramatic fall of Communism, the demise of Colonialism etc.

This First-World, global-scale perspective, however, does not always recognize the complexity of local effects – immediate and subsequent – on the inhabitants of the place where conflict occurs. From the wartime Australian public's perspective, the role that the PNG locals took on in the resistance to the Japanese invasion has recognized the efforts of the so-called 'Fuzzy-Wuzzy Angels' – the carriers without whom the campaign to push the Japanese out of PNG would have failed. These efforts were celebrated in Sapper Bert Beros's contemporary poem extolling the virtues of these 'angels,' a sentiment also picked up in numerous contemporary letters to the editors of Australian newspapers (Beros 1944). At about the same time, New Zealander George Silk shot an iconic photo of Orokaivan man Raphael Oimbari assisting a wounded Australian soldier, George 'Dick' Wittington through kunai grass, for medical treatment (Figure 3.1). This image of heroic, gallant, seemingly tireless and ever loyal locals dominated, and continues to dominate, Australian's image of the PNG population during the conflict. This image, I would argue, has an implicit corollary – that the colonial relationship between the Australian administrators and locals was positive, unproblematic and unvarying. This image of the carriers reflected the colonial relationship in a positive light to most of the Australian public during and after the war.

This essentialized view of a complex relationship has recently been countered by a number of writers who investigate and demonstrate more of the complexity of the relations between the Australian military, the Australian New Guinea Administrative Unit (ANGAU) and the locals.[3] The noted historian of the Pacific Hank Nelson reviewed the discontinuity between the history and politics of the Kokoda Track (Nelson 2003). He noted that Australians rightly recognize the sacrifices and support of the carriers during the fighting, but also that this gratitude overlooks important aspects of the carrier's experience – the fact that most were unwilling conscripts subjected to threats and corporal punishment from their ANGAU handlers. Nelson also highlights the misconception that the

**FIGURE 3.1** George Silk's photograph of Orokaivan Raphael Oimbari leading George Whittington back to medical care behind the lines. The photo had an enormous impact and resulted in Silk being hired by Life magazine shortly thereafter. Source: AWM 014028.

carriers on the Track were local Koiari men when most were from labour depots around Port Moresby (on the south coast) and later from Central District plantations. Another study of the participation of the Chimbu people of the highlands in the war paints a similar difficult picture of harsh conditions, forcible recruitment and substantial disruption to village life (Scheps 1995).

Riseman (2010) investigates this labour relationship in some greater detail. Conditions of carrying were harsh, i.e. poor food, hygiene, overwork and lack of adequate medical attention, which led many to desert. Riseman concludes that the attitudes of the Government, the military forces and ANGAU to the carriers during the war constituted a 'continuing colonial mindset and rac(ial)ist ideas, even as Australians grew to depend on Papua New Guinean support and participation.'[4]

Rogerson also reviews the 'myth' which colours the public perceptions of the motivations of the locals in PNG but also most tellingly our treatment of them (Rogerson 2012). The myth paints an unsophisticated picture of complex relationships. She concludes that 'Australia as a nation chooses to romanticize this past and its participants, rather than to acknowledge its own misdemeanours and confront the task of making amends for this part of the nation's history' (Rogerson 2012: 23).

The Japanese military also had a recruited labour for their forces, initially from New Britain, occupied since early 1942, but also later from the mainland. Some locals served the Japanese willingly but most notably those that served the *Nankai Shitai* from Buna to the Track were made up of about 2,000 men tricked into service and forcibly removed from New Britain. As Iwamoto (2006: 265) observes,

> In most cases the method of recruitment seems to have been compulsory and harsh, judging from numerous records and oral evidence that unanimously emphasise Japanese demonstrations of brutality such as beatings, torture, punishment and public execution of spy suspects and Allied air men.

The popular Australian perspective of the fighting along the Kokoda Track is therefore a generally circumscribed one born of our colonial involvement and current politics with simplified views of local involvement, motives and effects. In these popular and politicized accounts, local PNG people are rarely given a voice in respect of the Second World War and the relationship between them, the conflict's effects and our forces. This is not to say that occasional studies that view the conflict from the local perspective do not exist (Read 1947; White & Lindstrom 1989; Allen 2006; Kaima 2006). Only recently has a concerted effort been undertaken to record the rapidly fading voices of people from PNG about their experiences in the Second World War (Kokoda Initiative 2015).

For the local people, the effects of conflict on their doorstep had both immediate and longer-term results ranging from initial displacement and threat of death through an inherited status as refugees (sometimes in their own country), economic dislocation and loss, to a range of social and mental effects that can last for the rest of their lives. For many Papua New Guineans, for example, the war was a local affair that took no account of larger-scale politics – the rise of Fascism, the demise of colonialism (though they witnessed those effects first-hand) and the massive displacement of millions of people across the world. For those living along the Track, this global war was experienced at a more immediate and confined scale that is summed up by one elder who described the war experience as 'living in peace for generations, then one day the Australians and Japanese came, had a big fight in their backyards, caused a lot of damage in their villages, then went away!' (Lynn 2017: 254). The simple results of the war on their doorstep might be viewed in more quotidian terms. Some positive consequences resulted from involvement in the war – someone learnt carpentry, another learnt some English and perhaps another became more familiar with dealing with the local authorities. They of course could be countered by the bad – the death of a loved one, hunger though the destruction of a garden, uncertainty over who was now in charge, or doubt over when (and if) a loved one might return. The historic-political template that guides conflict archaeology's interpretation and assessment of the politics and historical consequences of war is not necessarily held by the local inhabitants of the landscapes and places that provide the setting for these events.

## Etoa Battlefield Project

The recent work in PNG, on which this chapter is based, has emphasized some of these issues as we deal with the Second World War conflict sites in both the Owen Stanley Ranges and the southern littoral areas of PNG outside Port Moresby. Our research into the campaign and its historical and social context has highlighted the narrow focus of most accounts of the events of the Kokoda Campaign, generally rendering the locals at best into passive support roles, and at worst as a mere part of the exotic backdrop to the events that occurred, lacking any sense of their own agency. The danger is that this views the locals as only passive elements of the Kokoda story. This project was undertaken as a commercial heritage consultancy for the PNG Government's Conservation Environment Protection Authority (CEPA) under the joint PNG and Australian agreement known as the Kokoda Initiative (Commonwealth Department of Agriculture Water and Environment: 2019).

Our work is focussed on two sites: a 1942 battlefield on the Kokoda Track, at Eora Creek, and a rest and recreation area just outside Port Moresby, known as Namanatabu or Blamey's Garden, which is associated with the Australian military supply and logistics sites supporting the troops to the north. Based on our archaeological surveys of these sites, we have completed two Conservation Management Plans that now form the basis for their future management by CEPA (AHMS 2016a, 2016b). The work at Eora Creek is focused on a specific part of the battlefield, named in the local Biage language, *Etoa*. It is located on the traditional hunting grounds of the people from nearby Alola village. The project has taken a multi-disciplinary approach and is based on a combination of archival research, archaeological ground survey and oral history.

## Historical Context

With the success of the attack on Pearl Harbor on the 7th of December 1941, Imperial Japanese forces moved swiftly into Southeast Asia with the attack in British-held Malaya and Thailand the next day. Singapore was captured by February 1942, and the Philippines were attacked and occupied by May 1942. Japanese forces had moved into the south-west Pacific by late January 1942 with the attack on the capital of Australian territory of New Guinea–Rabaul, on the island of New Britain.[5] This major deep-water port, Simpson Harbour, became the primary Japanese military base in the south-west Pacific. The 8th Area Army Headquarters, which was based here, would eventually control over

100,000 Japanese troops in the Solomons and PNG (Miller 1959: 47). This defeat directly threatened Papua – the other Australian territory, with its capital at Port Moresby. Concurrently, the Solomon Islands were attacked, initiating the fighting on Guadalcanal that was to eventually determine the outcome of the war in this part of the Pacific (see Gibbs et al., this volume).

The Japanese plan to capture Port Moresby on the south coast of PNG, Operation MO, was initially planned as a seaborne invasion. By capturing Port Moresby, the Japanese military hoped to protect their left flank in the Netherlands East Indies. This also had the benefit of interdicting supply and communications between the Australian mainland and the US. This invasion was prevented when the Japanese troop ships and escorting naval vessels were defeated in the Battle of the Coral Sea in early May 1942 (Lundstrom 1984). With this thrust thwarted, the Imperial Japanese forces resolved to undertake a difficult land-based operation in mid-1942.

This operation saw the Japanese South Seas Detachment (*Nankai Shitai*), which had previously taken part in the capture of Guam and Rabaul, landing on the north coast of the main island of New Guinea. The aim was for this force to cross the Owen Stanley Ranges via the old postal trail, known as the Kokoda Track, and thus take Port Moresby overland. The Kokoda Track (or Trail) is just that – a foot track across the Owen Stanley Mountains. It is a sinuous 96 km long track from the small town of Kokoda, in Oro Province, to Owers' Corner on the Sogeri Plateau, just 30 km north-east of Port Moresby.

The Kokoda Campaign lasted from July to November 1942 and initially resulted in successful Japanese attacks against militia units and ill-equipped, under-supplied Australian regular forces (McCarthy 1959; Williams 2012). These Australian Army units were forced into a fighting withdrawal south along the Track, suffering defeats at Isurava, Brigade Hill and Ioribaiwa. By the time the *Nankai Shitai* had advanced to within 40 km of Port Moresby it was a spent force, and a resurgent Australian force, now better supplied and trained, pushed it back out of the mountains and eventually to its base on the north coast, where it was overwhelmed by February 1943.

## The Fieldwork

The project work has focussed on an area of approximately one square kilometre, on the October 1942 Eora Creek battlefield, which represents only about 20% of the entire area fought over. The survey area lies 500 m west and upslope of the Kokoda Track, in rainforest between 1800 and 2100 m above sea level, on land traditionally owned by residents of the nearby village of Alola. This area is known as Etoa to the locals, and it forms only part of the larger Eora Creek battlefield. The site has been surveyed by archaeological teams over two seasons in conjunction with an oral history program focusing on the people of Alola and Abuari, the two villages nearest the site, which are inhabited by the Isurava Biage people (AHMS 2010, 2012; Connelly 2015). In two short seasons, the archaeological survey recorded 443 features consisting of weapons pits, individual artefacts, foot tracks, a horse track and two sets of human remains. There are anticipated to be up to sixty sets of human remains of the Japanese defenders still buried in their weapons pits on the site. From 2019, there has been a concerted effort by the Japanese Government, through the Japanese Association for Recovery and Repatriation of War Casualties, to retrieve these remains. This work is being co-ordinated through the PNG National Museum and Art Gallery. The complementary oral history program interviewed ten people from the two villages as primary informants, with numerous others making smaller contributions during group discussions or informal conversations.

The weapons pits recorded on the battlefield are evident as shallow depressions in the surface filled with rotting, spongy leaf matter. Single man pits (SMP) predominate on the site. These SMP are ovoid and usually measure about 1 m by 0.75 m. Two-man pits are typically 3 m long by 2 m wide, and they are usually oval shaped with a central earth baulk on the downslope side creating two separate fields of fire. The Japanese forces at Eora Creek consisted largely of the 144th Regiment, and portions of the 41st Regiment also deployed mountain artillery (both 70 and 75 mm guns). The mountain artillery positions are usually rectangular and measure up to 4 m long by 3 m wide.

In the course of the fieldwork, we have also been able to accession the local museum collection into a database to be included in the PNG National Museum database of historical artefacts. Most, if not all, of these items are from the battlefield at Eora Creek.

Our survey and recording work have added new information to that already understood about this 1942 battle and the campaign more generally. We have been able to establish that the battlefield was much larger than originally envisaged – so much so that the area in which we are working does not appear in the map detailing the battle in the Official Australian war history. We have recorded a significant new feature – known locally as 'Jap Track' – that demonstrates that the *Nankai Shitai* was improving a local track, which runs parallel to the Kokoda Track, through widening and levelling, thereby supplementing that track's limited supply capacity through the planned introduction of horse transport to the south. As supplementary evidence, we have been able to identify the use of horses or mules into the mountains by the Japanese, through historical research, the presence of characteristic artefacts at certain sites and through the oral history program. The Japanese use of horse/mule transport is well attested from the north coast to Kokoda, but its use in the mountains is usually discounted in analyses of the Japanese supply efforts during the Kokoda Campaign (Williams 2012: 155).

That the project has been successful is in no small part because the local people, the Biage of Alola and Abuari, are active participants in our work. We are at Eora Creek at their invitation. The site is on their traditional hunting ground and we are guided and assisted in our survey everyday by the owners of the land. Their support and physical guidance have been supplemented by anecdotes and stories of the places we visit on their land. Their presence and knowledge make it clear to us every day that while we investigate the circumstances of a battle between Australian and Japanese seventy years ago, we are also telling part of their story and their valley's story.

At an early stage, in addition to the archaeological survey, we initiated a focused oral history program with the people of Alola and Abuari (Connelly 2015). This oral history program has provided a local social context to particulars of the historic events of 1942 and the landscape of the battlefield – an alternative perspective to the standard western narrative of the campaign. It has highlighted the motives and effects of the battle on the forgotten actors of the historic events of 1942 – the indigenous locals. It has moved the locals from their place in the background of previous Australian narratives (see Figure 3.2). It has also broadened our perspective both geographically and temporally, providing an extended context for battles that lasted for hours (in the case of the August battle) or days

**FIGURE 3.2** An iconic image that reflects several tiers of colonial authority during the war, taken at Eora Creek by Damien Parer during the Australian retreat south along the Kokoda Track. In the foreground are the members of ANGAU. To the right, with rifles at the ready, is the Royal Papuan Constabulary who enforced ANGAU's authority. Lined up in several rows up the slope are the indentured native carriers. Scattered in the background are resting Australian soldiers. Source: AWM 013250.

(as in the case of the October battle). We can now view these events in the longer temporal framework of local engagement with outsiders (i.e. colonial relations) and the asymmetrical power relations that characterize these interactions. It has also helped to illuminate the indigenous landscape through the identification of places and stories associated with specific localities within the 1942 battlefield, over which the more recent historic events have been overlaid (see also Lindsay, this volume). One immediate result of this perspective has been the production of a local history component, in *Tok Pisin,* for the local primary school which introduces some of the events of the Second World War from the viewpoint of the people in the valley while demonstrating the effects of those events both on familiar places and the lives of the children's older family members.

## August to October 1942 in the Eora Valley

The narrative progress of phases of past battles, through both space and time, is often explained and demonstrated using maps of the battlefields, illustrating movement using symbols representing the combatants. The technical and ideological aspects of maps used in military planning and histories, however, are not within the scope of this chapter. (Harley 1988; Atkinson 1994; Kosonen 1999; Cosgrove & della Dora 2005). What is depicted, or in this case not depicted, will have an enormous influence on the perceptions of those viewing the maps about the various actors on the events represented.

Maps in existing histories of the Kokoda Campaign present just such information at varying levels of complexity, showing progress of the Japanese along the Kokoda Track and the reactions of the opposing Australian Forces (McCarthy 1959: 128, 210, 288; Williams 2012: 48, 186). Those that depict the actions of the belligerents in the Eora Creek valley saw fighting in two phases – August 1942, during the Japanese advance, and in October during the advance of the Australian forces. However, what is missing from these graphic depictions, as they are missing from all maps depicting military events, are the reactions and movements of the locals (Figures 3.3–3.6). Their presence and reactions to these events are unsuspected ad unrecorded. Despite this, we know from oral histories that the initial news of the Japanese advance was from the Local Australian Patrol Officer (known as a *kiap*), who travelled on foot around his mountainous bailiwick to simply announce that the villagers at Alola and Abuari should 'run away.'[6] This was a consistent approach by the Australian administration to the local people at the approach of the Japanese. While whites would be evacuated, locals would be expected to remain, endure Japanese rule and not collaborate. The local's loyalties were often questioned if they treated with the Japanese at all and ANGAU responses to suspicions of sympathy to the Japanese cause could be quite punitive (Powell 2003: 206–23).

The Biage people of Alola and Abuari did as told and abandoned their villages and gardens in advance of the Japanese as they pushed south (Figures 3.3 and 3.4). It is quite apparent from the oral history that the Biage were just as alarmed by the numbers of Australian soldiers walking north as they were by the threat of the Japanese heading south. The Japanese were described as numerous, 'like ants' and the Biage attempted to avoid both in their efforts to leave their villages.

The Australian attempts to hold the Japanese at Deniki and then Isurava were to no avail and they retreated in late August and early September 1942, through Alola on the Kokoda Track, and from Abuari lying on a subsidiary track on the eastern side of the valley. The Biage recount that after the initial dispersal, they camped at Eora Creek before crossing over the ridge near Abuari, past Mt

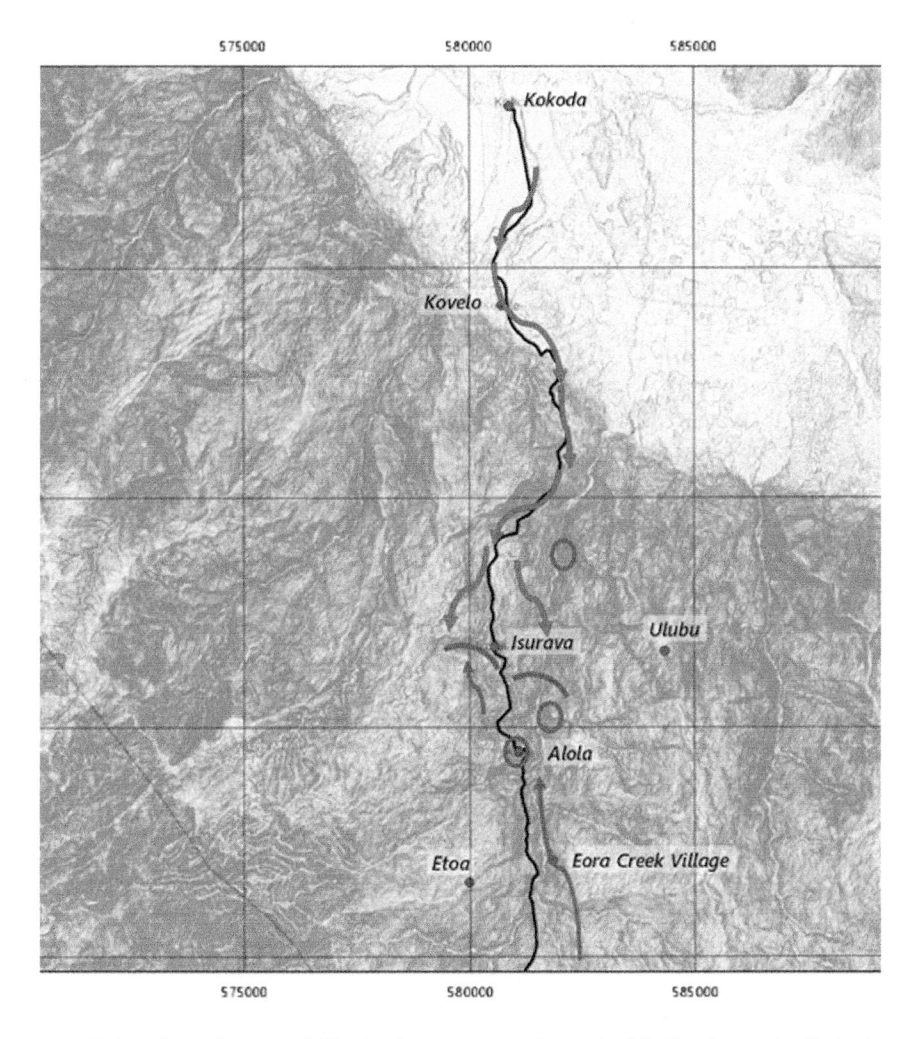

**FIGURE 3.3** Late August 1942: the Japanese attack south (black) along the Kokoda Track, from Deniki, and infiltrate on both sides of the Eora Creek valley. The Australian Forces (light grey) defend Isurava with the locals (dark grey) in their villages or isolated garden plots. Isolated encounters between Japanese and Biage. Map produced by Andre Fleury and Matthew Kelly.

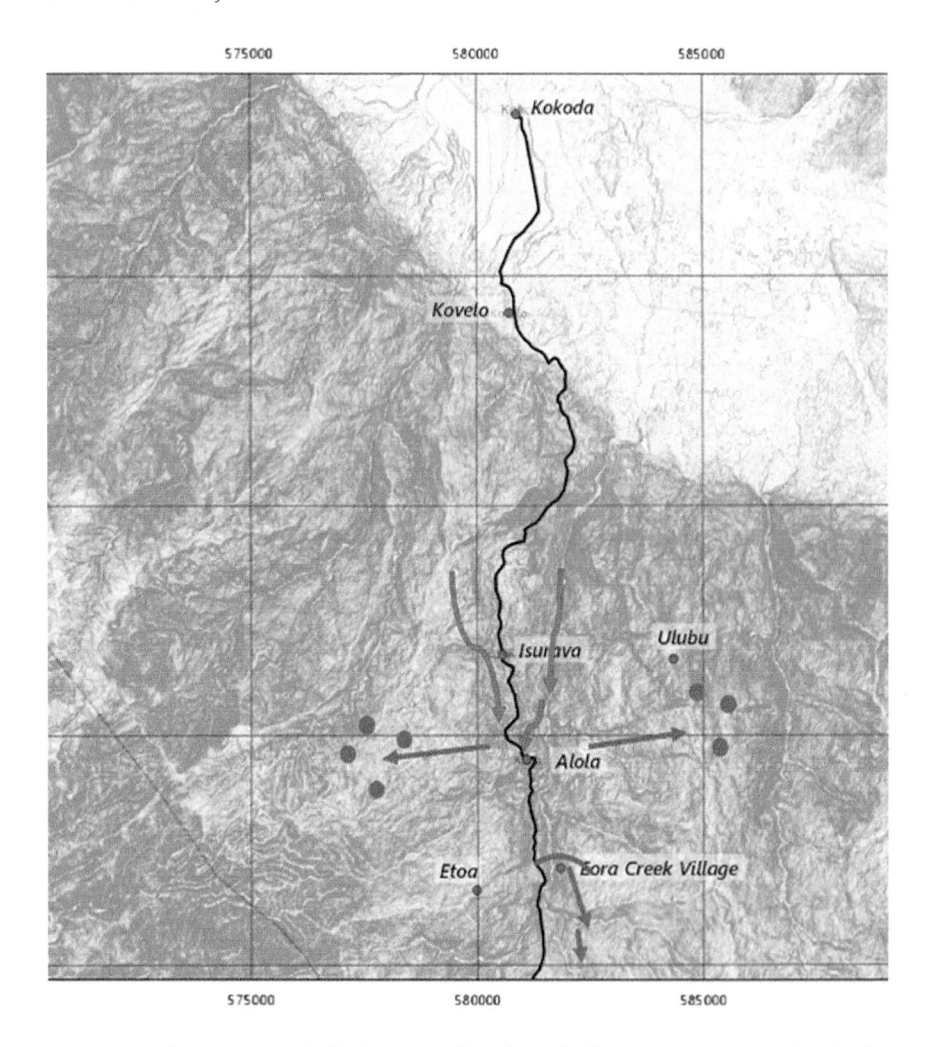

**FIGURE 3.4** Late August 1942: the Australians lose the battle at Isurava and begin the retreat south pursued by the Japanese. The Biage are told to 'run away.' They leave their villages and scatter to either side of the Eora Creek valley. Map produced by Andre Fleury and Matthew Kelly.

Ulubu, a large mountain that overlooked the east side of the valley to the range behind (Figure 3.5). They then made their way uphill behind this ridge east of the Eora Valley. After a time, they moved back down to try and cross Eora Creek near the village of the same name. This village no longer exists, as it was abandoned after the war. To cross Eora Creek, they had to filter through gaps in the advancing Japanese units (Figure 3.6). Miscalculations in these manoeuvres led to encounters that were almost always deadly, with one Biage account relating how some women were caught crossing the river, shot by Japanese soldiers and their heads mounted at the crossing on sticks to warn others of the consequences.

Despite this, the groups were able to gradually cross the creek line and camp temporarily at Etoa, near a water source on the traditional hunting ground on the west side of the valley, which is the focus of our battlefield survey. When the fighting overtook them there, many would move west and south-west over 'The Gap' to the vicinity of the village of to Seregena or Manumu, at the foot of Mt Victoria, taking refuge with kin (Figure 3.7). This was to avoid the area around the Kokoda Track which they recognized as the focus of Japanese movement. Some men were employed as carriers by Capt. Bert Kienzle of ANGAU, who had operated a plantation in the Yodda Valley before the war (Kienzle 2011).

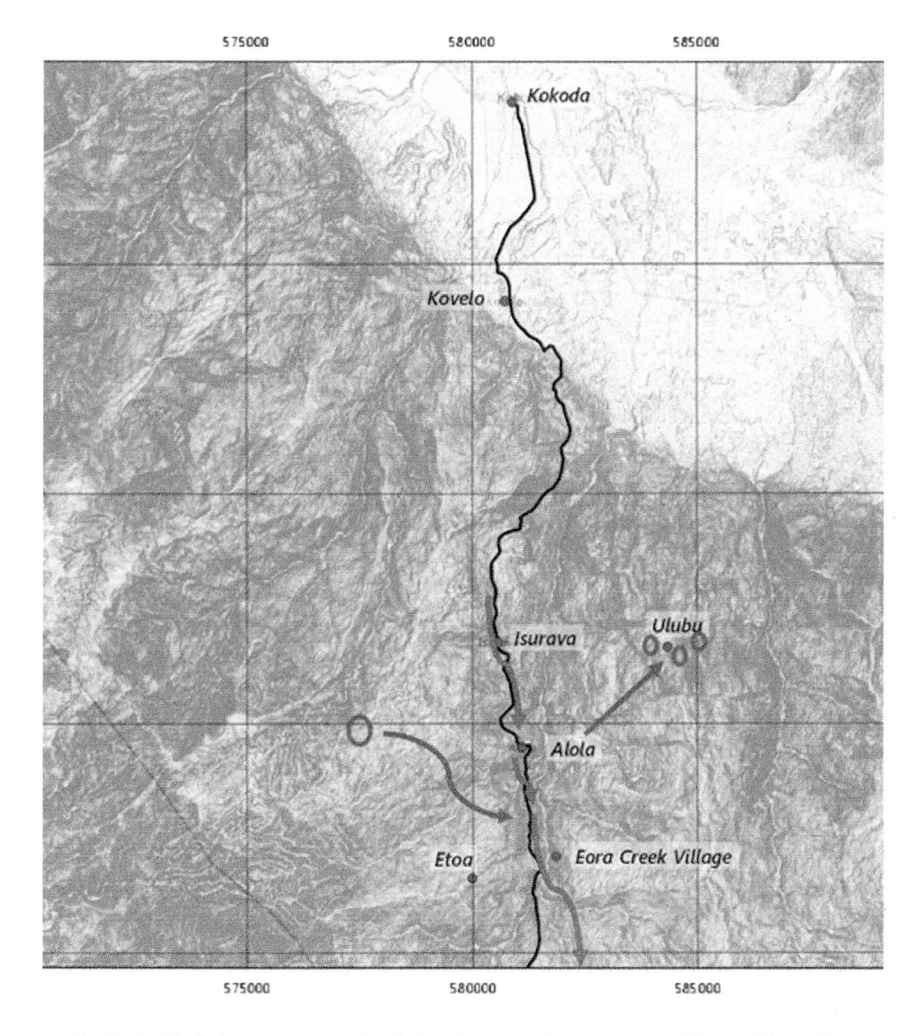

**FIGURE 3.5** Early September 1942: The Biage resolve to meet with the Abuari Biage behind Ulubu by crossing Eora Creek while the Japanese forces continue to move south. Map produced by Andre Fleury and Matthew Kelly.

Perhaps surprisingly, some elected to stay, living and sleeping in the bush with little to no shelter beyond pandanus mats, occasionally retrieving what food was left in their gardens. Some were simply curious about what was going on along the track. This curiosity again led to occasional contact with the Japanese, but it was not until the climactic events of October 1942 at the Second Battle of Eora Creek that the Biage witnessed the horror of a battle at first hand. Some saw the Japanese efforts to construct a defensive position and they maintained a watchful presence in the tree line as the Japanese worked. However, the sound of the gunfire and explosions convinced even these more curious locals to flee and await the end of the battle. They spoke of the aftermath as polluting the water and the water source running red from the blood of the combatants. The Australians for their part sought out the locals in the bush and required them to

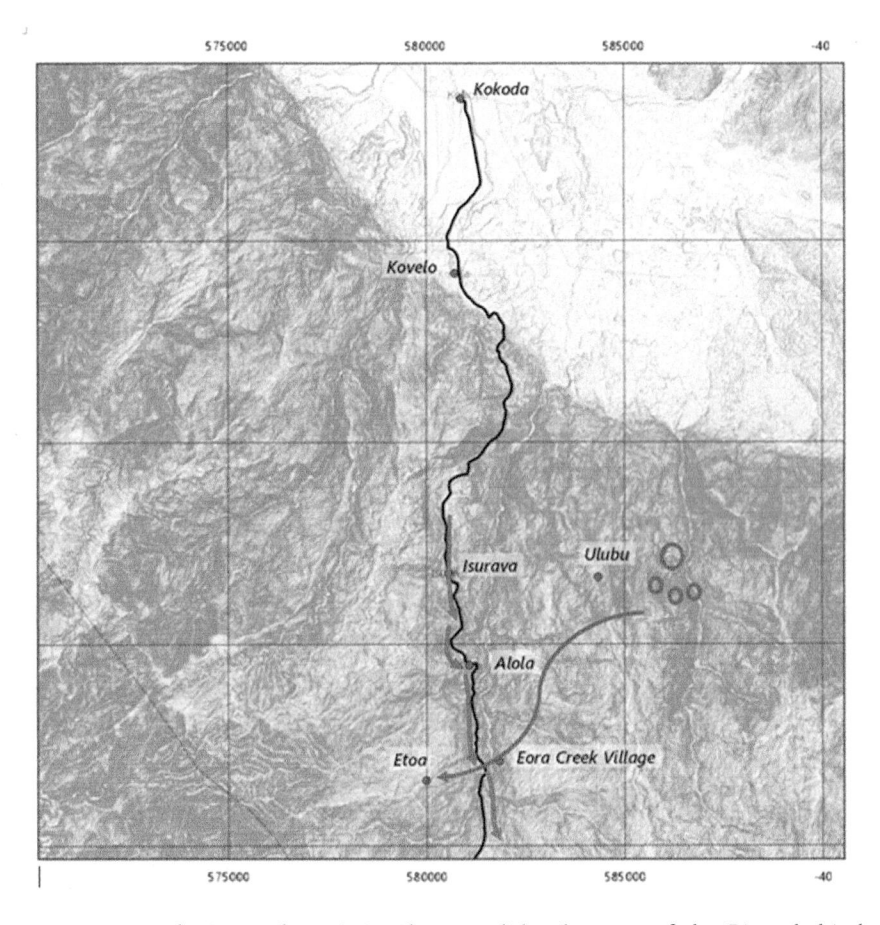

FIGURE 3.6 Early September 1942: The consolidated group of the Biage behind Ulubu then decide, under further pressure from Japanese encounters, to leave the valley, cross Eora Creek near the village of that name and stay at Etoa. Map produced by Andre Fleury and Matthew Kelly.

assist in body recovery, burial and, importantly for a returning colonial power, the recovery of all weapons from the field. After the war, when the Australian patrol officers were able to return to assess the effects of the war on the people of the Eora Valley, it was estimated that forty-nine Biage had been killed during the four months from July to November 1942 (Champion 1946). At the same time, £2,906.7.0 was paid out as compensation for damage from the fighting.

Considering the trauma of 1942, it might be easy to think that the Biage would actively try to erase the memories and ignore the physical remains of those events. However, they have incorporated some stories of that time into their longer-term myths of place. They have also recognized the presence of the physical remains of the dead Japanese on their hunting ground and assiduously guarded the secret of their presence for over seventy years. They now consider

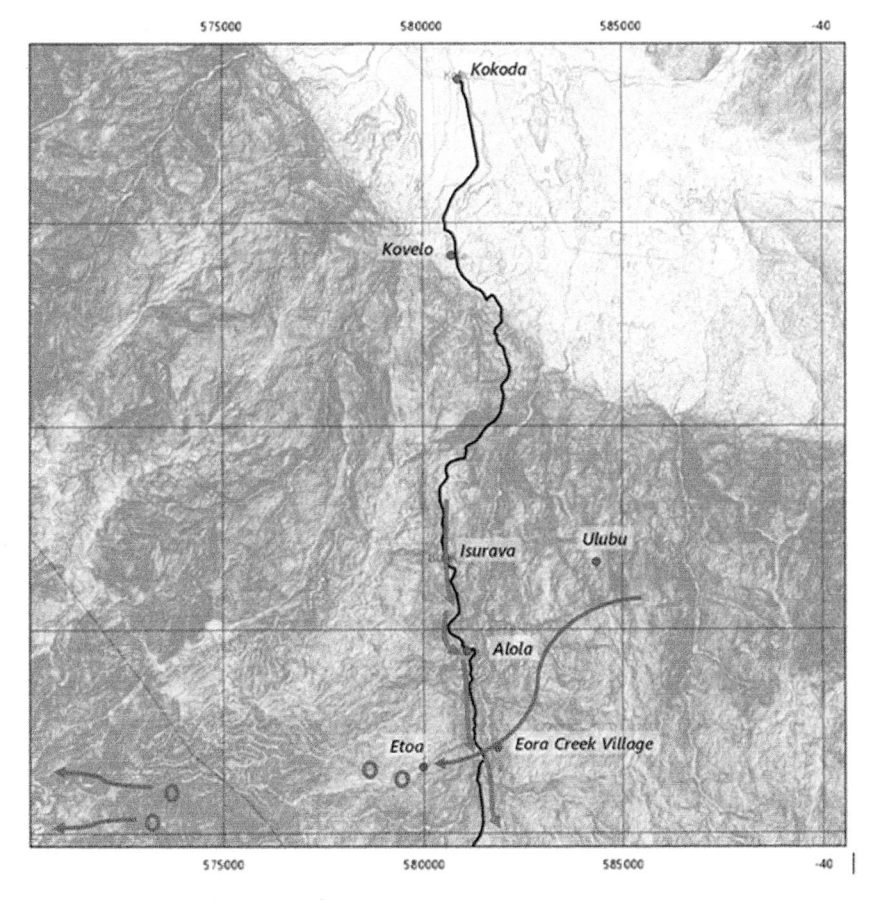

**FIGURE 3.7**  September to October 1942: Many of the Biage disperse to villages to the west but some remain at Etoa to witness the battle there in October 1942. Map produced by Andre Fleury and Matthew Kelly.

the dead as part of their landscape, a part of their valley, and they are happy to recognize that those that were once thought to be invaders can now be considered the sons of their valley.

## Conclusion

Typical accounts of battles provide narratives and depict opposing military forces across a particular time and space to detail the course of the conflict. All too often these accounts neglect other participants in these events, people who were still affected and participated and yet who also found themselves largely written out of history.

In this vein, many accounts of the campaign on the Kokoda Track ignore the effects of the conflict on the local people along the Track. Accounts that do portray local involvement employ the recurrent image of the helpful, beloved 'fuzzy-wuzzy.' The unthinking and repetitive use of that image tends to mask the terrible effects of the campaign on local communities. It only tells part of their story. It masks Australia's treatment of them as a colonial power and their use as a resource that could be mobilized to beat the Japanese. It masks the local's individual experiences as carriers, which were not unproblematic, and it masks the direct consequences of battle across their homelands, as well as the death and stress visited on individuals and communities. Many were killed and others became refugees in their own land. Our project at Etoa has provided us with an opportunity to investigate local community experiences, in a small part of the Kokoda Campaign, that continue to resonate in the community today through stories and personal memory. These memories are in turn continuously stimulated and disturbed through the presence of later interlopers. These include Australian trekkers seeking to 're-live' the military campaign or researchers, such as ourselves, tramping across their land for our own purposes. Our continuing archaeological work, investigating a short battle in October 1942 between Japan and Australian military, will have to remain cognisant of the third player in the drama of those war years.

## Acknowledgements

I would like to acknowledge the critical involvement of people involved in the project work at Etoa over the period of the last few years. They include Dr. Andrew Connelly, Military Heritage Advisor at the PNG National Museum and Art Gallery; Mr Mark Nizette, MBE, Strategic Advisor to the Kokoda Initiative; Mr Jon Sterenberg, archaeologist and colleague; Dr. Nalisa Neuendorf, social anthropologist; Mr James Sabi, PNG Department of Environment and Conservation and current and former work colleagues at Curio Projects and Extent Heritage who have all provided advice, support and encouragement during the life of this project. Primary thanks should, of course, go to the people of Alola and Abuari who have invited us into their places and shared their stories with us.

# Notes

1 Personal comments opening of 'Military Heritage Workshop investigating the options for a survey of the military heritage of the Kokoda Track', organized by Kokoda Initiative (November 2014).
2 Nearly 50% of the country's visitors are from Australia and again nearly 50% of those visitors are interested in the Kokoda Track or Second World War related sites: see International Finance Corporation, PNG Tourism, 2018.
3 ANGAU was the civil administration of the Territory of Papua and the Mandated Territory of New Guinea established in 1942. Its purpose was to provide civil services in areas of PNG not occupied by the Japanese and its focus was providing labour services and organize land to further the war efforts. Its members were often pre-War Patrol Officers. It's duties and purpose resulted in ANGAU's members being in immediate contact with and control of most of the local population.
4 The efforts of some ANGAU officers, and others, with quite different attitudes to relations with the locals should be recognized. Most notable in this respect on the Kokoda Track were Capt. H 'Bert' Kienzle of ANGAU, a former planter from near Kokoda, and Dr. G Vernon, Medical Officer of the 39th Battalion who both sought to improve conditions for the carriers.
5 The invasion forces consisted of the 3rd Kure Special Naval Landing Force, the 10th Establishment Unit, (construction troops) and the 144th Infantry Regiment.
6 The following account is condensed from the series of interviews conducted for the oral history program already noted.

# Bibliography

AHMS. 2010. *Lost Battlefield Site. Preliminary Site Survey and Future Work Program*. Report to the Lost Battlefield Trust.

AHMS. 2012. *Lost Battlefield, Eora Creek, Stage 2 Survey, Final Report*. Report to the Lost Battlefield Trust.

AHMS. 2016a. *Lost Battlefield of Etoa, Eora Creek, Papua New Guinea, Cultural Heritage Management Plan*. Report to PNG Department of Environment and Conservation.

AHMS et al. 2016b. *Blamey's Garden, Hombrom Bluff, Papua New Guinea, Cultural Heritage Management Plan*. Report to PNG Department of Environment and Conservation.

Allen, B. 2006. 'Remembering the War in the Sepik.' In: Y. Toyoda and H. Nelson, eds. *Pacific War in Papua New Guinea*. Tokyo: Rikkyo University Centre for Asian Area Studies, 11–34.

Atkinson, D. 1994. 'Arrows, Empires, and Ambitions in Africa: The Geopolitical Cartography of Fascist Italy.' In J.C. Stone, ed. *Maps and Africa: Proceedings of a Colloquium at the University of Aberdeen*. Aberdeen: University of Aberdeen Department of African Studies, 43–65.

Beros, H. 1944. *The Fuzzy Wuzzy Angels and Other Verses*. Sydney: F.H. Johnston.

Biskup, P., Jinks, B. & Nelson, H. 1970. *A Short History of New Guinea*. Sydney: Angus and Robertson.

Champion, F. 1946. *Patrol Report, Biage District Owen Stanley Range, No. 6-1946/47*. Unpublished report, National Archives of PNG.

Connelly, A. 2015. Eora Creek Oral History Report. Unpublished Oral History Report to AHMS.

Cosgrove, D. & Daniels, S., eds. 1988. *The Iconography of Landscape*. Cambridge, MA: Cambridge University Press.

Harley, J.B. 1988. 'Maps Knowledge and Power.' In: D. Cosgrove and S. Daniels, eds. *The Iconography of Landscape*. Cambridge, MA: Cambridge University Press, 277–312.

Iwamoto, H, 2006. 'The Japanese Occupation of Rabaul, 1942-1945.' In: Y. Toyoda and H. Nelson, eds. *Pacific War in Papua New Guinea*. Tokyo: Rikkyo University Centre for Asian Area Studies, 252-77.

Kaima, S. 2006, 'Kaiapit-Wantoat-Saidor Track: Villagers' Memories of the War in the

Kienzle, R. 2011. *The Architect of Kokoda: Bert Kienzle: the Man Who Made the Kokoda Track*. Sydney: Hachette Australia.

Kokoda Initiative. 2015. *Voices from the War – Papua New Guinean stories of the Kokoda Campaign, World War Two*. Canberra: Governments of Papua New Guinea and Australia.

Kosonen, K. 1999. 'Maps, Newspapers and Nationalism: The Finnish Historical Experience', *GeoJournal*, 48 (2), 91–100.

Lundstrom, J.B. 1984. *The First Team*. Annapolis, MD: Naval Institute Press.

Lynn, C. 2017. 'Trekking Kokoda.' In: K. James, ed. *Kokoda: Beyond the Legend*. Port Melbourne: Cambridge University Press, 52–64.

McCarthy, D. 1959. *South-West Pacific Area – First Year: Kokoda to Wau*. Canberra: Australian War Memorial.

Miller, J. 1959. *Cartwheel: The Reduction of Rabaul*. Washington, DC: United States. Department of the Army.

Nelson, H. 2003. 'Kokoda: The Track from History to Politics', *The Journal of Pacific History*, 38 (1), 109–27.

Nelson, H. 2008. 'Lives Told: Australians in Papua and New Guinea.' In: V. Luker and B. Lal, eds. *Telling Pacific lives: Prisms of Process*. Canberra: ANU E Press, 43–76.

Powell, A. 2003. *The Third Force: ANGAU's New Guinea War, 1942–46*. South Melbourne: Oxford University Press.

Read, K.E. 1947. 'Effects of the War in the Markham Valley', *Oceania*, 18 (2), 95–116.

Riseman, N. 2010. 'Australian [Mis]treatment of Indigenous Labour in World War II Papua and New Guinea', *Labour History*, 98, 163–82.

Rogerson, E. 2012. 'The "Fuzzy Wuzzy Angels": Looking beyond the Myth', *Australian War Memorial, SVSS Paper*, 1–24.

Scheps, L. 1995. 'Chimbu Participation in the Pacific War', *The Journal of Pacific History*, 30, 76–86.

Waiko, J. 2007. *Short History of Papua New Guinea*. Melbourne: Oxford University Press.

White, G. and Lindstrom, L. 1989. *The Pacific Theatre: Island representations of World War II*. Honolulu: University of Hawai'i Press.

Williams, P. 2012. *The Kokoda Campaign 1942, Myth and Reality*. Port Melbourne: Cambridge University Press.

## Web Pages

Commonwealth Department of Agriculture Water and Environment, 2022. International Projects, Papua New Guinea, Kokoda Initiative https://www.environment.gov.au/heritage/international-projects/papua-new-guinea/ (accessed 01/07/2022).

International Finance Corporation, 2019, PNG International Tourism Survey, 2018. https://www.ifc.org/wps/wcm/connect/6b704dcd-ec5b-4788-aa5d-ce63d8a2f79a/PNG-International+Visitor+Survey+2018+-+Infographic.pdf (accessed 01/07/2022).

# 4

# WORLD WAR II IN THE SOLOMON ISLANDS

## Conflict and Aftermath

*Martin Gibbs, Brad Duncan, Lawrence Kiko and Stephen Manebosa*

## Introduction

The Solomon Islands are notable as the region where Japanese and American forces first fully engaged in combat following the surprise raid on Pearl Harbor on 7th December 1941. Intense battles took place on land, sea, and in the air, with both sides formulating or trialling tactics and materiel for the first time. These conflicts left an immense body of sites, artefacts, and human remains across the islands, with lasting impacts on local cultural practices. There are also extensive bodies of primary literature which has survived from these conflicts, which represent an equally substantial resource of memoirs from all levels of combatant as well as post-war analyses and histories. Despite this wealth of documentary evidence, archaeological studies of the extensive physical remnants of World War II have been surprisingly limited, as have those of modern Solomon Islander engagements with these material legacies. This chapter provides an overview of archaeological investigations, current roles, and issues with the conservation and management of World War II heritage in modern Solomon Islander economy and society.

## Historical Background

There are numerous comprehensive histories of the opening stages of the Pacific conflict (e.g. Leckie 1965; Ambrose 2011; Toll 2011), so the following section offers only a thumbnail sketch. In the months following their successful attack on Pearl Harbor, Japanese forces swept through SE Asia and the Western Pacific, and by January 1942 they had established a major air and naval base at the former British settlement of Rabaul in New Britain. Japanese command had decided that it should capture British-held Port Moresby, with a forward base to be established

DOI: 10.4324/9780429270468-5

in the Solomon Islands, immediately to the east, prior to the assault (Figure 4.1). The new bases could then be used to protect newly conquered territories, project forces further if required, and disrupt communication and supply lines between the US and Australia, situated only 1,500 km south of the Solomons.

The Solomon Islands are an archipelago with six major and nearly 1,000 smaller islands, extending 1,700km south-eastwards from Buka in the north to the Santa Cruz Islands (Temotu) in the south. The central portion is arranged in a roughly parallel lines running NW-SE ('The Slot'). The major islands are volcanic and mountainous, covered in dense tropical forest on the slopes and with swamps and grasslands on the flatter coastal sections. The climate is tropical with a heavy rainfall monsoon season. The current political entity of the Solomon Islands, which forms the focus of this chapter, does not include the northernmost major islands including Bougainville and Buka.

Following a brief period of reconnaissance, Japanese forces arrived at the former British administrative hub of Tulagi (Florida Islands, now Nggela) in the heart of the Solomon Islands on the 3rd of May 1942. European civilians had mostly been evacuated several months earlier and the skeleton force manning the small RAAF Catalina base escaped as the fleet appeared over the horizon. Although US fighters bombed Tulagi the day after the invasion, they were immediately recalled to fight in what is now known as the Battle of the Coral Sea, south of the Solomon Islands. The only Europeans left behind in the Solomon Islands were a handful of missionaries and the Coastwatcher force, aided and supported by local people on each island (Horton 1970).

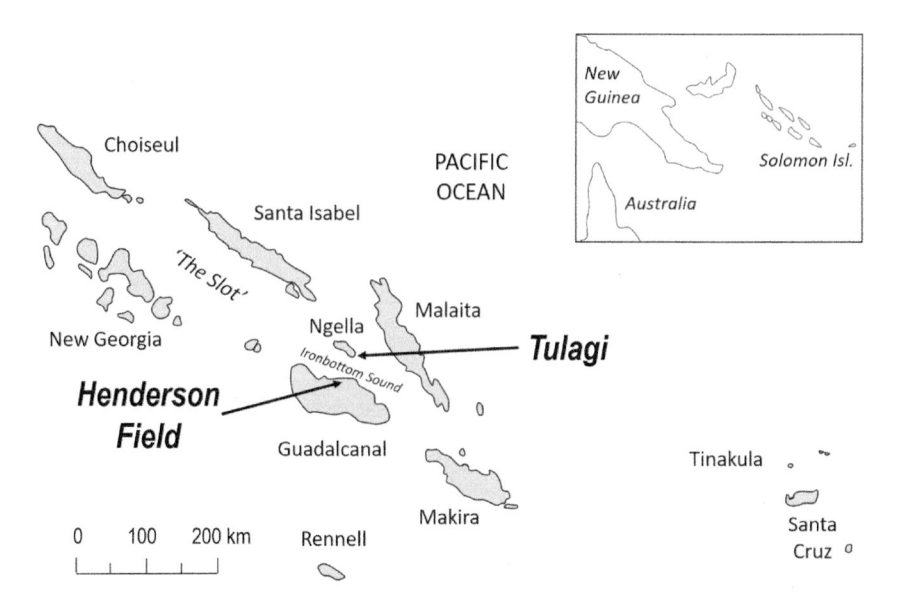

**FIGURE 4.1**  The Solomon Islands.

In the months that followed, the Japanese created a network of bases on Tulagi and nearby islands, including networks of tunnels, and had commenced construction of a conventional airstrip on the larger (and flatter) island of Guadalcanal, which lay 35km to the south. On the 7th of August, US marines launched counter-attacks against both Tulagi and Guadalcanal, which were immediately followed by the return of Japanese naval forces. A poorly advised retreat by the US Navy saw the Marines stranded without reinforcement or adequate supplies (Rottman 2005: 17). The Marines were able to complete the Guadalcanal airstrip – now Henderson Field – while defending it against daily bombing. Ground forces engaged in savage combat along the surrounding ridges and valleys (Leckie 2010). Neither side was familiar with this form of jungle fighting, let alone the difficult living and health conditions of the tropical environment. Casualties were at times horrifying, such as in October 1942 when the US 1st Battalion, 7th Marines, trapped the Japanese 2nd Battalion, 4th Infantry, in a wooded ravine near the Matanikau River. The US rained gun and mortar fire on to the Japanese troops and killed as many as 700 men in a single day. The battles of this period, such as that for Bloody Ridge (also Edson's Ridge or Raiders' Ridge), a critical position just west of the airfield, became almost legendary as evidence that the Japanese forces were not invincible (Leckie 1965).

Several major sea battles were also fought in the immediate area of Guadalcanal during the latter part of 1942, as each side tried to deny the other chance to resupply and reinforce their respective land forces. Savo Sound became known as Ironbottom Sound from the dozens of vessels including several aircraft carriers, destroyers, and submarines that were sunk or left abandoned on the shores (Ballard, Archbold and Minge, 1993). In December 1942, the Marines were finally relieved and the US Army was able to force the Japanese ground forces westward. Now also suffering from serious illness and lack of supplies, the Japanese command evacuated their soldiers from Cape Esperance in the first week of 1943. By this time, there had been several attempts at establishing new bases and airstrips in the western portions of the Solomon Islands, including at Munda, Ballalae, and Rakata Bay (Miller 1949). Guadalcanal now hosted major US supply bases and staging posts, with extensive infrastructure for a range of bases and several major airfields for bombers and combat aircraft. The sheltered bays around Tulagi were used as refuelling bases or warships, as well as a base for PT boats.

Solomon Islanders were an integral part of the Allied military operations from the outset, assisting Coastwatchers, providing reconnaissance intelligence on Japanese troop movements, rescuing pilots, and castaways, and taking prisoners if they encountered them in the field (Horton 1970). Most commonly, Solomon Islanders were utilized as part of the Labour Corps, signing one-year contracts to assist in logistics and the construction of airfields and bases (Laracy & White 1988; White & Lindstrom 1990). There was also significant population movement as coastal communities fled inland to escape hostilities.

Over the following months, American forces pushed the Japanese northwards through the Solomons, employing an island hopping (or leapfrog) strategy that involved the isolation and bypassing of Japanese-held islands which offered no immediate threat, thus allowing these stranded groups to 'wither on the vine.' This loss of supply, including of essential foodstuffs, was the source of immense suffering for the abandoned Japanese forces. The successful Allied offensive against Rabaul on the 30th June 1943 was the end of the major threat in the Solomon Islands, although fighting continued on Bougainville until the end of the war. Different sources provide very different counts of total losses in the Solomons conflict, but the number of Japanese deaths from injury and illness numbers over 30,000, with Americans close to 8,000. More than sixty large vessels and submarines were sunk or beached, plus unknown numbers of smaller craft and upwards of 1,200 aircraft (e.g. Leckie 1965; Twining 2007). We have not been able to find an accounting of total deaths of Solomon Islander combatants and civilians, or a clear accounting of the extent of loss of property (although see Laracy & White 1988; Gegeo 1991; Kwai 2017).

## Depicting the War

While the processes of military engagement generated a massive volume of primary documents and still and movie imagery, this was supplemented by a formidable body of biographical accounts and secondary analyses in the years following the war. The dominant perspective on the events of World War II in the Solomon Islands is provided by the accounts of US personnel, ranging from those tasked with the oversight of major operations to individual experiences of regular soldiers, sailors, and airmen in the field (Rasor 1997; Jersey 2008). Popular imagination continues to be captured through semi-fictionalized accounts of the Solomons campaign such as Jones' (1962) *Thin Red Line* and its 1998 film adaptation, or Robert Leckie's books based on his Guadalcanal experiences (Leckie 1965, 2010), which more recently formed the basis of the 2010 television mini-series *The Pacific*. Japanese perspectives have been significantly more limited, although there have been recent attempts to expose those that exist to non-Japanese speakers via translations (e.g. Sakai 1978; Bullard 2007). Solomon Islander participation, particularly of the Scouts working with the Coastwatchers, is recognized in some but certainly not all official, biographical, and popular accounts (Miller 1949). In many instances, attention has focussed on the heroism of a small number of individuals such as the conduct of Sir Jacob Vouza (MacQuarrie 1946). There are also extensive photographic records of interactions between Islanders and both the US and Japanese servicemen (White 1987; White & Lindstrom 1990). Broader Solomon Islander memories and perspectives on World War II have been captured belatedly from the 1970s onwards through a series of oral historical and anthropological studies (e.g. White 1987, 1988; White et al., 1988; White & Lindstrom 1989, 1990; Bennett 2009).

## The Physical Legacy of World War II

Despite over seventy years having passed, the physical evidence of World War II is still evident on many of the islands in the central and western parts of the Solomon Islands. Following the end of the war, there were formal salvage operations for materiel as part of war reparations, with Solomon Islanders also extensively salvaging and incorporating discarded materials of various kinds in ways documented for many Pacific Islands (See Spennemann 1992). The ubiquitous Marsden matting from airstrip construction and repair is still a common sight around the north coast Guadalcanal.

Following the end of the war, the US base at Point Cruz on Guadalcanal, with its extensive maritime, building, and road infrastructure and its proximity to the airstrip at Henderson Field, was re-named Honiara and became the new seat for the post-war British administration, replacing Tulagi. Many of the wartime Nissen huts and structures were reoccupied and incorporated into government and private usage, while the former US 9th Army Field Hospital became the National Referral Hospital (locally referred to as No. 9) and includes some original structures which are still in use (Figure 4.2). It has only been in the last several years that these corrugated galvanized iron structures have reached their structural lifespan and have been demolished. It is worth noting that concrete fortifications and emplacements are rarely seen in the Solomon Islands, and those which exist tend to be quite small. Henderson Field is now the Solomon Islands International airport, although the several other fighter and bomber airstrips and bases near Honiara have generally been overtaken by urban development. There are notable sites nearby such as Tetere, east of Honiara, which has several dozen first-generation Amtraks neatly parked in rows above the beach (Figure 4.3). On nearby Tulagi and its neighbouring islands, Gavutu and Tasamboko, there are readily visible sites from the initial stages of the conflict, including the 1942 tunnel system dug by the Japanese prior to the American counter-attacks (Figure 4.4), as well as foundations and emplacements from the later US naval supply bases. Elsewhere across the Solomons, there is a network of bases, often attached to airstrips or flying boat landing areas, as well as ancillary sites for lookouts, radar, and gun emplacements. Some of the strips and bases further afield are still legible in the landscape, with several also being used as the basis for modern airfields. The former Japanese strip at Ballalae in the Shortland Islands to the far northwest is perhaps most famous for its collection of rare Japanese aircraft, still in situ in the World War II parking bays. The site of the Prisoner of War and slave labour camp associated with its construction is situated nearby.

The remains of World War II vessels and maritime infrastructure can be found along the shorelines in many of the main battle zones and especially near to former bases. Some of these vessels were wrecks, sunk near shore at moorings by bombing or deliberately stranded during and after the war in order to prevent sinking or to expedite salvage (Figure 4.5). Various types of pontoons, barges,

**FIGURE 4.2** Nissen hut in Chinatown area, Honiara. Photo: Martin Gibbs 2015.

**FIGURE 4.3** Amphibious landing vehicle, Tetere, Guadalcanal. Photo: Martin Gibbs 2015.

and temporary wharfs and jetties used for fuelling and other operations are also evident and have sometimes been repurposed as landfill or erosion devices. There is also the rich resource of deep-water wrecks for which Ironbottom Sound is named. World War II shoreline infrastructure has usually been seriously battered by the regular cyclonic surges and tsunamis.

**FIGURE 4.4** Japanese tunnel. Photo: Martin Gibbs 2015.

**FIGURE 4.5** World War II pontoon, Tulagi. Photo: Martin Gibbs 2015.

## Archaeological Research

Despite the significance of the Solomon Islands in the Pacific war, systematic archaeological research has been very limited. The passing of the 1980 *Protection of Wrecks and War Relic Act* saw the creation of a World War II Officer position attached to the Solomon Islands National Museum (SINM), which has monitored export of relics and assisted with various related activities, although this is largely un-resourced and unable to undertake independent research. Various terrestrial World War II sites have been recorded by SINM staff while assisting with other projects including environmental impact and mitigation surveys prior to logging developments, with sites being entered on the archaeological sites register.

The highest profile and best resourced World War II archaeological investigations in the Solomon Islands have been on the deep-water wrecks of Ironbottom Sound, by Robert Ballard (Ballard et al. 1993), and more recently around Savo Island in expeditions funded by the late Paul Allen (Kozak 2015). The less spectacular but far more numerous shallow water wrecks, abandoned barges, landing craft, and maritime infrastructure are almost completely unrecorded (see also Drew 1998). However, it is also the shallower wrecks and crashed aircraft that are also the focus for the burgeoning tourist dive industry.

At this time, the most detailed but not strictly archaeological research on sites has been done by avocational enthusiasts. These are usually historians whose interests have tended to towards the identification of historic features and landscapes, often with the intention of being used as tourism resources rather than as part of problem-oriented studies (e.g. Margry 1980; Innes 2012). Avocational research into World War II archaeological sites and objects is by far the most consistent driven by specific themes, especially the relocation of crashed aircraft and/or shipwrecks by extremely dedicated enthusiasts, undertaking intensive historical and oral historical research. This has included attempts to relocate sites, sometimes with large-scale and elaborate expeditions. The results of these efforts are often made available via web pages and reports (e.g. Stephenson 2022). These provide a valuable resource upon which to build the research and management platforms, offering as they do a longitudinal insight into site deterioration and loss.

Since 2014, the authors, who represent a collaboration between SINM staff and Australian-based university researchers, have begun pilot studies exploring the World War II landscapes and sites of the Guadalcanal and Tulagi area, in the first instance to develop a basic inventory of sites for the purposes of further research and heritage management. Details of this survey will be made available in a future publication, although in summary a variety of World War II landscapes, structures, sites and artefacts survive, albeit under increasing pressure from salvage, collectors, and development as described below.

## What does World War II Represent for Solomon Islanders?

Part of the authors' current collaborative project is a dialogue about what the World War II legacy represents for the Solomon Islands as a nation, and in consequence what to do about that legacy with regard to both future research and management of landscapes, sites, and objects. It is also worth stressing that at this stage there is currently no formal collaboration or relationship between the authors and either the US or Japan, although the staff of the SINM have regular interaction with the relevant authorities from both countries (see below).

An abiding question is what the majority of Solomon Islanders made of the war at the time during which it was fought. The various recorded oral histories, including the author's own discussions with elderly men and women who remember the war, often suggest a level of confusion as to why a war between two nations with whom they had previously had little direct involvement was taking place in their islands (Laracy & White 1988: 10; Zoleveke 1988; Kwai 2017). Early reports of the Pacific War were mostly dismissed or had limited context for most Solomon Islanders. Then, literally overnight, communities who had never seen a seagoing vessel larger than a schooner were cast into a situation where sizeable fleets including destroyers and aircraft carriers were engaged in full-scale air and sea battles on their doorstep. The not unexpected response of most civilians was to flee inland to safety. Having been a Christian nation and a British protectorate for more than two generations, much store was put in the guidance from missionaries and administrators urging assistance for the Allied forces, while active propaganda also played its part (Horton 1970: 10–11, in Kwai 2017: 57). As mentioned above, c.3,500 men worked heroically as scouts, spies, and guerrilla fighters for the Coastwatcher network and the Solomon Islands Labour Corps (SILC).

Labour, economic, and social relationships were also formed with Japanese occupiers of the various islands, although in later periods these deteriorated as the Japanese, cut off from supplies, began to demand food and labour (White 1989: 69). Most accounts make it clear that Solomon Islanders as a whole approached both sides with humanity, with many of the stories celebrating not only heroism but also relating a 'trickster' aspect enjoying the deception of the Japanese forces, without bloodshed (White 1987, 1988; White et al. 1988; White & Lindstrom 1989). Stories recorded by the authors repeated some of the themes in these previous volumes which, with the exception of the more recent work by Kwai (2017), were exclusively with men who had direct involvement with the conflict. However, interviews with women solicited complementary perspectives and included details of the meals enjoyed by rescued airmen, the discomforts of fleeing to (and living in) the bush away from village comforts, but also the thrill of receiving goods from either side, including salvage from shipwrecks.

There is not sufficient scope here to critically review the literature on the influences on or consequences of the war for Solomon Islanders. There was social and economic disruption as a result of displacement of people and destruction of property, and also a re-opening of some traditional rivalries and enmities during periods of instability. However, some writers have also discussed it in terms of a broadening of world views and political consciousness thanks to an increased exposure beyond those mediated by (British) missionaries and administrators (Gegeo 1991). This included seeing the abandonment of the islands by the

British, different relations offered through contact with the American servicemen including seeing African American GIs being treated as equal, glimpses of new technologies, and access to a wider range of material goods (White 1988; Gegeo 1991; Kwai 2017). Others have mapped out a larger post-war trajectory towards self-determination and the independence of the Solomon Islands. The emergence of the pro-nationalist *Maasina* (Marching) movement in Malaita, with its overtones of a US cargo cult, has also been suggested (Laracy 1983; Bennett 1987, 2009). Independence from Britain was, however, achieved in 1978 as part of a peaceful transition.

So, we return to asking what the significance of World War II archaeological landscapes, sites, and objects might be for modern Solomon Islanders. The short answer is possibly 'not much,' or at least not in direct terms. The outlines of the history of World War II are taught within schools, and there has in recent years been a celebration of the role of the Solomon Islander Scouts and Coastwatchers as part of a rebuilding of a post-colonial national narrative (Kwai 2017). The SILC has not come in for similar plaudits and might plausibly be seen as creating a stronger link between the contemporary Solomon Islands communities and the sites they helped to construct. But what of the value of rusting helmets, decayed landing barges, or disused airstrips? Some of the points below are as much a factor of the interests of our Solomon Islander colleagues and co-authors, themselves trained archaeologists, with legislative responsibilities under the 1980 Act and a broad world view as internationally travelled professionals on the long-term necessities for preserving heritage items. Many of these themes are also familiar from the various writings of Dirk Spennemann on the World War II legacy in Micronesia (see, e.g. Spennemann 1992, 2006). However, it is a starting point.

As for many places throughout the Pacific, the immediate wartime and post-war period can be linked to a range of physicalities, including social and economic disruption from movements of populations to 'safe' areas, the loss of land and possessions, and access to material items from both nations as gifts, payments, or small- and large-scale salvage (Spennemann 1992, 2001, 2006). The re-appropriation and re-purposing of sites and buildings also followed the war, as ownership of land and a revived British administrative framework were re-established. This direct economic benefit has understandably diminished over time but has increasingly been replaced by indirect values as tourism 'product.'

The potential of World War II sites and objects has long had a recognized value for tourism in the Solomon Islands, initially via their use as a focus for commemoration by former Allied and Japanese servicemen and their families (see Lipscomb 2003). As generational changes occurred, this has increasingly shifted to recreational wreck diving and more distanced forms of historical tourism have increasingly emerged (TRIP Consultants 2016). Alongside this, the erection of formal memorials in the Solomon Islands has been ongoing and often the source of tension at both local and international levels, in particular with regards to the choices of location and the ongoing maintenance of these commemorative places and items. Anthropologist Geoffrey White (1996, 2015) and more recently Solomon Islander historian Annie Kwai (2017) have both explored the longer-term relationships between Solomon Islanders and World War II relics, memories, and memorialization, as well as some of the problems with the uneven representations presented by them (Figure 4.6). There has been limited analysis of the potential damage to World War II sites as a consequence of tourism, and in balance the benefits to community and local interest in preserving viable product for tourists are more likely to afford some protection and encourage transfer of local knowledge.

There are several privately owned museums ranging from the extensive collection of aircraft parts and artillery at Vilu (west of Honiara) down to smaller holdings of objects that are shown to the visitors of nearby World War II sites. Almost none of these objects have been conserved or treated and most are deteriorating rapidly. There is currently no coordinated approach to World War II tourism and limited assistance towards conservation and heritage planning beyond advice from largely un-resourced the SINM World War II Officer. The SINM has a small World War II collection (c.1,000 items), established in 2009 largely as a result of purchases from people who had come forward with heirlooms or salvaged items. With the exception of mounting a small display of

**FIGURE 4.6** Solomon Scouts and Coastwatchers Memorial, Honiara, Guadalcanal. Photo: Martin Gibbs 2015.

these items in its Honiara gallery, until now SINM has largely left World War II museum display to private interests.

Broadly related to the nexus between commemoration and recognition or conservation of the archaeological resource are the activities of the US *Defense POW/MIA Accounting Agency* and Japan's *Ministry of Health, Labor, and Welfare*, both of which continue to send teams to undertake the recovery of human remains from the Solomon Islands. While the former nation removes remains for identification at a centralized facility in Hawaii, the latter has pursued a policy of cremation within the Solomon Islands that sees only the ashes returned to surviving relatives (if the remains can be firmly identified). SINM staff have assisted with these processes, although the recording and sharing of information has been very much skewed towards the repatriation process rather than archaeological or heritage value. While the US recoveries tend to be professional investigators and tightly focussed on particular sites, there are emergent concerns surrounding more recent work by the Japanese teams, which are starting to encourage a broader volunteer base of untrained enthusiasts. These volunteers have engaged with recovery as a laudable cross-generational commemorative process (Fackler 2014) but reportedly have limited concern with recording where human remains and objects are recovered from. At this time, neither group release the details of their recoveries as research outcomes, although the intention is to see whether this information can be obtained for incorporation into current projects.

It is worth noting that several times during conversations or interviews regarding World War II sites, local people on Guadalcanal, Santa Isabel, and Tulagi have mentioned a sense of unease about the presence of such large numbers of dead foreigners on their lands. Although most people were at pains to stress that these concerns were now largely in the past (usually with reference to the fears of their grandparents), they did note the potential problems of 'uneasy' spirits. Foreign voices coming from the bush at night were seen as just one marker of this, although sometimes this also blended into stories about 'holdout' Japanese soldiers. Removal and proper burial or treatment of foreign remains was seen as a positive step. Similarly, as for many Pacific nations impacted by World War II, unexploded ordnance remains a serious danger and there are frequent discoveries of live munitions (Safeground 2016). The Australian and New Zealand militaries continue to make regular tours to defuse and destroy, such as through *Operation Render Safe*. Many areas still have warning posters with advice on marking and avoiding sites should people encounter explosive materials.

A more difficult situation has been the long-term pressure from collectors wanting to remove World War II relics, especially the rarer forms of aircraft crashed or abandoned on various islands (such as at Ballalae). The 1980 *Protection of Wrecks and War Relic Act* was passed in response to several specific threats and acted to provide some protection for significant sites by restricting export without a formal license, as well as to establish full exclusion zones around wrecks (White 1996; Forrest & Corrin 2013). Ironically, this heritage legislation significantly pre-dated any laws protecting sites of local cultural significance. In some instances, avocational enthusiasts and visitors have acted to remove significant relics, avowing that they are attempting to protect or conserve important heritage sites and objects which they perceive as unmanaged and/or at risk of destruction (see Forrest & Corrin 2013).

The salvage or removal of World War II materials was compounded by the c.1998–2003 period of civil unrest known as 'the [Ethnic] Tensions,' which saw the weakening or collapse of many government controls as well as significant economic and social disruption. During this period, there was recovery and repurposing of World War II materiel (guns and munitions) for use in the conflict, samples of which were collected during the disarmament process of the mid-2000s. The strained financial circumstances of many Guadalcanal residents also led to the large-scale salvaging of World War II-era metals from aircraft, wrecks, and buildings for sale to Malaysian Chinese scrap merchants, although SINM staff were partially successful in stemming this by deploying the export restrictions afforded by the 1980 Act. There is strong suspicion that some of the exported 'scrap' was also being directed to foreign collectors. Recovery of small World War II items from battlefields for sale to tourists was also taking place, as was more overt and large-scale disturbance of sites in search of 'treasure.'

Following the cessation of civil hostilities, there has been a significant population boom around Honiara, partially a function of renewed economic investment and a desire by young Solomon Islanders to be nearer to the opportunities this offers. However, this has also seen significant formal and informal urban and industrial development across many of the areas which were once the iconic battlefields of the Guadalcanal conflict. None of these sites have yet been the subject of archaeological recording. In 2018 the iconic site of Bloody Ridge (Edson's Ridge) was declared a 'National peace park' in a bid to prevent illegal squatter settlement and farming from extending up the sides of the hills and destroying this significant cultural landscape.

## The World War II Legacy in the Solomon Islands – Ways Forward

In many respects, the Solomon Islands is still recovering from the civil unrest of the 'Tensions,' with the project of nation building being very much in the mind of government. The 2011 unveiling of memorial to the Coastwatchers did include a short resurgence of interest in World War II, but the largely foreign conflict still holds a somewhat ambiguous place in the national psyche, as does the value of the remnants of this now several generations old conflict. The SINM continues building relations with communities who own World War II heritage sites and have regular interactions with salvage yards, exporters, and other government departments to try to stem the flow of World War II exports. There are also still opportunities for direct and indirect oral histories from those who remember the war, or to receive accounts of local activities from their elders.

For the authors as archaeologists, our collaborative project has already engaged with a traditional process of survey, identification, and recording of the sites around the Guadalcanal-Tulagi area and in the future will consider what these can tell us about the evolution of military doctrine and strategy, as well as a battlefield innovation and the evolution of the conflict landscapes in this first open struggle between the US and Japan. However, we are also pursuing a broader strategy, using students and volunteers in Australia and the Solomon Islands in order to draw together a much wider range of historical and other sources in a desktop study of World War II sites throughout the Solomons. There have been dozens of articles in tourist and dive magazines locating, describing, and photographing World War II sites. Similarly, there are the formal US and Japanese lists of wrecks and aircraft crashes, as well as the various avocational and archaeological research projects that can also provide information on terrestrial and marine sites. Through the collaborative process, we hope to generate a database and some understanding of the conservation status of the World War II legacy which can then be used in SI National and Provincial government and tourism planning.

## Acknowledgements

Our thanks to Director Mr Tony Heorake for the continuing support of the SINM, to Dr. David Roe for his advice and assistance, Ewen Stephenson (Archaeohistoria) for generously providing information, and to the late John Keopo (archaeologist – SINM) and John Innes (historian) in recognition of their pioneering work in the field.

## References

Ambrose, H. 2011. *The Pacific: Hell Was an Ocean Away*. New York: New American Library.

Ballard, R., Archbold, R. & Minge, U.D 1993. *The Lost Ships of Guadalcanal*. New York: Warner Books.

Bennett, J. 1987. *The Wealth of the Solomons: A History of a Pacific Archipelago*. Honolulu: University of Hawaii Press.

Bennett, J. 2009. *Natives and Exotics: World War II and Environment in the Southern Pacific*. Honolulu: University of Hawaii Press.

Bullard, S., trans. 2007. *Japanese Army Operations in the South Pacific Area: New Britain and Papua Campaigns 1942–43*. Canberra: Australian War Memorial. [Translated Extracts of Bōeichō Bōei and Kenshūjo Senshishitsu, eds. 1968. *Senshi sōsho: Minami Taiheiyō Rikugun Sakusen*. Tokyo: Asaguma Shinbusha].

Drew, T. 1998. 'Solomon Islands: Guadalcanal Shipwrecks Revisited', *Bulletin of the Australasian Institute for Maritime Archaeology*, 22, 71–74.

Fackler, M. 2014. 'Japanese Unearth Remains, and Their Nation's Past, on Guadalcanal', *New York Times*, Nov. 29, 2014 [WWW] https://www.nytimes.com/2014/11/30/world/japanese-unearth-remains-and-their-nations-past-on-guadalcanal.html (accessed 29/08/2018).

Forrest, C. & Corrin, J. 2013. 'Legal Pluralism in the Pacific: Solomon Island's World War II Heritage', *International Journal of Cultural Property*, 20, 1–21.

Gegeo, D.W. 1991. 'World War II in the Solomons: Its Impact on Society, Politics, and World View.' In: G. White, ed. *Remembering the Pacific War.* Occasional Paper series 36. Honolulu: Center for Pacific Islands Studies, 27–35.

Horton, D. 1970. *Fire over the Islands: The Coast Watchers of the Solomons.* Sydney: Reed.

Innes, J. 2012. *Guide to the Guadalcanal Battlefields.* Research Notes Provided by Mr John Innes.

Jersey, S.C. 2008. *Hell's Islands: The Untold Story of Guadalcanal.* Houston: Texas A&M University Press.

Kozak, G. 2015. 'Mapping the Ghost Fleet of Iron Bottom Sound', *Ocean News and Technology Magazine* Monday, 01 June 2015, GK Consulting. [WWW] https://www.oceannews.com/feature-story/2015/06/01/may-feature-story (accessed 29/08/2018).

Kwai, A. 2017. *Islanders in the World War II: An indigenous perspective.* Canberra: Australian National University Press.

Laracy, H. 1987. *Pacific Protest: The Maasina Rule Movement, Solomon Islands, 1944–52.* Suva: Institute of Pacific Studies.

Laracy H. & G. White, eds. 1988. *Taem Blong Faet: World War II in Melanesia.* Special Issue of *'O'o: Journal of Solomon Islands Studies.* No. 4. Honiara: Solomon Islands Centre.

Leckie, R. 2010. *Helmet for My Pillow.* New York: Bantam Books.

Leckie, R. 1965. *Challenge for the Pacific: Guadalcanal, the Turning Point of the War.* New York: Doubleday.

Lipscomb, A. 2003. 'Village-Based Tourism in the Solomon Islands: Impediments and Impacts.' In: E. Laws, B. Faulkner and G. Moscardo, eds. *Embracing and Managing Change in Tourism: International Case Studies.* New York: Routledge, 185–201.

MacQuarrie, H. 1946. *Vouza and the Solomon Islands.* Sydney: Angus and Robertson.

Margry, K., ed. 1980. *Guadalcanal: After the Battle No. 108.* London: After the Battle UK.

Miller, J. 1949. *Guadalcanal: The First Offensive.* Washington, DC: Centre for Military History.

Rasor, E. 1997. *The Solomon Islands Campaign, Guadalcanal to Rabaul: Historiography and Annotated Bibliography.* London: Greenwood Press.

Rottman, G. 2005. *Japanese Army in World War II. Conquest of the Pacific 1941–42.* Oxford: Osprey.

Safeground. 2016. *Safeground: Reducing the Impacts of War.* [WWW] https://safeground.org.au/project/solomon-islands/ (accessed 29/08/2018).

Sakai, S., Caidin, M. & Saito., F. 1978. *Samurai!* New York: Bantam.

Spennemann, D.H. 1992. 'Apocalypse Now? The Fate of World War II Sites on the Central Pacific Islands', *CRM Bulletin: A National Park Service Technical Bulletin,* 15 (2), 15–22.

Spennemann, D.H. 2001. 'Secondary Use World War II Equipment in the Marshalls. Japanese Rice Cookers — A Photo Essay.' [WWW] http:/marshall.csu.edu.au/Marshalls/html/WWII/RiceCookers.html (accessed 29 August 2018).

Spennemann, D.H. 2006. 'Examples of Adaptive Re-Use of World War II Artefacts in Micronesia', *Micronesian Journal of the Humanities and Social Sciences,* 5 (1/2), 268–84.

Stephenson, E. 2022. *Archaeohistoria.* [WWW] https://archaehistoria.org/ (accessed 29 August 2018).

Toll, I. 2011. *Pacific Crucible: War at Sea in the Pacific, 1941–1942.* New York: W. W. Norton & Company.

TRIP Consultants. 2016. *The Solomon Islands National Tourism Development Strategy 2015 – 2019.* Report for the Pacific Regional Tourism Capacity Building Programme (PRTCBP). [WWW] http://macbio-pacific.info/wp-content/uploads/2017/08/National-Tourism-Strategy-2015.pdf (accessed 29/08/2018).

Twining, M.B. 2007. *No Bended Knee: The Battle for Guadalcanal*. New York: Random House.

White, G. 1987. *Pacific Encounters: Island Memories of World War II*. Honolulu: East-West Center.

White, G. 1988. 'The Big Death: What Pacific Islanders can teach us about World War II.' In: H. Laracy and G. White, eds. *Taem Blong Faet: World War II in Melanesia*. Special Issue of *'O'o: Journal of Solomon Islands Studies*, 4, 75–78.

White, G. 1989. 'Wartime Encounters in Santa Isabel.' In: G. White and L. Lindstrom, eds. *The Pacific Theater: Island Representations of World War II*. Honolulu: University of Hawaii Press, 43–72.

White, G. 1991. *Identity through History: Living Stories in a Solomon Islands* Society. Cambridge, MA: Cambridge University Press.

White, G. 1996. 'War Remains: The Culture of Preservation in the Southwest Pacific', *Cultural Resource Management*, 24 (5), 9–13.

White, G. 2015. 'The Coastwatcher Mythos: The Politics and Poetics of Solomon Islands War Memory.' In: G. Carr and K. Reeves, eds. *Heritage and Memory of War: Responses from Small Islands*. London: Routledge, 194–218.

White, G., Akin, D., Gegeo, D. & Watson-Gegeo, K., eds. 1988. *The Big Death: Solomon Islanders Remember World War II*. Suva: University of the South Pacific.

White, G. & Lindstrom, L. 1989. *The Pacific Theater: Island Representations of World War II*. Honolulu: University of Hawaii Press.

White, G. & Lindstrom, L. 1990. *Island Encounters: Black and White Memories of the Pacific War*. Washington: Smithsonian Institution Press.

Zoleveke, G. 1988. 'The War Was Not Our War', In H. Laracy and G. White, eds. *Taem Blong Faet: World War II in Melanesia*. Special Issue of *'O'o: Journal of Solomon Islands Studies*, 4, 75–78.

# PART 2
# 1944

# 5

# CHUUK LAGOON WORLD WAR II UNDERWATER CULTURAL HERITAGE

## A Divers' Paradise, a Chuukese Dilemma?

*Bill Jeffery*

## Introduction

World War II was a terrible time for the indigenous people of Micronesia. Many lives were lost; islands, villages, traditional sites, and ways of life were greatly impacted. The aftermath brought new colonial rulers. It also brought many foreign tourists to visit the region, some to view the remnants and reminders of World War II. Contemporary management and interpretation of these historic sites is primarily based on foreign interests.

This chapter investigates and compares the research and management of the World War II underwater cultural heritage in Chuuk, Federated States of Micronesia (FSM), with its terrestrial World War II heritage. An analysis of historical information, oral histories, and the results of a number of site surveys is brought together in considering how Chuukese were impacted by the war and how and why they now 'use' the World War II sites. The aims of this investigation are to consider the various values of the World War II cultural heritage, and to consider a way forward in their research, management, and interpretation, which incorporates a multi-vocal and locally relevant approach.

## Chuuk Lagoon

Chuuk Lagoon (formerly known as Truk Lagoon) is the central and most populated region of Chuuk State, one of four states of the FSM, the other three being Pohnpei, Kosrae and Yap. It is located 3,700 km south-east of Tokyo and 4,000 km north of Sydney.

Chuuk Lagoon is enclosed by a circular shape barrier reef of approximately 63 km in diameter and encompasses an area of 2,125 km². The lagoon contains eighteen inhabited high volcanic islands and is the fourth largest atoll in the

DOI: 10.4324/9780429270468-7

FSM. The barrier reef contains sixty-nine low-lying coralline islets and a limited number of passes for ships to sail through. Inside the lagoon, the depth of water can reach seventy metres. Outside, it drops off very quickly, reaching 1,000 m within one km of the barrier reef.

## Indigenous History

The first inhabitants of Chuuk, from about 2,000 BP, were initially coastal dwellers living in stilt houses (Rainbird 2004: 51–69). Around 500 years ago, hilltop occupation and more sedentary settlement on the coast and hill slopes appeared. The hilltop settlements were characterized by shell middens, wooden meeting houses (*wuuts*), and stone forts which 'created a perception of territoriality, this in turn seems to have caused friction which led to intra and inter-island warfare, as is suggested by the numerous forts' (Rainbird 1993: 17).

Chuuk society is structured around matrilineal clans which were ranked according to their time of settlement, numerical strength, knowledge and skills, amount of land ownership, and success in battle. Ownership of a piece of land also meant ownership of the adjacent reef and its resources and for a clan or village, this could extend to a section of the barrier reef. Chuukese have spiritual and customary associations with whole and parts of islands, which can reflect their cultural identity and inform a sense of place. An ethnographic study revealed that some islands were named according to their shape and in some cases, such as on Tonoas the various features of the islands symbolized, as well as influenced the spiritual and physical characteristics of their inhabitants (Young et al. 1997: 16–17).

## Colonial History

The first foreigners to make contact with the inhabitants of Chuuk were Spaniards in 1565. They were reportedly harassed by Chuukese in canoes throwing spears and attempting to cut lose the ship's launch (Hezel 1973: 52–53). It could be that this hostility was a major reason the next Spaniard did not enter Chuuk Lagoon until 1814. Chuuk was not part of the Spanish plans for the region, despite the superb anchorage that the lagoon afforded, given it was south of the trading routes for the galleons sailing between Mexico, Guam, and Manila.

Further foreign contact came from British, German, French, Japanese, Russian, Australian, and American explorers, traders, black-birders, whalers, and missionaries. These foreign contacts were deadly for many indigenous inhabitants—particularly from introduced diseases—and many died. A British trader named Andrew Cheyne (1852: 126–27) noted that the population of the whole group in 1844 was about 15,000–20,000 and warned anyone sailing past the area not to have anything to do with the inhabitants, given their treacherous nature. Others, such as the French Captain Dumont d'Urville who visited Chuuk Lagoon in 1828, had observed Chuukese women had been secreted out of sight. Harassment of Chuukese women and the introduction of diseases gave Chuukese good reason to be hostile to foreigners and to keep them away.

While Spain claimed sovereignty over Chuuk and the rest of the Caroline Islands from 1885, their impact was limited in comparison with following rulers. Following the Spanish-American War, Germany acquired the Caroline Islands in 1899, with the United States of America holding onto Guam. German administration was much more 'hands-on' across the FSM. In attempting to stamp out the violence and unrest in Chuuk, a number of Japanese were expelled, hundreds of guns were confiscated, and a German warship shelled and totally destroyed a small islet as a show of strength (Jeffery 2007: 79–82). In 1901, they initiated the appointment of regional chiefs over six areas of Chuuk Lagoon, 'each of them given a flag as a symbol of his share in the imperial authority of Germany' (Hezel 1995: 98).

With the outbreak of war in Europe in the summer of 1914, Britain requested Japan's help to counter the German Navy in the East China Sea. Within eleven days, Japanese forces occupied all of the major Micronesian islands, except Guam and the Gilbert Islands, and the Navy 'made it plain that it did not welcome the entry of any other ships into Micronesian waters, even those of its allies' (Peattie 1988: 44). After the war, Japan ruled over Micronesia under a Class C Mandate under conditions from the League of Nations. This was a time of great upheaval for all Micronesians. Japan wanted economic development of the islands but also to 'Japanize the islanders through education, propaganda, intermarriage, and in general the promotion of cultural changes' (Mirrer 1971: 23). In 1940, there were 14,735 Chuukese and about 4,000 Japanese; in 1945, the population was 9,082 Chuukese and 39,945 Japanese.

## World War II in Chuuk

Japan occupied the islands in FSM until 1945, establishing many military fortifications and facilities, particularly in Chuuk where Japan established one of its four regional offices. Chuuk was the Fourth Fleet Headquarters and the base for Imperial Japanese Navy Combined Fleet from 1942 to 1944. The Japanese military established over 1,200 buildings on the island of Tonoas alone. They were used as offices, warehouses, magazines, personnel shelters, barracks, government buildings, maintenance and repair facilities, Dublon Town for civilians, a fish cannery (which was established by Okinawans and *Nan'yō-chō*), a saltwater distiller, and hospital facilities (JICPOA, 1944: 10). Many of the lagoon islands were heavily fortified and four airfields were established.

Immediately following the attack on Pearl Harbor, the Japanese Fourth Fleet departed Chuuk and captured American bases in Guam (10th of December 1941). On the 21st of January 1942, a Japanese Taskforce departed Chuuk to invade Rabaul, landing on the 23rd of January and taking Lae and Salamaua on the 8th of March that year. The main Japanese motives for taking Rabaul, Lae, and Salamaua early in the war were to enforce a blockade of supply routes between the US and Australia, and to protect Chuuk from southern approach Allied air attacks (Bailey 2000: 13). From Chuuk, a Japanese fleet departed to invade New Guinea, which led to the Battle of the Coral Sea (7th–8th of May 1942), in which both the Japanese and Americans lost an aircraft carrier.

With Rabaul in Japanese hands, Chuuk became the advance base for operations in the southeastern Pacific, and with the landing of Japanese forces on Guadalcanal in the Solomons in July 1942, Chuuk became the rear-area naval and defence headquarters for the Imperial Japanese Navy Combined Fleet. The fleet operated between Chuuk and Rabaul, and supplies, materiel, aircraft, ships, and military personnel came from Japan through Chuuk to Rabaul. In Chuuk, the fleet replenished, rested, and was repaired to the extent that Chuuk's facilities could handle. New pilots also received their latest training before heading onto the frontlines.

In August 1943, Chuuk was designated as a Key Advance Base in which the Combined Fleet assembled and other bases were used to defend the area 'from the Kuril Islands in the north, through the Marshalls and the Gilberts down to the sea north of the Solomons' (USN 1952a: 12). Each island base was left to defend itself, leaving the Combined Fleet to conduct its own decisive battle (USN 1952a: 9). This was the time when the Chuuk base was heavily fortified with the arrival of more than 14,000 army personnel and equipment.

## Operation Hailstone

During late 1943 to early 1944, American Carrier Task Force 58 moved through the Pacific conquering all ahead of it, landing in the Gilbert Islands on the 21st of November 1943 and in Kwajalein in the Marshalls on the 1st of February 1944. The Japanese Navy had failed 'to force a decisive navy battle when Americans invaded the Gilberts and the Marshalls largely because of the shortage of carrier-born air strength' (USN 1952a: 15). As it pushed further west, Task Force 58 launched an attack on Chuuk, beginning on the 17th of February 1944. Hesitant about Chuuk's defences but armed with photographs of the base from a fly-over earlier in February, they decided not to launch an amphibious invasion but instead a series of aircraft attacks to neutralize the four airstrips and destroy the aircraft and ships stationed there.

A US photo-reconnaissance flight on the 4th of February 1944 observed and documented about sixty large ships (half being naval vessels) in Chuuk Lagoon. Also located in the lagoon were a number of smaller vessels including fifty sampans, fourteen tugs, three 500-ton fuel barges, three water lighters, and seventeen smaller vessels (USSBS, 1947: 3). Task Force 58, comprising four large aircraft carriers, thirteen light carriers, six battleships, six heavy cruisers, twenty-seven destroyers, ten submarines, and a number of support ships, lying about 160 km to the north and east of the lagoon, sent out a continuous wave of aircraft on the 17th and 18th of February 1944 in an aerial bombardment campaign known as 'Operation Hailstone.'

A total of '1,250 combat sorties from the carriers dropped over 500 tons of bombs and torpedoes' (Carrell 1991: 237) over the two days, with the attacks including 'the first US carrier aircraft night attacks against enemy shipping' (Bailey 2000: 153). Japanese Monograph No. 173 (USN 1952b: 109a–109e) identified fifty-three ships and submarines sunk or destroyed inside and outside of the lagoon during the 17th and 18th of February 1944.

About 250,000 tons of merchant ships were sunk in Chuuk in February 1944, and together with a similar amount being sunk by US submarines in the same month, the total Japanese losses amounted to 548,376 tons; 'over 10% of all the merchantmen afloat when the month began. It was a disastrous month for Japan's merchant marine' (Parillo 1993: 137). It was the largest loss of merchant marine tonnage for any one month for the whole war (USN 1952c: 171–240). This lack of an effective strategy to defend the merchant marine and the continual bickering between the Japanese Army and Navy seem to have played a role in the loss of Japanese merchant ships throughout the Pacific, including at Chuuk.

To the US, the attack of Chuuk was highly successful. The US Navy's historian Samuel Eliot Morison (1975: 329–32) stated that: 'The strike on Truk demonstrated a virtual revolution in naval warfare; the aircraft carrier emerged as the capital ship of the future, with unlimited potentialities.' Japanese military personnel were recorded after the war as noting: 'The big air strike on Truk by the planes of an American striking Task Force on 17 February took such a heavy toll that it was called "Another Pearl Harbor" by the Japanese forces' (USN 1952a: 29). The US plans were to neutralize the Chuuk base so Japanese aircraft could not play any role in attacking the Carrier Task Force operating in the Marianas and New Guinea (Poyer et al., 2001: 144).

The Japanese Army, which had reached its full complement by April 1944, implemented much of the fortification work at Chuuk, as they were in command of the defences. The large coastal defence guns and anti-aircraft guns that were positioned on most hilltops used a system of connecting tunnels as major transport routes. Denfield (1981: 17) carried out a survey of the World War II remains in Chuuk in 1979 and found 101 Army guns (75–105 mm), eighty-five Navy guns (75–200 mm), and about 302 automatic weapons of smaller calibre. By April 1944, the fortifications were thought to be in good shape but a revision of plans and additional facilities were added right up until the end of the war.

On the 30th of April and 1st of May 1944, the US Carrier Task Force 58 carried out another attack of Chuuk as Japanese Army troops and aircraft from Rabaul had been sent to strengthen the defences. The USSBS (1947: 9) noted that eight aircraft remained serviceable after the February attack and just prior to the April attack, there were between eighty-one and 104 aircraft in Chuuk. A total of 2,200 US sorties being flown during this attack led to the dropping of 748 tons of bombs. A further ninety-three aircraft were destroyed, '423 buildings and six hangers were destroyed and 44 buildings were damaged … This carrier attack virtually nullified Truk's value as a supply and airbase' (USSBS 1947: 14).

Denfield (1981: 51) calculated that 6,878 tons of bombs were dropped in total, killing 499 Japanese Army and Navy personnel and wounding 572; and killing sixty-three and wounding sixty Chuukese; with a further 4,000 lost on the ships. A secret US document that was declassified in 1985 records that the Japanese fleet in Chuuk was initially selected as a target for the atomic bomb, the reasoning being that if the bomb failed to explode, it would be lost in the lagoon, thus 'preserving the secrets of US nuclear weaponry' (Stewart, 1989: 97).

## Impact of the War on the Chuukese

Poyer *et al.* (2001) in *The Typhoon of War,* which was based on interviews with many Micronesians about their war experiences, found that Chuukese were greatly impacted when the Japanese Army arrived in January 1944. They found that up until that time much of the hard work was done by civilian or foreign prisoner labour and that travel and food continued normally (Poyer *et al.* 2001: 49). When the Japanese Army arrived, life changed and Chuuk was turned into a fortress by the Army using Chuukese labour and according to one informant, Mori Masataka, 'that's when the war started' (Poyer *et al.* 2001: 49).

In discussions with the Chiefs on Tonoas in 2001–02, I was told about the changes in many Japanese-Chuukese relations particularly with the Japanese Army in January-February of 1944. The Army commandeered Chuukese homes, Japanese civilian homes, and schools. They also tore homes down, built new ones or cleared the land for military facilities (Poyer *et al.* 2001: 82–84). The Army greatly increased the use of Chuukese labour (men and women) to drag large coastal defence guns up to the strategic hilltops, killing some Chuukese in the process (Aisek, Gradvin pers comm. 2002). In addition, Chuukese historic sites on many islands, such as Fauba on Tol, which were positioned in strategic locations on hilltops, were interfered with by the Japanese (Craib 1997: 7).

Tonoas, being the headquarters for the Navy in Chuuk, was most heavily impacted, as people had to leave their villages and were relocated in other Tonoas villages or on other islands in order to make way for the military facilities. In 1935, the indigenous population of Tonoas and Etten was 1,293, in 1945 it was 296 (Thompson 1945: 2). Tong Misa, Chairman of the Chiefs of Tonoas in 2002, worked as a deckhand on the small supply ships for the Japanese Navy and told me that if he missed work, Navy personnel would come and search for him, violently rebuking him, and because much of the island had been cleared, there was nowhere to hide (Misa, Tong pers comm. 2002). In other cases, 'people were beaten, stripped naked, and hung in public to shame them when they missed work' and children were conscripted to work on farms and in military constructions (Poyer *et al.* 2001: 103, 109).

Joshua Suka, a Chuukese man I met on Tonoas in 2001 and who was used to make seals for the Japanese before the war, had fond memories of the Japanese facilities in Dublon Town on Tonoas, which included theatres, ice-cream shops, and all other kinds of stores (Suka, Joshua pers comm. 2002). The war changed

Joshua's world—he was sent away from Tonoas to live elsewhere but returned after the war. A number of years later, when Japanese returned to honour their fallen comrades, Joshua received many visitors. Other Chiefs of Tonoas whom I met in 2001 and 2002, and who were young men during the war and 'worked' for the Japanese, all relayed similar stories of good pre-war and bad war times in Chuuk, especially when the Japanese Army arrived. Many were used as slave labour during the war to help with establishing Japan's military facilities on the islands.

In addition to the constant bombing for eighteen months, US submarines sunk many transport ships to Chuuk, which stopped much needed supplies and equipment reaching the base. This very limited transport into Chuuk caused a severe shortage of food for all of the nearly 50,000 inhabitants and placed great pressure on the continuing supply of local foods—taro, breadfruit, coconut, and bananas (which had been decimated by removal and bombing). Japanese military personnel had already dug up some taro patches and replaced them with watercress and sweet potato. They threatened to shoot any Chuukese who took coconuts and breadfruit (that traditionally belonged to them) and Stewart (1989: 71) notes an occasion when one Chuukese man was shot during an attempt to take some potatoes grown on his own land.

It is unknown how many Pacific Islanders were killed during the war in the Pacific. While the numbers would be comparatively small, it was not a war that was of their making, and those who survived were greatly impacted. Turner and Falgout (2002: 112) concluded: 'Those who experienced the intense suffering during the Japanese military buildup and the American campaign describe it as the greatest hardship they ever endured.' Similarly, Poyer *et al.* (2001: 14) found that 'World War II in Micronesia meant, in short, both terrible suffering and momentous change. Nothing would ever be the same again.'

Japanese surrender of the Chuuk base and its territory took place on the USS *Portland* on the 2nd of September 1945. While US plans for Chuuk had not been formalized, 'it was understood that Truk was to be used as a fleet anchorage and recreation centre' (Blake, 1945). A survey of the facilities in Chuuk found that they were either very limited, such as no deep-water wharves; or were destroyed and inoperable, as in the case of the navigation aids, piers, wharves, and airfields; or undeveloped, as with the recreation facilities. A total of eighteen recommendations were made about the major work required, including salvage of the shipwrecks, and the need for 2,952 officers and enlisted men. No mention was made about Chuukese interests or land ownership in this discussion on creating a US recreation centre in Chuuk.

## Truk Atoll Advisory Council Meetings

An initial activity for the US administrators in Chuuk was to establish a series of formal weekly meetings with representatives of various lagoon islands, initially called the 'Meeting of Truk Atoll Advisory Council'. A review of the minutes of the first few meetings provides some interesting details on the major issues that Chuukese and the US Navy administrators faced in Chuuk. Some of the early issues discussed at the first meeting on the 13th of December 1945 included: improvement of sanitation; for Chuukese to start farming to provide food; confirmation of the appointment of Chuukese Police; and information on Chuukese skilled and unskilled labour to help the American rebuilding efforts (Lands 1945a). To the Chuukese, the main points they made to the US administrators included: their desire to reclaim their land and homes and to have Japanese moved away as quickly as possible to stop them from destroying their property; concern over money placed into Japanese postal savings; to obtain more food (especially pigs and chickens); and the need for schooling in the English language. Chief Moses from Tonoas spoke of how the Japanese had dynamited a church on his island and one of his houses during the two weeks prior to the meeting and when challenged, they stated 'we blew it up because Americans must clean the shore' (Lands 1945a). Chief Albert Mailo from Weno also complained about similar destruction of his property.

The US Navy administrators stated that all the Japanese military should be off the islands within a month (although some were still working for the Americans one year later) and landowners could start to move back to their islands as the Japanese moved. At the second meeting of Truk Atoll Advisory Council on the 20th of December 1945, considerable anger was expressed by the Chuukese about the Japanese presence, about them using Chuukese boats without payment, the need for compensation for Japanese occupying their land, cutting down their trees, pulling down timber houses and burning the timber, and the lack of help in rehabilitating their land, houses, and facilities (Lands, 1945b).

An important issue that pervaded many of the meetings, particularly in the first couple of months was the need for Chuukese to reclaim their land, their houses, and boats, in addition to controlling Japanese interfering in this process. Within a few months of the US arriving in Chuuk, the US Navy administrators had also established some health care, schools, and jobs for Chuukese. However, they had also alienated some Chuukese from their land, re-established a whole-of-the-lagoon chief similar to that established by the Germans, introduced a tax system on each and every person to help pay for public works, and criticized the work ethic of some Chuukese though they were keen to assist them in various commercial ventures, which some Chuukese saw as problematic.

## Chuukese Views on the US War Victory

While the immediate post-war period was welcomed and had a positive evaluation throughout Micronesia, a number of Chuukese interviewed by Poyer et al. (2001) were openly critical of this period compared to the pre-war days under the Japanese stating:

> When they [Americans] came, they brought corned beef and distributed it to the people for a few months. After that, it stopped. And there were not

enough jobs to go around. On the other hand, during the Japanese time, there were more jobs than there were workers.

*(Ichios Eas interviewed and reported in Poyer et al. 2001: 292–93)*

On the 1st of October 1945, when the 'US Military Government Unit, Truk' was first commissioned, thirty-one officers and eighty-three enlisted men were assigned duty (McCarley 1945a: 16). In 1946, only fifty-five US Navy personnel were based there, which greatly contrasted with Japanese pre-war days when many Japanese civilians and Chuukese worked and lived side by side and many were fluent in the Chuukese language. This would have contributed to the feeling amongst Micronesians that Americans were more bureaucratic and less keen to befriend Chuukese (Poyer *et al.* 2001: 292). Coupled with the fact that a number of Chuukese and Japanese married and had children, some of whom fought for the Japanese outside of Micronesia, this level of 'sentiment and emotion was not easily forgotten or overcome by American liberation of the islands' (Hanlon 1998: 25).

Lieutenant John Useem (1945) of the US Naval Reserve wrote a number of reports and journal articles about American military rule in Micronesia, the reactions of the Micronesians to American rule, and the war and relations between American, Micronesians, Japanese, and Koreans. In September 1945, he concluded: 'Micronesians do not regard the Americans as liberators who saved them from an awful fate'. In fact, he saw the welfare of the people as much poorer given the Japanese had 'provided a high material standard of living and security' (Useem 1945: 100). Hanlon (1999: 70) also cites further work by Useem about Micronesian resistance against Japanese colonialism before and during the war and how Micronesians maintained a 'viable cultural identity that allowed for survival even in the face of a world war.'

In 1951, civilian administrators from the US Department of Interior replaced the US Navy. The *1985–1989 FSM First National Development Plan* (OPS 1985: 4) referred to the Navy period as a time when 'there was virtually no internal development, either economically or politically' and which produced the term 'rust territory' (Hezel 1992: 16). While a 1950 report from the 'High Commissioner of the Trust Territory of the Pacific Islands to United Nations Trusteeship Council' identified some gains such as 'thriving local wholesale companies in Truk', it also found a number of problems that put the blame on Micronesians, 'the basic characteristics of its people … language and ethnic barriers … extensive transportation requirements; and a dearth of economic resources' (UNTC 1950: 1). For a further ten years under civilian administration, the area continued to languish until a 1961 United Nations Visiting Mission's report concluded in strong anti-colonial language that the US neglect must end and that they must prepare Micronesia for self-government (Hanlon 1998: 91).

Chuukese would have been very relieved to have gained US support immediately after the war. However, initial US plans for Chuuk were for a fleet anchorage and recreation centre with no reference to Chuukese people and their ownership of the land (Blake 1945). Within a short time, and a change of plans not to proceed with the recreation facilities, US impacts and aims became similar to earlier Japanese times—imposition of another official language, alienation of the Chuukese from their land, manipulation of the traditional political and social structures, and acquisition of the territory through a United Nation's system leading to independence with strings attached. Japanizing Micronesia was replaced with Americanizing Micronesia. In the words of a post-war US administrator in the Marshall Islands:

> What the United States wants of Truk and like islands was presented quite succinctly by the Subcommittee of the House Naval Affairs Committee in presenting the Navy's plans for bases in the Pacific, to the effect that Truk was to be held to keep other powers out.
>
> *(Pomeroy 1970: 73)*

## Chuuk Lagoon's World War II Landscape and Seascape (Underwater Cultural Heritage and Terrestrial Cultural Heritage)

An investigation of documentary sources revealed 113 Japanese ships were sunk or damaged in and around Chuuk Lagoon during the war (United States Joint Army-Navy Assessment Committee (JANAC) 1947; Figure 5.1). One American vessel, the submarine *Corvina*, is reported to have sunk on the 16th of November 1943, at about 190km south of Chuuk Lagoon with the loss of eighty-two lives. The submarine has not been found.[1] A total of fifty-two shipwrecks have been located inside the lagoon. There are other newly acquired historical sources that suggest further, smaller vessels could be located in the lagoon (Jeffery 2007). There also remains the potential for up to 453 aircraft losses to be found in and around Chuuk Lagoon, and from secondary historical sources and site surveys, eleven have been identified in the lagoon.

In a series of site surveys, I documented the identity, condition, integrity, and uses of twenty sites: nine were transport vessels (converted and armed merchant ships), two tugs, two oil tankers, two submarine tenders, one destroyer, one store-ship, one gunboat, one dock boat, and one war-debris accumulation. It was considered to be a fair cross section of the site types in the lagoon that could provide a range of information on the research and underwater cultural heritage management issues. A number of the smaller shipwreck sites, not dived by tourist divers, were found through talking to local people. One such site, which was named the 'Dock Boat' appears to be the intact remains of a bonito fishing vessel, an industry that was prominent before World War II, and which was modified by the Japanese for war use.

The ships and aircraft sunk in the lagoon were manned by Japanese military personnel. Some Chuukese visited the ships when working in the *gunzoku*, Japanese civilian military, and it is unknown if any died when they were bombed. The commencement of the bombing in Chuuk on the 17th of February 1944,

**FIGURE 5.1**  Fujikawa Maru, a 7,000 ton aircraft transport vessel, and the most popular shipwreck dive in Chuuk Lagoon. Photograph by Greg Adams, 2002.

the date on which many ships sunk, is remembered by some Chuukese as the day that the war came to Chuuk (Poyer *et al.* 2001: 139–44). For others, the war was perceived as arriving with the Japanese Army and the removal of the Chuukese from their homes in January 1944 (Poyer *et al.* 2001: 83). Chuukese war memories primarily relate to how Chuukese were impacted by the bombing or by the behaviour of the Japanese Army. There is some Chuukese emotional attachment to the ships, such as through the loss of Japanese friends or family members from those who married and had children, but it is not the same attachment or loss that occurred on the islands.

During fieldwork in Chuuk, I spoke to a number of younger Chuukese men who had Japanese ancestry from the war but limited knowledge of their Japanese parents. This could in part be associated with the repatriation of all Japanese and Okinawan nationals from Chuuk after the war (Peattie 1988: 308–10). All of the Chuukese men knew of the shipwrecks and the terrestrial military remains, from a tourism or fishing perspective, but expressed little interest in them as historic sites, preferring to talk about tuna fishing, folklore, or traditional cultural sites.

From a diving tourism perspective, the submerged World War II sites and associated marine life are potentially unrivalled elsewhere in the world. While human remains are not obvious, they are an attraction for some diving tourists, but not for those who regard the submerged World War II sites as gravesites.

Diver souveniring and dynamite fishing are two other issues that were recorded during the site surveys, something which has been carried out for over

FIGURE 5.2  'Diving group…black and white shots of diving the wrecks of Japanese ships in Truk Lagoon. Some skin diver magazine shots. Undated but about 1972'. Source: Trust Territory Photo Archives, University of Hawaii–Mānoa Library (N-1887b.01).

FIGURE 5.3  Aircraft parts in one of the holds in Fujikawa Maru. In 2019, it was found that these aircraft are deteriorating and collapsing. Photograph by Bill Jeffery, 2004.

forty years (Figure 5.2). The first corrosion survey conducted in 2002 indicated that some of the shipwrecks could start to collapse in ten-to-fifteen years which is a concern from the diving tourism viewpoint and environmentally, especially if they contain oil or gasoline and the release is uncontrolled (MacLeod, 2003). From 2012 to the present day, shipwreck collapse is accelerating (Figure 5.3).

## Terrestrial World War II Surveys

The terrestrial surveys on Tonoas and the opportunistic surveys I implemented on the islands of Weno, Etten, and Uman place the submerged World War II sites in context with the broader Chuuk World War II landscape. Many other islands in the lagoon contain similar sites. Many have been appropriated into use by Chuukese, such as the former Japanese Navy radio transmitting station on Weno, which took a direct hit by a bomb that is still evident today, and is used as Xavier High School. Others, such as the 26th Air Flotilla Headquarters on Etten, which was hit by bombs, lies abandoned, although it was used immediately after the war as a church (Rudolph, Arimichy pers comm. 2007). The terrestrial site surveys also place the submerged World War II sites in context with the social history of the war from a Chuukese perspective.

The terrestrial World War II surveys consisted of reconnaissance surveys of over 200 sites comprising documentation of site locations and descriptions, and oral histories. An interesting aspect that became apparent in the surveys implemented during the documentation of terrestrial and submerged World War II sites was that terrestrial sites were valued differently to the submerged World War II sites. When asked about the value of the submerged World War II sites, all Chuukese participants replied 'tourism,' and a small number referred to historic value through association with the commencement of the bombing in Chuuk. When asked about the value of the terrestrial sites, it was the reverse, they were seen as representing a time of hardship and suffering and provided a sense of place to some Chuukese. Today many have been appropriated and used in a practical manner by Chuukese land owners, but many of those that are of limited practical use have been left abandoned, allowing the jungle to consume them. This could also be as a result of land owners not having the finances to utilize the remains or, as it has been suggested, Chuukese are keen to forget this painful period in their history. Rainbird (2000: 46–47), in his study of views of a Chuukese-Japanese site and a Japanese World War II memorial on Fefan—one of the lagoon's major islands—noted that the landscape surrounding the site and the memorial has been ignored by Chuukese. He concluded that

> a landscape with its associated remembrances may be intensified by its abandonment, by its discontinuity in its use. In fact, the abandoned landscape may be as much a memorial as is the structure erected for the purpose by the Japanese.
>
> *(Rainbird 2000: 46–47)*

During my survey of the terrestrial sites on Tonoas, a Chuukese emotional attachment to the sites was apparent as well as a lack of desire to change their status quo through site conservation and restoration. However, some have an interest in promoting the sites for tourism because of the economic benefit. Some land owners and their families today simply want to maintain their rights to the land and the food that grows on it, and given the intensity in guarding traditional land ownership and the competitive and disruptive nature of tourism, do not or cannot promote tourist activities (Figure 5.4).

One of the most heavily damaged areas was Dublon Town, located in the south-east corner of Tonoas. The Japanese made Dublon Town into a thriving little town of about 800 inhabitants (Peattie 1988: 184) and at the time of the bombing, it contained all the stores, cafes, repair shops, movie theatre, laundry, and dentist that residents needed, including Joshua Suka's seal maker's shop. While many of the buildings have gone today, some concrete buildings, foundations, and stairways, such as the Chuuk hospital, Chuuk Shinto shrine, schools, comfort houses, and pre- and post-war memorials can still be seen (Figure 5.5). Joshua Suka lamented the good pre-war times in Dublon Town, the availability of food (mostly fresh fish), services, and electricity compared to today's inadequate and poor conditions on Tonoas. On the 25th of January 2022, electricity finally returned to Tonoas, the first time since Japan lost control in 1945.[2]

**FIGURE 5.4** Sapuk Lighthouse on the island of Weno. Built by the Japanese in 1937 and containing a powerful searchlight, it still shows the scars of strafing by the British in 1945. The lighthouse was placed at the location of a fortified residence of a Chuukese Chief. Photograph by Bill Jeffery, 2020.

**FIGURE 5.5** Remains of the Chuuk Hospital on Tonoas. Built by the Japanese in the 1930s, it was the only hospital available to the indigenous community. The gardens still contain Japanese flowering plants. Photograph by Bill Jeffery, 2002.

In a questionnaire I developed and distributed to staff of Chuuk HPO and College of Micronesia students, the importance of the submerged World War II sites in the tourism industry was noted, but they considered cultural practices, folklore, and associated sites to be the most significant. One of the reasons provided was 'because some of the things we are still using', another, 'because that is what have been there for many generations till today and it is very important to remind us of our heritage and culture'. This Living Heritage, the traditional cultural practices, sites, and stories considered as significant include dancing, canoe making, weaving, *wuut* (meeting house) making, and stories associated with spiritual beings.

## Interpretation of the World War II Landscape and Seascape

While the submerged World War II sites are used as mnemonic devices for accessing war memories, this research has shown that they do not provide a sense of place or belonging for Chuukese. There are many military sites on the lagoon islands that do this, having tangible connections to Chuukese people and the terrible impacts of the war.

Some Japanese use the submerged World War II sites as mnemonic devices to remember their fallen comrades and the war, while others choose to forget the painful memories (Figure 5.6). Younger Japanese are slowly starting to take an interest in the sites, which prompts them to think about the futility of war and the need for peace, a feeling that I found pervaded many divers' reminiscences from diving the shipwrecks.

US war veterans do not revere Chuuk as they do other battlefields, such as Guadalcanal, Saipan, Iwo Jima, and other sites where American human losses were high. There are no substantial US memorial services in Chuuk as there are in other US battlefields in the Pacific. The bombing of the Chuuk military base and the sinking of the shipwrecks are remembered as a pay-back for Pearl Harbor, as a demonstration of the power of aircraft carriers, and as a great tactical success in driving the Japanese back to their homeland. As such, the Chuuk campaign was a significant event in winning the war. This is in stark contrast with how Japanese value the sites, as open war graves, and where Japanese ceremonies are held annually in Chuuk.

To Chuukese, the tourism industry centred on the submerged World War II sites brings economic benefit to the government and tourist operators, as does

**FIGURE 5.6** 'Silver banded bamboo flute from Shinohara,' Japanese submarine I-169, sunk in Chuuk on April 4th 1944. The flute was recovered in 1973 when the remains of about 100 crew and workmen were recovered and cremated. Source: Trust Territory Photo Archives, University of Hawaii-Mānoa Library (N-2987.09).

dynamite fishing and artefact recovery to some Chuukese families. Although these latter activities can conflict in relation to the management and longevity of the sites, the government appears powerless to stop it. It could also be indicative of Chuukese not perceiving the submerged World War II sites as part of their heritage. Heritage to Chuukese can include tangible material culture where it is associated with traditional cultural practices but much of it is intangible—Living Heritage—found in the cultural practices and connections of people, family, food, land, and sea.

The Chuuk Lagoon World War II landscape and seascape is an example of a complex and contested cultural arena: it has a number of meanings for the Japanese, Chuukese, and Americans. During the war, the military landscape overlaid, dominated, and in some cases destroyed the traditional landscapes from which Chuukese gained a spiritual, personal, and collective identity. Chuukese ambivalence about a tourism industry on their land, and in how the jungle is left to reclaim Japanese military sites, could be associated with Chuukese re-establishing their traditional meanings in the landscape, and in regaining their identity.

The current approach to managing the Chuuk Lagoon shipwrecks is from a tourist management perspective. The shipwrecks provide an important benefit to Chuuk, although in comparison with its neighbour Guam, where over $50 million is gained from the diving industry, Chuuk's economic benefit is much smaller, although in comparison with Guam's World War II sites, it has much more to offer.

A law designed to control access and stop souveniring of the shipwrecks was enacted in 1971, being *Chapter 8, Chuuk Lagoon Monument* of *Title 25, Maritime and Marine Resources*, but many artefacts have been taken from the shipwrecks. Scuba divers need to have local guides when visiting the shipwrecks, and to pay an annual license fee of $50. The shipwrecks have also been placed on the US National Register of Historic Places in 1976, and are recorded as a National Historic Landmark (NHL), one of only two NHL sites in the FSM. In 1989, the US explored different approaches to management, including recommendations as either a Chuuk State, or FSM, or US National Park, but this study and report were never acted upon (USNPS 1989).

## Conclusions

There is little ongoing historical, anthropological, or biological research implemented on the shipwrecks or the terrestrial World War II sites, research that would help to further highlight the various values. The impact of the oil that has leaked since 1944 into the marine environment and surrounding islands also has not been mitigated until recently. In 2017, a Japanese NGO—the Japanese Mine Action Service (JMAS)—gained funding from the Japanese government and is recovering oil from some of the shipwrecks, and in April 2022 an Australian consortium of the Secretariat for the Pacific Regional Environment Program and the Major Projects Foundation gained funding to assist the FSM and JMAS in this endeavour. The stability and longevity of the shipwrecks has been an area of research that Ian MacLeod began in 2002, and it is an important issue that needs an accelerated level of commitment given the increasing deterioration of many of the shipwrecks (MacLeod 2003, 2006, 2016). Their collapse will potentially be a catalyst for further oil pollution and for the demise of the already fluctuating and fickle tourism industry, an industry that in 1975 had 4,026 visitors, and in 2019 5,045 visitors.

The legislation and the approach used in management up until today is not greatly inclusive. The dive industry (dive shops and live-aboard operators) has provided moorings for dive boats at their own expense, which has stopped the large boat anchors hitting the shipwrecks. But apart from this aspect, site management and research has not been collaborative, with the government seemingly uninterested, as evidenced from not investing the c. $200,000 gained annually from the license fees into submerged site management. The current management approach is not broad and multi-vocal, the focus is primarily on the economic gain received from tourism, which benefits the Chuukese government and some local and foreign businesses, whereas the general community and Japanese interests are marginalized.

The impact of the war on Chuukese, using the combined terrestrial and underwater World War II landscape as a focus, needs to be realized. In 2018, the FSM ratified the UNESCO Convention on the Protection of Underwater Cultural Heritage 2001 (the first country in Oceania, with Niue ratifying in 2019), and through UNESCO Partnership funding the first capacity building training in maritime archaeology of staff from the FSM, Palau, Marshall Islands HPOs, and some University of Guam students took place in Chuuk in June 2019. It is hoped that this will be a catalyst for local people investigating local heritage values and issues in underwater cultural heritage across Micronesia. As mentioned above, this is best undertaken in combination with researching terrestrial World War II heritage, in addition to traditional indigenous sites and histories and how the people, their lives, and their cultural heritage were impacted by the war.

## Acknowledgements

There are many people to thank for their help in this work in Chuuk, too many to name them all but I would like to thank in particular Gradvin Aisek, Mayor of Tonoas, the traditional chiefs of Tonoas particularly Tong Misa, Chairman of the traditional chiefs, and Joshua Suka former interpreter in Chuuk during World War II. I would like to acknowledge the great help I received from Chuuk State Historic Preservation Office, particularly Arimichy Rudolph, Anerit Mailo without whom I would not have been able to implement the terrestrial and underwater surveys, Chuuk State Historic Preservation Officers David Welle, Dickenson Dois, Tracy Meter, and at the National Federated States of Micronesia level, Dr Rufino Mauricio and Gus Kohler, and Paula Creech, formerly the

American Samoa and Micronesia Program Manager from the US National Park Service. Finally, I would like to thank colleagues from Australia who came to help in various aspects, Ian MacLeod, Jeremy Green, Corioli Souter, Vivenne Moran, Andy Viduka, Nic Bigourdan, and Ed Punchard and Rhian Skirving from Prospero for their amazing documentary.

## Notes

1 See United States Submarine Losses World War II, Corvina (SS 226). Source, US Naval History and Heritage Command, https://www.history.navy.mil/research/library/online-reading-room/title-list-alphabetically/u/united-states-submarine-losses/corvina-ss-226.html (accessed 13/04/2022).
2 Tonoas has Electricity. Source, FSM Public Information, Embassy of the Federated States of Micronesia. https://fsmembassy.fm/tonoas-has-electricity/ (accessed 13/04/2022).

## Bibliography

Bailey, D.E. 2000. *World War II Wrecks of the Truk Lagoon*. Redding: North Valley Diver Publications.

Blake, R., & Brigadier General. 1945. Engineering Assistance, Truk. Memorandum from Prospective Island Commander to Island Commander, Guam. 2 September 1945. NARA Project No. NW 23238. Record Group No. 313. Washington: NARA.

Carrell, T. 1991. *Micronesia: Submerged Cultural Resources Assessment*. Submerged Cultural Resource Unit. Santa Fe, NM: National Park Service.

Cheyne, A. 1852. *A Description of the Western Pacific Ocean, North and South of the Equator with Sailing Directions*. London: J.D. Potter.

Craib, J.L. 1997. *Truk Archaeology: An Intensive Archeological Survey of Pwené Village, Dublon, Truk State, Federated States of Micronesia*. Micronesian Resources Study. Micronesian Endowment for Historic Preservation.

Denfeld, D.C. 1981. *Field Survey of Truk: World War II Features*. Micronesian Archaeological Survey Number 6. Saipan: Historic Preservation Office, Trust Territory of the Pacific Islands.

Hanlon, D. 1998. *Remaking Micronesia*. Honolulu: University of Hawaii Press.

Hanlon, D. 1999. 'Magellan's Chroniclers? American Anthropology's History in Micronesia'. In: Kiste, R. and Marshall, M., eds. *American Anthropology in Micronesia*. Honolulu: University of Hawaii Press, 53–79.

Hezel, F.X. 1973. 'The Beginnings of Foreign Contact with Truk', *Journal of Pacific History*, 8, 51–73.

Hezel, F.X. 1992. 'The Expensive Taste of Modernity: Caroline and Marshall Islands'. In: Robillard, A.B., ed. *Social Change in the Pacific Islands*. New York: Kegan Paul International, 203–19.

Hezel, F.X. 1995. *Strangers in Their Own Land: A Century of Colonial Rule in the Caroline and Marshall Islands*. Honolulu: University of Hawaii Press.

Jeffery, W.F. 2007. *War Graves, Munition Dumps and Pleasure Grounds: A Post-Colonial Perspective of Chuuk Lagoon's Submerged WW II Sites*. PhD dissertation, James Cook University. [WWW] http://eprints.jcu.edu.au/2068/ (accessed 13 May 2019).

Joint Intelligence Center Pacific Ocean Areas (JICPOA). 1944. Information Bulletin, General Survey Truk Islands, No. 41–44, April 1, 1944. *Military Intelligence in the Pacific*

*1942–46: Bulletins of the Intelligence Center, Pacific Ocean Area; Joint Intelligence Center, Pacific Ocean Area; and the Commander-in-Chief, Pacific Ocean Area*. Microfilm Roll 10. Canberra: Australian National University Library.

Lands, J.A., Lt (jg) USNR. 1945a. First meeting of Truk Atoll Advisory Council. Memorandum to Commanding Officer, USN Military Government Unit, Truk and the Central Carolines, 13 December 1945. NARA Record Group No. 313. San Francisco: NARA.

Lands, J.A., Lt (jg) USNR. 1945b Second meeting of Truk Atoll Advisory Council. Memorandum to Commanding Officer, USN Military Government Unit, Truk and the Central Carolines, 20 December 1945. NARA Record Group No. 313. San Francisco: NARA.

MacLeod, I.D. 2003. *Metal Corrosion in Chuuk Lagoon: A Survey of Iron Shipwrecks and Aluminium Aircraft*. Chuuk: Chuuk Historic Preservation Office.

MacLeod, I.D. 2006. 'In-Situ Corrosion Studies on Wrecked Aircraft of the Imperial Japanese Navy in Chuuk Lagoon, Federated States of Micronesia', *International Journal of Nautical Archaeology*, 35 (1), 128–36.

MacLeod, I.D. 2016. 'In-Situ Corrosion Measurements of WWII Shipwrecks in Chuuk Lagoon, Quantification of Decay Mechanisms and Rates of Deterioration', *Frontiers in Marine Science*, 3 (38), 1–10.

McCarley, H.H. 1945a. Military Government Truk – Monthly Report of Activities. Memorandum from the Commanding Officer to Commander Marianas, 30 November 1945. NARA Record Group No. 313, San Francisco: NARA.

Mirrer, B.M. 1971. *Educational Change in Truk, Micronesia*. Master of Arts dissertation, University of Ohio.

Morison, S.E. 1975. *History of United States Naval Operations in World War II. Volume VII: Aleutians, Gilberts and Marshalls, June 1942–April 1944*. Boston, MA: United States Navy.

Office of Planning and Statistics (OPS). n.d. *Federated States of Micronesia. First National development Plan 1985–1989*. Kolonia: Government of the Federated States of Micronesia.

Parillo, M.P. 1993. *The Japanese Merchant Marine in World War II*. Annapolis, MD: Naval Institute Press.

Peattie, M.R. 1988. *Nan'yō: The Rise and Fall of the Japanese in Micronesia, 1885–1945*. Honolulu: University of Hawaii Press.

Pomeroy, E.S. 1970. *Pacific Outpost: American Strategy in Guam and Micronesia*. New York: Russell and Russell.

Poyer, L., Falgout, S. & Carucci, L.M. 2001. *The Typhoon of War: Micronesian experiences of the Pacific War*. Honolulu: University of Hawaii Press.

Rainbird, P. 1993. *Report on the Cultural Resource Management in the Coastal Area of Chuuk Lagoon*. Chuuk: Chuuk Historic Preservation Office.

Rainbird, P. 2000. 'Round, Black and Lustrous: A View of Encounters with Difference in Truk Lagoon, Federated States of Micronesia.' In: R. Torrence and A. Clarke, eds. *The Archaeology of Difference: Negotiating Cross-Cultural Engagements in Oceania*. London: Routledge, 32–50.

Rainbird, P. 2004. *The Archaeology of Micronesia*. Cambridge, MA: Cambridge University Press.

Stewart, W. 1989. *Ghost Fleet of Truk Lagoon*. Missoula, MT: Pictorial Histories Publishing Co.

Thompson, A.W., Lt Comdr., USNR 1945. Preliminary Report on Negotiations Relative to the Surrender of Areas under the Jurisdiction of Truk. Memorandum to the

Deputy Chief Military Government Officer, 31 August 1945. NARA Record Group 313/ 344/6943. Washington, DC: NARA.

Turner, J.W. & Falgout, S. 2002. 'Time Traces: Cultural Memory and World War II in Pohnpei', *The Contemporary Pacific*, 14 (1), 101–31.

United Nations Trusteeship Council (UNTC). 1950. Major Problems of Administration in the Trust Territory of the Pacific Islands. NARA Record Group No. 313. Washington, DC: NARA.

United States Joint Army-Navy Assessment Committee (JANAC). 1947. *Japanese Naval and Merchant Shipping Losses during World War II by All Causes*. Washington, DC: US Government Printer.

United States National Park Service (USNPS). 1989. *Truk Lagoon Historical Park Study. Draft report for Federated States of Micronesia, State of Truk*. Pohnpei: Photocopy from Micronesian Seminar.

United States Navy (USN). 1952a. *Outline of Third Phase Operations, February 1943 – August 1945, Defense Operations*. Japanese Monograph 117. Microfilm. Canberra: Australian National University Library.

United States Navy (USN). 1952b. *Inner South Seas Islands Area, Naval Operations, Part II, Marshall Islands (December 1941 – February 1944). Defense Operations*. Japanese Monograph 173. Microfilm. Canberra: Australian National University Library.

United States Navy (USN). 1952c. *The Imperial Japanese Navy in World War II. A Graphic Presentation of the Japanese Naval Organization and List of Combatant and Non-Combatant Vessels Lost or Damaged in the War*. Japanese Monograph 116. Microfilm. Canberra: Australian National University Library.

United States Strategic Bombing Survey (USSBS). 1947. *The Reduction of Truk*. Pacific War Series No. 77. Washington, DC: US Navy.

Young, J.A., Rosenberger N.R. & Harding, J.R. 1997. *Truk Ethnography*. Micronesian Resources Study. San Francisco: United States National Park Service.

Useem, J. 1945. 'The American Pattern of Military Government in Micronesia', *The American Journal of Sociology*, 51 (2), 93–102.

## Personal Communications

Mr. Gradvin Aisek, General Manager/Owner, *Blue Lagoon* dive shop, Mayor of Tonoas, Chuuk, FSM.

Mr. Tong Misa, Chairman of the Chiefs of Tonoas, Chuuk, FSM.

Mr. Arimichy Rudolph, Technical Assistant, Chuuk State Historic Preservation Office.

Mr. Joshua Suka, Interpreter, Tonoas, Chuuk, FSM.

# 6

# SEEKING A SHARED CONNECTION AND SHARED HERITAGE THROUGH WORLD WAR II UNDERWATER CULTURAL HERITAGE IN THE PACIFIC

*Jennifer F. McKinnon*

## Introduction

The cultural heritage of World War II is ever present on Pacific Islands. This is most obvious through the tangible remains of Japanese and US vehicles of war that litter the shoreline and interior landscape. World War II underwater cultural heritage (UCH), which can be described as 'out of sight and out of mind,' is less well known and more removed from the civilian non-combatant experiences of the war and the contemporary non-diving communities that live on the islands. As such, it presents an interesting case study in examining how as archaeologists we might explore meaning and create shared connections between difficult heritage and communities of all kinds including Pacific Island non-combatant communities and veterans of contemporary wars.

For nearly a decade, I've wrestled with the personal and professional ethics of studying World War II conflict heritage in Pacific Island nations, particularly Saipan, Commonwealth of the Northern Mariana Islands (CNMI). Seeing the tragedy that descendant communities suffered at the hands of warring colonial nations (one of which I am associated with) impacted my research at an early stage and set the pace for the projects I have developed or worked on over the years. It has led me to question my intents, the ethics of such work, and the impacts of that work on the communities and pushed me towards using a Community Archaeology framework. In more recent years, my work with veterans of contemporary wars on World War II conflict heritage in Saipan has presented a different set of ethical considerations to be contemplated. One concern related to how veteran work can be perceived of as popular and attention-grabbing, and as such, may be idealized and misunderstood. Nevertheless, I have tried to check myself regularly through questioning the motives that drive my interest to work with these different communities and constantly assessing and reassessing the

DOI: 10.4324/9780429270468-8

structural and historically colonial foundations of my field and academic institution. Have I always been successful in questioning, recognizing, and assessing these issues? Surely not. Do my efforts to do so contribute to a better outcome for those descendant communities who trust me to conduct research on their history and island or those veterans willing to work with me in the field? I hope so. What follows is a description of one of the more current areas of interest I have in exploring how the experience of World War II and resulting conflict heritage can be considered shared through a multiplicity of connections with communities – specifically through those who have engaged in war and conflict, veterans.

## Brief Overview

The island of Saipan is part of the larger Mariana Islands chain is in the western Pacific. Approximately 21 km long and 6.5 km wide, Saipan is the capitol of the CNMI and has a diverse community including the descendant Indigenous Chamorro who migrated and populated the islands 3,500 years ago and the Indigenous Carolinians from the Caroline Islands (Russell 1998). The island and its people have been the subject and location of numerous episodes of colonial aggressions and resistance from the Spanish colonization in the 17th century, to German occupation in the 19th century, followed by Japan and US occupations in the 19th and 20th century. However, none of those historical periods, or occupations, left as much material culture on the island and in its waters as the World War II battle for Saipan.

The US plan to take control of the Marianas from Japanese forces was code-named Operation FORAGER and included the island of Guam. The plan to invade and take control of Saipan was called Operation TEARAWAY. Air attacks were the first phase of Operation FORAGER. In response, Japanese forces prepared 'Operation A-Go,' which relied upon the Imperial Japanese Navy to support troops on the ground in the Marianas. Air raids began in February on Saipan striking Japanese shipping and support installations on the 22nd and 23rd of February 1944. Marie Soledad Castro, a young girl whose father worked at the docks related 'That area was all in flames because the Japanese had a lot of storage tanks there,' and another, Vicky Vaughan said, 'One of my older brothers, Shiuichi, was killed during one of these air raids...We never found his body...like so many, he just disappeared' (Petty 2002: 18; Goldberg 2007: 23; Farrell 2009: 277). These pre-invasion attacks caused a considerable amount of damage to property including the sinking of most Japanese ships operating in the waters. US forces attempted to gain as much information about the island and Japanese forces by flying reconnaissance missions in April and May 1944. These missions collected aerial photographs of Japanese troop defensive measures and weaponry (Goldberg 2007: 23). Additional reconnaissance work included Underwater Demolition Teams whose mission was to blast obstructions and record the depth of the lagoon to determine which vessels could be used during the invasion (Kauffman

1986: 237). For those civilians who knew of or suspected an impending invasion, preparations were made in order to ensure their survival. Indigenous families stocked caves and shelters with goods such as food, water, clothing, and even buried valuables. Sister Asuncion 'Chong' Demapan (2018) recounts, 'My father and mother had prepared a cave for our family beforehand with breadfruit, water, food that wouldn't spoil, and clothing.'

Operation FORAGER was in full swing by June 1944 when the invasion of Saipan was planned. On the 11th of June, Rear Admiral Marc Mitscher ordered all four carrier groups to launch their planes and attack the Marianas including aircraft from USS *Enterprise, Essex, Cowpens,* and *Langley.* A total of 208 fighters and eight torpedo bombers flew that afternoon (Tillman 2005: 55). Air raids continued on the 12th of June, and on the 13th and 14th of June, US battleships began bombarding the island offshore (Russell 1994: 88). As a result of this bombardment, roughly 150 Japanese aircraft were destroyed (Wheeler 1996: 244). This had a significant effect on Japanese forces preventing an air attack on incoming US troops. 'The din robbed us totally of all sense of hearing,' wrote Maashi Ito, a Japanese soldier, in reference to the bombardment; 'It wasn't the same as a boom or a roar that splits the ears: it was more like being imprisoned inside a huge metal drum that was incessantly and insufferably being beaten with a thousand iron hammers.'

As the sun rose on the 15th of June, the enormous US amphibian force was assembled for the invasion. AMTRACS and DUKWs were unloaded and LSDs (Landing Ship, Dock) launched LCMs (Landing Craft, Mechanized) that held tanks. Battleships, cruisers, and destroyers closed in on the invasion beaches with aircraft screaming overhead toward the shore. With nearly 1,500 vessels in all, this great unpacking of men, weaponry, and ammunition was surely an intimidating sight for the Japanese forces and civilians. Meling Chargualaf (2018) recalls, 'My brother remembers when the American ships came in, he was saying how exciting it was. They looked like little toys. But then everyone started running, and things got serious, because they were starting to bomb us.'

Awaiting the arrival of the invading US force were over 32,000 Japanese troops, double what was anticipated (Spector 1984: 302). Japanese forces were skilled at using the local terrain to their advantage and the use of caves and high ground gave them a considerable advantage in spotting and attacking US invading forces. The battle raged for many days moving from south to north including engagements in dense jungle settings, wide open sugarcane fields, valleys and caves, and the metropolitan town of Garapan. By the 7th of July, the US had secured most of the island and the remaining Japanese troops were fortified in the hills and caves to the north. As morning broke, under the command of Lt. General Yoshitsugu Saito, and in keeping with the shogun code of Bushido and the philosophies of State Shinto, a counterattack was the only way to save face (Cabrera 2015: 22). With approval from mainland Japan, Saito gave orders for the *Gyokusai* and stressed adherence to the battle ethics known as *Senjinkun* where honor is achieved by taking one's own life as opposed to suffering the disgrace of surrender or capture. Saito committed himself to the *Senjikun* while the remainder of his troops surprise-attacked the 1st and 2nd Battalions of the 105th Infantry in the final *Gyokusai* (Cabrera 2015: 22). Over 4,300 Japanese were killed in this attack while the US lost approximately 650 men (Goldberg 2007). On the 9th of July, US Admiral Turner announced that Saipan was officially secured (Hoyt 2000: 404). Shortly after the announcement, suicide jumps began by Japanese civilians that had taken heed of their military's propaganda about US soldiers raping and killing women and children. Jumps took place at Suicide Cliff and Banzai Cliff, but also at any other cliff available along Marpi Point. It is not known how many Japanese civilians perished of their own accord (Cabrera 2015: 23–24). Mop-up efforts for Japanese troop holdouts continued through July and well into August, conducted solely by the 27th Army Infantry Division.

The loss of life was tremendous. Approximately, 3,500 of over 67,000 US troops who participated in the battle were killed or reported missing in action, and four times this number were wounded. Japanese losses were far greater still. Of the approximately 31,000 Japanese troops who participated in the battle, 29,500 were killed (Rottman 2004). Japanese sources estimate the total number killed on Saipan to be well over 40,000 (Bulgrin 2005). Over 900 Chamorro and Carolinian people and an unknown number of Japanese, Korean, and Okinawan civilians were killed (Cabrera 2015). Additionally, over 14,000 civilians (Chamorro, Carolinian, Japanese, Okinawan, and Korean) were placed in internment camps and an additional unknown number of civilians committed suicide (Willmott 1999: 147).

The battle was a significant win for the US as it placed US forces within reach of the Japanese homeland. The capture of Saipan and the Mariana Islands paved the road for more decisive battles at Okinawa and Iwo Jima and eventually led to the atomic bombings which hastened the end of the Pacific War.

## Challenges for UCH and World War II Heritage in the Pacific

UCH by its very nature of being located underwater is an 'out of sight and out of mind' heritage. If it cannot be seen or interacted with, an awareness and recognition will fail to develop. This inaccessibility situation sets up challenges with regards to protection of UCH. We can see this readily in the history of legislative protection of underwater sites developing much later than terrestrial heritage legislation, the continued cottage industry of treasure hunting in remote places around the globe, and even the pillaging and overnight disappearance of World War II war graves for steel supplies (Ridwan 2019: 1625).

In addition to the out of site/out of mind nature of UCH, accessing underwater sites typically requires one to have an income that can support expensive training courses in SCUBA, the purchase of recreational equipment and associated maintenance fees, and finally a boat or charter, tanks fills, and other costs. This limits access to these sites to a small, privileged set of individuals with the economic status to accommodate their activities (Ransley 2007). That set of privileged is further defined by their physical ability to swim and SCUBA dive. For many, the ability to swim is not a reality and for others the physical fitness requirements to dive are beyond their capabilities, leaving a large percentage of the population unable to access UCH.

Relevance is yet another key restriction to recognition and protection, particularly for conflict sites such as World War II-related UCH. The role of war and the warrior in most societies has been relegated to men. Conflict and violence, valor, and courage are intimately related to the roles of men in both social and military affairs. As such, war and the technological machines of war have been and continues to be a male-dominated predilection. It comes as no surprise that women, 50% of the population, are typically less drawn to the subject and objects of war, with exceptions such as women's roles in the support or action of combat or immediate familial connections to combatants.

When considering World War II-material in the Pacific that is related to either colonial Japanese or US forces, we see that it has little relevance to Pacific Islanders upon which the war happened, and they had no choice but to endure. This sentiment is best summed up by Genevieve Cabrera (2015: 24) in the first published account of the battle for Saipan from an Indigenous female perspective when she related,

> The war and the battle come to life with each vivid recounting of those that fought it and those that survived it. The extant remnant features that comprise the battle sites out in Saipan's lagoon and surrounding waters, as well as those that riddle the island itself, are reminders of this devastating segment of native island history. Regrettably, the ravages of the battle rage on in the memories of the families of the 933 native men, women, and children that died in a conflict not of their making. For these departed, there would never be resolution. They neither died fighting for principles of freedom nor defense of country. They simply died and ostensibly are categorized as *collateral damage*, but yet even this descriptor was never theirs for the choosing.

Furthermore, western styles of cultural heritage preservation tend to focus on tangible heritage such as the colonial buildings, structures, and sites while Pacific Islanders have stronger ties to and a preference for their intangible heritage including traditional skills and knowledge, oral history, dance, and music (Chapman & Lightner 1996; O'Neill 2005; King 2006; Marsh 2013). While World War II in the Pacific and its associated heritage is a momentous event in world history from a western perspective, it is yet another destructive colonial interlude in the long Indigenous history of Oceania (Underwood 1977; Murray 2006; Falgout et al. 2008; Camacho 2011; Cabrera 2015). As Poyer et al. (2001: 337) found, World War II remains are of little interest to most, 'but they want to preserve this history and to correct the imbalance that makes Islanders nearly invisible in American and Japanese accounts of the Pacific War.' As such, relevance in relation to recognition and stewardship will always be an issue unless archaeologists can bridge that gap and help identify common interest and understanding in a shared past.

## Shared Heritage and Shared Experience

One of the ways in which archaeologists and heritage practitioners have fostered recognition and stewardship is through the idea of 'shared heritage.' Shared heritage is a concept that has been utilized both explicitly and implicitly in many ways within the field of archaeology and heritage preservation including identifying a shared connection within a community with their past and heritage, describing a heritage shared by multiple communities, for the purpose of a common preservation need, and promoting heritage diplomacy (Winter 2019). The concept of shared heritage has even been explored explicitly to overcome conflict and achieve consensus when heritage represents conflicts of interest, such as the *Promoting Dialogue and Cultural Understanding of our Shared Heritage* project that brought together Israeli, Jordanian, and Palestinian researchers to advance peace within the region (Ya'ari 2010: 9).

Within the field of maritime or underwater archaeology, the concept of shared heritage has been utilized through the capacity building schemes of UNESCO and by other associated programs such as the *Center for International Heritage Activities* in regions like Southeast Asia and Africa (Parthesius 2011). Within these programs, there was early and continued emphasis on colonial shipwreck research and protection in post-colonial waters, but that shifted in some cases to the need for recognizing pre-colonial histories and the experience and heritage of the colonized as equally important and relevant (Parthesius 2011). Shared heritage has also been employed in pragmatic ways such as in nation-to-nation memorandum of agreements for supporting the protection and management of shipwrecks that lie in waters outside of the national state, including the case of the Dutch wrecks off Australian and Sri Lankan coastlines (Australia-Netherlands 2017; Dwyer & Klimis 2019).

The concept of 'shared heritage' and how it has been used by archaeologists and heritage professionals is not necessarily synonymous with 'shared experience,' but it can be. Shared experience, as defined in this chapter and related to heritage, is a connection with heritage either through personally experiencing the historical event that created the heritage or sharing an experience similar to the historical event(s) that create a heritage. In other words, shared experience can lead to shared heritage either as a natural progression or through an exploration of that shared experience connection. This chapter explores the concept of a shared experience of war which may lead to a shared heritage of conflict. It specifically focuses on two projects that incorporated veterans of contemporary war in the exploration and study of heritage of war. The first project was a 2017 National Endowment for the Humanities (NEH) Dialogues on the Experience of

War project called *War in the Pacific: Difficult Heritage*, hereafter referred to *War in the Pacific* (McKinnon et al. 2019). The program engaged Pacific Islander veterans of contemporary wars, non-combatant civilian survivors of World War II, and military families in considering how war and conflict is universal to humanity and how conflict heritage can be considered shared heritage. Indigenous Pacific Islander veterans are a poorly represented and supported veteran community despite being proportionally 'overrepresented in the US Army by 249%, compared to 43% of black, 44% of whites and American Indians/Alaskan Natives 53%' (White House Initiative on Asian Americans & Pacific Islanders n.d.). The second project is the development of the Joint Recovery Team (JRT), an ongoing collaboration between East Carolina University (ECU) and the non-profit organization, Task Force Dagger Foundation (TFDF), which offers rehabilitative therapy events to medically retired Special Operation Forces (SOF) veterans (David et al. 2020). Specifically, the JRT was created by training SOF veterans in archaeology and World War II history and incorporating them into current archaeological survey and research of World War II sites in the Mariana Islands.

## War in the Pacific: Difficult Heritage

According to NEH (2019), the funding scheme Dialogues on the Experience of War, 'supports the study and discussion of important humanities sources about war, in the belief that these sources can help US military veterans and others think more deeply about the issues raised by war and military service.' This idea that humanities sources, including archaeological sites and heritage, can be explored and discussed to examine the issues raised by war and military service was the emphasis for developing a program that further explored how the shared experience of war can lead to the heritage of war being perceived as shared heritage. The idea follows that if contemporary veterans experienced and know war, then they may have a connection with and understanding of the heritage of past wars. Further, Pacific Island veterans may have an even stronger connection to the historic conflicts that took place within their islands, including those in which their ancestors and immediate family may have been involved, either willingly or inadvertently.

Invasions, battles, and colonial aggressions have been waged with and on top of the first Indigenous peoples, the Chamorro, and the Carolinians who immigrated to the Marianas from the Caroline Islands for centuries. As such, the land and seascape represent in both tangible and intangible ways the cultural heritage of those conflicts, the oldest of which are the Spanish-Chamorro Wars of the 17th century and the most recent and prominent is the World War II battle for Saipan. Today, Pacific Islanders navigate daily through their island reminded of the battles and wars that have both defined and challenged who they are and where they are going. But what do they think of this conflict heritage? How do they relate to it and their ancestors who were involved? Is it their history or some colonial aggressors' history and heritage?

*War in the Pacific* focused on two wars: the Spanish-Chamorro Wars and the World War II battle for Saipan as bookends to the history of resistance and aggressions in the islands. The Spanish colonization of the Marianas in the late 17th century represents the 'discovery' of the islands and the 'fatal impact' of Europe on a Pacific island culture. It began with cultural suppression, a depopulation and consolidation of island peoples, and religious fanaticism and conversion through missionization. Although these events, which spanned over a century, were tragically catastrophic for the Chamorro, they were met with resistance and agency in what has become known as the Spanish-Chamorro Wars. These wars are little understood historically and archaeologically, and in some ways they are overlooked because their related heritage is ephemeral. The history, furthermore, has been written primarily from a Spanish perspective. However, they are beneficial for exploring and understanding how Indigenous peoples and warriors both resisted colonial powers and acted as their own agents negotiating allegiances for their benefit (Camacho 2008). Additionally, they provide an opportunity to examine how war can be complex and have multiple viewpoints through exploring the relationship between Spanish state and church and their often-conflicting agendas. The wars also serve to explore themes around modern resistance to colonialism and military build-up, which is an intense current affairs topic since the US and Asian nations are presently using Pacific islands for staging military activities.

The World War II battle for Saipan was an intense aerial, amphibious, and terrestrial battle fought during June/July of 1944. It involved the warring Japanese and US forces, as well as Chamorro, Carolinian, Japanese, and Okinawan civilians, and conscripted Korean soldiers. The US capture of the Marianas was a decisive turning point in the war as it put US bombers within reach of the Japanese home islands and served as a staging area for the deployment of the atomic bombs that ended the war. The use of the World War II battle for Saipan as a case study is valuable to participants for exploring civilians' experiences during war because it was the first time in the Pacific Theater that a large population of civilians of several ethnicities were inadvertently involved. It is also useful for identifying what struggles and opportunities the post-war period (1945–78) brought to the island that reach past today and impact the future of the islands. Finally, it affords an opportunity to contemplate the most obvious and tangible conflict heritage that covers the island through an existing World War II Maritime Heritage Trail and the most personalized Indigenous heritage of World War II – the caves civilian families used for protection during the invasion. As a more recent war of living memory, it provides a stronger connection to the past and the present for veterans who have served in contemporary wars.

Using these two battles, *War in the Pacific* identified five intersecting themes for their association with Saipan's colonial history, its difficult heritage, and the veteran's experience. These include Veteran and Indigenous Identity, The Enemy, The Civilian, Memorialization, and Conflict Heritage. Artifacts and archaeological sites, both terrestrial and underwater, were the foundational humanities content with supporting humanities sources such as film, poetry, art, and literature rounding out the content. Through these themes and humanities content, Saipan's veterans, World War II survivors, and veteran families undertook a one-week program to explore the experience of war.

It was important to situate the beginning of the program with the earliest conflict, the Spanish-Chamorro Wars, and end with the more recent battle of World War II. Starting with an Indigenous/colonial conflict served to draw the veterans back in time and consider how their ancestors were warriors and how they might consider their own Indigenous and warrior identity. Within the 'Veteran and Indigenous Identity' theme, it was useful to recognize their status as a warrior and how the history of conflict has transcended generations from the first resistance against the Spanish to their contemporary service in the US military. Veterans had the opportunity to explore the archaeological record of the Spanish-Chamorro Wars through the study of prehistoric weapons including sling stones, adzes, and axes. These early weapons of war allowed veterans to reflect upon how they are similar to and different from the modern weapons of war they have utilized. This exercise was a powerful experience for some who wondered what the history of those weapons were and how they became part of the archaeological record. They also reflected on the difference between past warriors creating their own weapons by hand versus the modern military practice of being issued a weapon. Participants were then taken to the location of archaeological sites associated with the colonial period and Chamorro struggle for resistance including a Spanish period cemetery site and caves utilized by their ancestors. At the sites, they reflected upon how subsequent colonial activities and invasions have impacted these early sites of resistance up to and including World War II and modern commercialization.

In addition to Spanish-Chamorro War sites, veterans visited a range of terrestrial and underwater World War II sites. A visit to The Last Command Site allowed veterans to reflect upon the theme 'The Enemy' through the Japanese and US perspective. Although misidentified, this tourist site is interpreted as the last stronghold held by Japanese forces prior to the last counterattack. *Gyokusai*, which translates to 'the crushing of the jewel,' is the event in which Lt. General Yoshitsugu Saito encouraged the nearly 3,000 remnant troops to attack the US troops during a night raid, while he committed ritual suicide in the last command. The significance of this site as a tourist destination that draws hundreds of tourists per day is important to consider because it represents the final struggle of brutal hand-to-hand combat between the Japanese and the US soldiers. For the veterans, it allowed them to consider the differing underlying codes and principles of war from both US and Japanese perspectives.

Veterans also visited several archaeological caves in exploring the theme 'The Civilian' which allowed them to appreciate the Indigenous experience of war and their use of the caves during the battle. Cave visits included storytelling by the landowners, occupants during World War II, or family members of occupants on site. Experiencing the cramped quarters, seeing the artifacts that remain on the cave floor and walls, and hearing the firsthand accounts was a palpable reminder of civilian experiences and hardships. In addition to the World War II context, some of the caves contain ancient rock art and burials that precede the Spanish colonial period. Viewing and discussing Indigenous history as told through pictorial representation created by Chamorro ancestors served to draw a line from the pre-contact past through to the present and solidify veteran understanding of how their ancestors have used these caves over time for protection. Also discussed was the impacts World War II had on ancient heritage including the destructive use of flamethrowers and grenades to clear caves and subsequent damage to ancient rock art and burials. In many cases, the participants had heard about these caves but had not had the opportunity to visit them. Veterans spoke about how their family members passed along the stories of hiding in the caves and were grateful for being able to see them firsthand.

As part of the theme 'Memorialization,' veterans visited Banzai Cliff, the site of many Japanese civilian suicides that are now marked by numerous individual, group, and official monuments and the National Veterans' Cemetery nearby to Banzai Cliff where veterans of modern wars are now buried. Both these visits served to broaden veterans' understanding of memorialization, of the types of memorials present, for whom and by whom they are created, the permanence and ephemerality of memorials and offerings, and the differences and similarities between national cemeteries and places of commemoration. Visits to underwater archaeological sites that include memorials were undertaken via snorkel. The sites included a wrecked Kawanishi H8K (allied code name 'Emily') seaplane on which two, Japanese and Korean, underwater monuments are situated, and a Korean monument on the sunken Japanese freighter thought to be *Shoan Maru*, which was bombed while transporting Korean conscripts (Figure 6.1). Visits allowed veterans to view the wide range of memorialization and how memorialization of the past can be political in nature in the case of the Korean conscript monument on the sunken Japanese aircraft site.

During the 'Conflict Heritage' theme, visits to underwater World War II sites were accompanied by viewing the eighteen-minute interpretive film *Battle of Saipan: WWII Maritime Heritage Trail* and reading the guides, posters, and trail website. Site visits included underwater Japanese and US submerged aircraft, sunken amphibious vehicles, and shipwrecks lost during the battle for Saipan (Figure 6.2). Visits to sites were conducted on snorkel for those who felt comfortable. Veterans were encouraged to explore questions related to how the sites relate to their own experience of using vehicles of war and how they reflect changes in war technology. While underwater sites are more removed from the Indigenous experience of World War II, veterans still viewed them as both interesting from a historical perspective and important to the island's cultural heritage tourism sector.

Between the two one-week discussion sessions, a total of sixty participants were involved in the program, with an additional thirty reached on the night the program opened to the general public for a film viewing (Figure 6.3). These totals

FIGURE 6.1   Monument on Japanese freighter dedicated to Korean conscripts during World War II. Photograph by J. McKinnon.

FIGURE 6.2   A group participant diving down to visit a Japanese landing craft. Photograph by J. McKinnon.

far surpassed plans to reach a total of twenty-to-thirty participants. Participants included veterans from the Vietnam, Korean, Afghanistan, and Iraq wars. There were also survivors of the battle for Saipan, active service and veteran family members, and general members of the public interested in veterans, heritage, and the humanities. Participants were from Saipan and neighboring Tinian and ages ranged from thirteen-to-eighty-five with an equal gender ratio.

The program was evaluated using pre- and post-program surveys. Initial analysis of the surveys indicates that participants gained specific knowledge about the program themes and increased value of heritage sites on the island, including preservation efforts. Some post-program responses to the question, 'How did the program meet your expectations?' included 'far beyond my initial expectations/ deeply exhilarating in many ways' and 'I think it went beyond 'discussion' as I expected, into discovery and some sort of therapy for some.'

Through the selected themes and humanities sources including heritage sites, film, poetry, art, and literature, veterans and the public gained a meaningful and relevant understanding of war as a shared human experience and came to see the associated cultural heritage of war on their island as shared cultural heritage. These personalized interactions with both the physical, tangible remains of heritage sites and humanities sources provided a new or in some cases renewed sense of historical and cultural value for both the veterans' experiences and the local conflict heritage. Additionally, it assisted participants with developing a

**FIGURE 6.3** A group of War in the Pacific participants. Photograph by J. McKinnon.

sociocultural position of knowledge and authority on the history of their island and the Pacific war, one which they endeavored to share with their families and others.

## Joint Recovery Team

TFDF is a non-profit organization that 'provides assistance to wounded, ill, or injured US Special Operations Command members and their families. We respond to urgent needs, conduct Rehabilitative Therapy Events, and provide next-generation health solutions for issues facing our service members. We are a rally point to combat traumatic brain injury, Post-Traumatic Stress, and environmental exposures' (Task Force Dagger Foundation 2019). The organization has extensive knowledge and experience in providing rehabilitative therapy events including SCUBA diving programs and has a medical advisory team that includes services from mental health to rehabilitation.

The JRT program developed when a TFDF veteran applied to ECU's Maritime Studies Program and connected TFDF and ECU. Conversations began about a veteran's program that would augment the annual TFDF dive rehabilitative therapy event by training veteran divers in archaeology and taking them to the Pacific to conduct underwater archaeology on World War II sites. In addition to this development, ECU developed a Memorandum of Understanding (MOU) with the Department of Defense's Defense POW/MIA Accounting Agency (DPAA) to assist in their mission of accounting for lost service members from past conflicts. TFDF desired to become involved in DPAA work as well, given the mission's alignment with their own oath of 'never leaving a fallen soldier behind.' Together ECU and TFDF applied for and received a grant through the National Park Service Maritime Heritage Grant Program in partnership with the Florida Public Archaeology Network (FPAN) to develop and run a pilot maritime heritage and archaeological training program for veteran divers. Additional support for the program was provided through private funding and donors to TFDF, in-kind staff and equipment by ECU and FPAN, and funding from DPAA. Committed project partners also included Saipan's NPS American Memorial Park and Historic Preservation Office and Naval Facilities Engineering Command Marianas on Guam. What developed was a reciprocal relationship whereby archaeologists may benefit greatly from the extensive background and knowledge of veterans in understanding war, combat, and battlefields and veterans may benefit through the archaeological training, physical fitness, comradery, and mission-based program.

The JRT project initially had two main objectives: (1) to develop a maritime heritage and archaeological education program designed specifically for medically retired veterans about World War II maritime heritage and (2) to implement this hands-on, participatory program in Saipan on World War II sites. FPAN, which provides education and outreach in archaeology for the public in Florida, has an existing training called Submerged Sites Education and Archaeological

Stewardship (SSEAS) in Florida. SSEAS in its current format was tailored to the veteran group and the location of Saipan making the delivery and program more effective for the goals of the field work.

TFDF recruited and selected veterans through existing networks, particularly through their annual SCUBA event, but also through need-based searches within their organization (Figure 6.4). Selected veterans received a comprehensive review of mental and physical needs by a diverse team including but not limited to members of the TFDF Board of Directors, medical specialists, maritime archaeologists, and dive trainers. The team also reviewed the experience veterans would be exposed to, decided upon the task load for individual veterans with varying capabilities, and set guidelines for the fieldwork. Introductions and briefing materials were held through online meetings in preparation for travel to Saipan. TFDF provided all SCUBA and diving equipment to the veterans and ECU supplied all archaeological survey gear. Travel to Saipan included a stopover in Hawaii to visit the DPAA lab. At the lab, the veterans were provided with a tour of the facilities and briefing about the mission of DPAA. From there, they traveled to Saipan and prepared for the training and field work.

The training was modified specifically for JRT to include content on the maritime heritage of the Mariana Islands, historical context of World War II in the Pacific Theater, and local Indigenous history and culture. The training took place over two days with the first being a classroom day and hands-on practice of

**FIGURE 6.4** Joint Recovery Team, 2018. Photograph by J. McKinnon.

archaeological skills. The second day was an in-water day in which the veterans practiced the skills they learned on land in a pool. In addition to the training, veterans visited historical and cultural sites including museums, underwater sites on the World War II Maritime Heritage Trail: Battle of Saipan, local cultural markets, Indigenous canoes and traditional seafaring demonstrations, and World War II civilian caves and military tunnels.

Veterans conducted archaeological search and survey of World War II underwater sites following the training. They tested magnetometer and side scan sonar survey targets identified during previous surveys using visual circle searches and metal detectors and recorded cultural material on a proforma and via photography (Figure 6.5). Veterans participated in all aspects of the survey and recording for a total of ten days. They kept personal journals that included daily archaeological field notes, but also reflections about the work they were undertaking. Briefings were held each night to discuss the day's activities, plan for the following day, but also reflect upon their experience in the mission. Days off the water were planned and rotated when members became fatigued, evenings included some site tours and social activities, and weather days were also utilized for topside site tours.

**FIGURE 6.5** A TFDF veteran conducting circle searches on a target. Photograph by N. Grinnan.

An assessment of the program was undertaken including a questionnaire survey of participants about the training, the fieldwork, and their experience. Comments from the survey indicate that the program was meaningful personally and connected veterans with the process of archaeology and study of conflict sites. Examples of comments included, 'It was more than I could have imagined. Emotionally made me cry several times. Real world mission! Mission that needs to be done,' and 'The fieldwork side is certainly the rewarding side of things and I am thankful to have been part of it.'

The development team assessed the program and discussed the strengths and weaknesses making some adjustments for future iterations. And the program was run a second time in summer 2019 as part of a second DPAA mission in Saipan. The second mission was a follow-up on a specific aircraft found during the 2018 mission. Currently, the plan is to run the program annually, pending funding and support, with new recruits feeding in while trained veterans act in leadership roles. Additionally, TFDF signed their own MOU with DPAA allowing them to support both organic missions (i.e. those run in-house by DPAA) and those run by other DPAA partners. These connections are critical to sustaining an ongoing archaeological veterans' program.

The results of the JRT are both tangible and intangible. The program created an underwater maritime heritage and archaeological education program aimed at veterans who can engage in learning about the significance of maritime heritage through the exploration of World War II underwater archaeological sites. It allowed veterans with the opportunity to investigate World War II archaeological sites and aided in the location and recording of new sites with potential for DPAA recovery missions. It provided veterans with a physical fitness opportunity to continue to improve upon their recovery. It provided a new mission, purpose, and focus of working toward a goal of bringing closure to the families whose loved ones have never been accounted for after being declared MIA during World War II. Finally, it fostered an appreciation for World War II archaeological sites as share heritage through existing shared experiences by veterans.

## Conclusion

Despite the challenges of World War II UCH in the Pacific being 'out of sight and out of mind,' this chapter has outlined how it still can be considered shared heritage through the shared experience of war. There are few communities around the world that have not experienced or been impacted by regional and world wars within the last century. Whether as a soldier, a veteran, a non-combatant, or a family member, many of us have been touched by war. Recognizing these commonalities of experience can help us draw connections between each other, between the past and present, and with the conflict heritage that surrounds us and lurks beneath the waters.

## Acknowledgements

I would like to thank the participants in both veteran programs for their participation, enthusiasm, and support for learning more about our difficult, but shared, conflict heritage. I would like to particularly thank the War in the Pacific Leaders, Dr. Anne Ticknor and Dr. Anna Froula and the Discussion Leaders, Eulalia V. Arriola, Jim Pruitt, Genevieve Cabrera, Tina Sablan, Fred Camacho, and Leila Staffler for helping put together and run a successful program that created new historical and cultural meaning and connection to war and conflict heritage for those of Saipan. I'd also like to thank the leadership of Task Force Dagger's Joint Recovery Team, particularly Mark Stephens, Keith David, and Alan Williams, as well as all veteran participants, for continuing the oath of never leaving a fallen soldier behind and giving everything they have to offset the ultimate sacrifice our past service members made and bring closure to families who have been waiting for decades. I'm continually inspired working with veterans and Pacific Islanders and feel incredibly lucky to be accepted by those communities to work with them on their past.

## References

Australia-Netherlands. 2017. 'Memorandum of Understanding between the Cultural Heritage Agency of the Netherlands and the Australian Government Department of the Environment and Energy.' [WWW] www.environment.gov.au/system/files/pages/7e5adec7-b7a0-4d42-9cd4-11d99c2b733f/files/mou-netherland-australia-2017.pdf (accessed 13/11/2019).

Bulgrin, L.E. 2005. 'The Tudela Site: Fire and Steel over Saipan, 15 June 1944', *The Journal of Conflict Archaeology*, 1, 1–17.

Cabrera, G. 2015. 'A Historical Overview of the Battle for Saipan.' In: J.M. McKinnon and T. Carrell, eds. *Underwater Archaeology of a Pacific Battlefield: The WWII Battle of Saipan*. New York: Springer Press, 15–26.

Camacho, K.L. 2008. 'The Politics of Indigenous Collaboration: The Role of Chamorro Interpreters in Japan's Pacific Empire, 1914–45', *The Journal of Pacific History*, 43 (2), 207–22.

Camacho, K.L. 2011. *Cultures of Commemoration: The Politics of War, Memory, and History in the Mariana Islands*. Honolulu: University of Hawai'i Press.

Chapman, W. & Lightner, D. 1996. 'Historic preservation training in Micronesia: An assessment of Needs', *CRM: The Journal of Heritage Stewardship*, 2, 11–14.

Chargualaf, M. 2018. *Interview with Meling Chargualaf. Interview Collected by Stephanie Soder on 25 July*. Greenville: East Carolina University.

David, C.K., Smith, P. & McKinnon, J. 2020. 'The Journey Home: Recovering Self and Those Who Gave All', *Journal of Community Archaeology and Heritage*, 7 (4), 234–38.

Demapan, Sister Asuncion "Chong." 2018. *Interview with Sister Asuncion "Chong" Demapan. Interview collected by Stephanie Soder on 20 July*. Greenville: East Carolina University.

Dwyer, G. & Klimis, S. 2019. 'Full Steam Ahead: Recent Developments Concerning Australia's New Legal Regime for Regulating Underwater Cultural Heritage', *Australian & New Zealand Maritime Law Journal*, 33 (2), 12–24.

Falgout, S., Poyer, L. & Carucci, L.M. 2008. *Memories of War: Micronesians in the Pacific War*. Honolulu: University of Hawai'i Press.

Farrell, D. 2009. 'Operation Tearaway and Tattersalls.' In: T. Carrell, ed. *Maritime History and Archaeology of the Commonwealth of the Northern Mariana Islands*. Santa Fe: Ships of Exploration and Discovery Research, Inc., 269–343.

Goldberg, H.J. 2007. *D-Day in the Pacific: The Battle of Saipan*. Bloomington: Indiana University Press.

Hoyt, E.P. 2000. *How They Won the War in the Pacific: Nimitz and His Admirals*. Guilford: The Lyons Press.

Kauffman, D. 1986. 'The UDTs Come of Age at Saipan.' In: J. Mason, ed. *The Pacific War Remembered: An Oral History Collection*. Annapolis: Naval Institute Press, 236–45.

King, T.F. 2006. 'How Micronesia Changed the US Historic Preservation Program and the Importance of Keeping it from Changing Back', *The Micronesian Journal of the Humanities and Social Sciences*, 5 (1), 505–16.

Marsh, K.G. 2013. *An Exploration of Indigenous Values and Historic Preservation in Western Micronesia: A Study in Cultural Persistence*. Unpublished Doctoral Dissertation, Charles Sturt University, Thurgoona, NSW.

McKinnon, J.F., Ticknor, A.S. & Froula, A. 2019. 'Engaging Pacific Islander Veterans and Military Families in Difficult Heritage Discussions', *Journal of Maritime Archaeology*, 14, 167–81.

Murray, S.C. 2006. *War and Remembrance on Peleliu: Islander, Japanese, and American Memories of a Battle in the Pacific War*. Unpublished Doctoral Dissertation, University of California, Santa Barbara, CA.

National Endowment for the Humanities. 2019. Dialogues on the Experience of War. https://www.neh.gov/grants/education/dialogues-the-experience-war (accessed 01/11/2019).

O'Neill, J.G. 2005. *Historic Preservation in Post-Colonial Micronesia*. Unpublished Doctoral Dissertation, Charles Sturt University, Thurgoona, NSW.

Parthesius, R. 2011. 'Shared Heritage? Shared Responsibility? Reflections on the Role of 'Shared' Colonial Heritage Within Capacity Building Programs in the Postcolonial World.' In: M. Staniforth, ed. *Proceedings of the Inaugural Asia-Pacific Regional Conference on Underwater Cultural Heritage*. Manila: Asian Academy for Heritage Management, 641–51.

Petty, B.M. 2002. *Saipan: Oral Histories of the Pacific War*. Jefferson: McFarland & Company Inc.

Poyer, L., Falgout, S. & Carucci, L.M. 2001. *The Typhoon of War: Micronesian Experiences of the Pacific War*. Honolulu: University of Hawai'i Press.

Ransley, J. 2007. 'Rigorous Reasoning, Reflexive Research and the Space for "Alternative Archaeologies." Question for Maritime Archaeological Heritage Management', *Journal of Maritime Archaeology*, 36 (2), 221–37.

Ridwan, N.N.H. 2019. 'Vulnerability of Shipwreck Sites in Indonesian Waters', *Current Science*, 117 (10), 1623–28.

Rottman, G.L. 2004. US *World War II Amphibious Tactics: Army & Marine Corps, Pacific Theater*. Oxford: Osprey Publishing.

Russell, S. 1994. *Operation Forager: The Battle for Saipan*. Saipan: Division of Historic Preservation.

Russell, S. 1998. *Teimpon I Manmofo'na*. Micronesian Archaeological Survey, No. 32. Saipan: Division of Historic Preservation.

Spector, R.H. 1984. *Eagle against the Sun: The American War with Japan*. New York: Viking Penguin. Task Force Dagger Foundation. 2019. Task Force Dagger. [WWW]https://www.taskforcedagger.org/ (accessed 01/11/2019).

Tillman, B. 2005. *Clash of the Carriers: The True Story of the Marianas Turkey Shoot of World War II*. New York: NAL Caliber.

Underwood, R.A. 1977. 'Red, Whitewash and Blue: Painting over the Chamorro Experience', *Pacific Daily News, Islander*, 17th July.

Wheeler, R. 1996. *A Special Valor: The US Marines and The Pacific War.* New York: Meridian.

White House Initiative on Asian Americans & Pacific Islanders n.d. 'Fact Sheet: What You Should Know about Native Hawaiians and Pacific Islanders.' [WWW] https://www2.ed.gov/about/inits/list/asian-americans-initiative/what-you-should-know.pdf (accessed 21/02/2020).

Willmott, H.P. 1999. *The Second World War in the Far East.* London: Weidenfeld & Nicolson.

Winter, T. 2019. 'Heritage and the Politics of Cooperation.' In: A.M. Labrador and N.A. Silberman, eds. *The Oxford Handbook of Public Heritage Theory and Practice.* Oxford: Oxford University Press, 65–72.

Ya'ari, E. 2010. 'Promoting Understanding of Shared Heritage (PUSH)', *Museum International*, 62 (1–2), 9–13.

# 7

# 'YOU'VE COME A LONG WAY TO STUDY SOMETHING THAT IS BAD'

## Human Remains, Ethics and Community-Based Research in Conflict Archaeology in the Pacific

*Julie Mushynsky*

## Introduction

This chapter focuses on using community-based research strategies during a conflict archaeology project on World War II in the Pacific Theatre, specifically on Saipan, United States (US) Commonwealth of the Northern Mariana Islands (CNMI) (Figure 7.1). From 2013 to 2015, I partnered with local community members to record a series of World War II caves and tunnels, or 'karst defences' (Mushynsky et al. 2018; Mushynsky 2019, 2021). The goals of the project were to analyse the defence strategies and tactics used by both civilians and military forces during the Battle of Saipan, which took place between June 15th and July 9th 1944. A second aim was to understand the contemporary significance of these sites to local stakeholders. We recorded seventy-three caves and tunnels, over 4,000 artefacts and interviewed four civilians who survived the battle by sheltering in caves.

During the project, I interviewed Rosa T. Castro, who was fourteen years old during the Battle of Saipan (Mushynsky 2021). Rosa remembered the US arrival to Saipan and the sound of air-raid sirens and Japanese people yelling that everyone needed to run and hide. 'I was small…we see [*sic*] the ships and heard the bombs…there was no time to get things…get [*sic*] ready to run' (Castro pers comm. 2014). At that time, Rosa and her family left their home in Tanapag—a village on the north western coast of Saipan, and headed north towards the caves on Mount Tapochau, Saipan's highest point. As the battle moved from the southern portion of the island to the north, Rosa's family moved from cave to cave, sheltering within each for a few days at a time (Mushynsky 2021). The caves were big enough that several families hid within a single cave together. Often, the Japanese military forced civilians out of their cave and took it for themselves. During the twenty-five-day battle, civilians were under constant threat of dying

DOI: 10.4324/9780429270468-9

from starvation, dehydration and bombardment. Luckily, Rosa never lost any family members during the war, but she told me that, at the time, she truly felt that she was going to die. Towards the end of the interview, Rosa told me, 'I feel sorry for you because World War II is not happy' (Castro pers comm. 2014). Knowing I was not a local, she thought that it was unfortunate that I had come such a long way to study and learn about something that is bad. Rosa passed away two months after I conducted the interview.

There were devastating levels of violence and suffering experienced by both civilians and military forces during the Battle of Saipan. In total, the Japanese military lost at least 27,000 soldiers, the US lost 3,000 and at least 900 civilians died (Henshall 2013: 325; Cabrera 2015: 24). Many of these individuals lost their lives within karst defences. Karst defences were used by civilians as shelters and by the Japanese military as combat positions, command posts, hospitals, storage units and for shelter (see Figure 7.2; Mushynsky et al. 2018; Mushynsky 2021). As a result, much of the hand-to-hand combat during the battle occurred between Japanese and US troops at these sites. The US military attacked the Japanese at karst defences with grenades and flamethrowers (106th Infantry 1944: 11). At some caves, the US military attempted to get civilians to surrender by calling out to them or dropping leaflets, but if they suspected that Japanese soldiers were inside, they would seal the cave shut burying people alive (106th Infantry 1944: 11). Rather than risk being captured, a number of Japanese soldiers hiding out in caves and tunnels took their own lives, especially during the last few days of the battle (Harries & Harries 1991: 432; Denfeld 1997: 87, 89). Japanese soldiers told civilians that, if captured, the US would torture and mutilate the women and children (North 2004: 352; Mushynsky 2021). Consequently, many civilians killed themselves and their families within caves. Death within karst defences continued post battle. 'War souvenir hunting,' where soldiers would remove militaria and body parts from Japanese corpses as a personal souvenir, to trade with other soldiers or as a gift for friends or relatives back home, was a common practice among US soldiers throughout the Pacific Theatre (Sledge 1981: 120; Weingartner 1992; Harrison 2006: 824, 2008: 775; Price et al. 2015: 224–25). Upon entering caves in search of such souvenirs, Allied troops were sometimes killed by concealed traps or armed Japanese survivors (27th Infantry Division G-2 Section 1944: 229; Price et al. 2015). The evidence of violence still exists within karst defences and in Saipan, I recorded 216 elements/fragments of human bones within eleven different sites in unburnt, burnt and calcined forms. Whether these remains are a result of the battle or post war was determined through the analysis of artefacts and evidence of post-depositional disturbance.

As Rosa's interview conveys, projects that involve death and violence still within living memory can re-open old wounds. As a result, research on modern conflict has the potential to become emotionally and politically charged, especially for stakeholders (Camp 2018: 605; Harrison & Schofield 2010: 5). Scholars argue that conflict archaeologists must manage potential unease and discord by employing community-based methodologies (Schofield et al. 2002: 1;

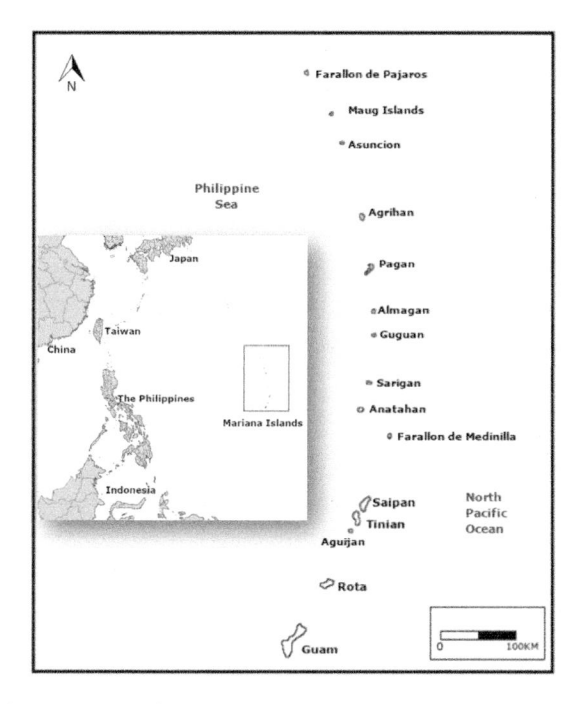

**FIGURE 7.1** The Mariana Islands in the Pacific. Figure previously published in Mushynsky, J. 2021. *The Archaeology, History and Heritage of WWII Karst Defenses in the Pacific: Cultures of Conflict.* Springer Nature: 2, reproduced with permission of the publisher.

**FIGURE 7.2** Interior of Japanese tunnel.

Moshenska 2009: 49–51). However, how modern conflict archaeologists conduct community-based research on topics involving death and violence and its ethical challenges has not been sufficiently addressed. This is largely because archaeological research on conflict in the recent past is still relatively new (Price 2005: 7; Moshenska 2008: 160). The archaeological literature needs more explicit discussion on this topic in order to guide and prepare archaeologists for some of the challenges they may encounter. This chapter is a contribution to that discussion. Using the Saipan Karst Defence Project as a case study, I examine some of the ways I addressed the challenges of conducting community-based conflict archaeology.

In this chapter, I focus on the sensitivities surrounding and the methods of dealing with human remains from World War II. I wish to focus on this because public engagement on projects involving human remains is difficult to navigate and can present serious ethical problems. Moreover, in the Pacific, encountering human remains on conflict archaeology projects is almost inevitable. Thus, researchers in the area need to be aware of what to expect during their projects. Ultimately, I advocate for a methodology that incorporates both bottom-up and top-down strategies to ensure public involvement and the ethical treatment of archaeological materials related to death and violence.

## Modern Conflict Archaeology, the Present and Ethics

Post-processual paradigms assert that archaeological interpretations are always bound up in the politics of the present (Harrison and Schofield 2010: 22; Johnson 2011: 11, 15). Some scholars argue, however, that modern conflict archaeology is even more entrenched in contemporary matters because of its temporal proximity (Buchli & Lucas 2001a: 8–9; Harrison & Schofield 2010: 4–5; Camp 2018: 605). Consequently, modern conflict archaeology can significantly affect stakeholder communities. During Renshaw's (2011: 52, 76) work on the mass graves of the Spanish Civil War of the 1930s, for example, community members rejected involvement because the past was too painful for them or they feared hostility from people who disagreed with the study. Renshaw (2011: 80) explains that during the project, archaeologists received phone calls and emails from opponents threatening to harm the archaeologists and damage the site. Similarly, Sturdy Colls' (2015: 106) work on Holocaust archaeology attracted the attention of Holocaust deniers and fascist and nationalist organizers who opposed the work.

Conflict archaeologists argue that in order to effectively deal with the implications of conjuring up violent pasts, they must conduct their research ethically (Moshenska & González-Ruibal 2015: 1). There is no specific standard or code of practice for conflict archaeologists to follow, so establishing right and wrong practices is situational and context specific (Moshenska 2008: 172; Giblin 2015: 44). Some archaeologists argue that ethical modern conflict archaeology must be community-based (Schofield et al. 2002: 1; Moshenska 2009: 49–51). Engaging with local communities has several benefits. Collaboration helps achieve a primary aim of historical archaeology, which is to understand the lives of those often ignored in recorded histories. Working with communities can help add that neglected information from historical accounts and establish more multivocal and inclusive histories (Buchli & Lucas 2001b:171; Harrison & Schofield 2010: 13–14; Mushynsky 2021). Secondly, working with local communities allows archaeologists to address any ethical issues in advance which can then be considered during research design, fieldwork and follow up (Moshenska 2015: 174; Mushynsky 2021). Sturdy Colls (2015: 89) agrees and urges that, prior to embarking on a modern conflict project, archaeologists should dedicate a considerable amount of time to identifying possible sensitivities and the political, social and cultural landscapes surrounding the research.

Community engagement comes in various forms that differ in the level of non-archaeologist involvement and control (Colwell-Chanthaphohn & Ferguson 2008: 1; Kador 2014: 35–36). Public engagement can be understood as a spectrum with superficial public involvement through publications, websites and public talks at one end and full-fledged, community-run archaeological initiatives at the other (Figure 7.3; Kador 2014). These methods are also referred to as 'top-down' or 'bottom-up' approaches, respectively (Thomas 2014: 25–26). Due to the nature of modern conflict and the potential social, political and cultural sensitivities, archaeologists may find that purely bottom-up strategies are not appropriate in certain instances. Forensic anthropology projects on human remains, for example, require the highest level of competency when recording and recovering. In this instance, if the public cannot meet such standards, they may need to be excluded from fieldwork (Sturdy Colls 2015: 106; Congram et al. 2016: 569).

Scholars argue that modern conflict archaeologists must go beyond methodological concerns and also consider the ethics of their interpretations and how they fit into political landscapes. There are several examples of political uses and abuses of archaeological interpretations (Fowler 1987; Meskell 1998), one of the most sinister being the Nazis who used archaeology to construct racial identities which became the basis for genocidal actions later on (Arnold 2002). More recently, archaeologist, John Giblin was concerned that his research on a burial from the Rwandan genocide which showed physical evidence of a violent death and possible dismemberment could be used to incite violence (Giblin et al. 2010; Giblin 2018). The concern is not unfounded as according to official histories, anthropological reinforcement of ethno-racial stereotypes between the Twa, Tutsi and Hutu was a contributor to the genocidal violence that occurred between these groups in Rwanda in 1994 (Krüger 2010: 8). Giblin (2015: 47) suggests that conflict archaeologists be explicit in the potential political uses of their findings in order to guide the direction and intention of their interpretations.

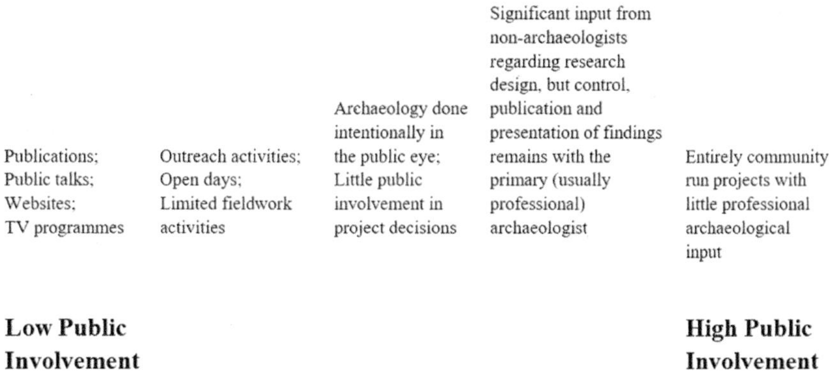

| Publications;<br>Public talks;<br>Websites;<br>TV programmes | Outreach activities;<br>Open days;<br>Limited fieldwork<br>activities | Archaeology done<br>intentionally in<br>the public eye;<br>Little public<br>involvement in<br>project decisions | Significant input from<br>non-archaeologists<br>regarding research<br>design, but control,<br>publication and<br>presentation of findings<br>remains with the<br>primary (usually<br>professional)<br>archaeologist | Entirely community<br>run projects with<br>little professional<br>archaeological<br>input |
|---|---|---|---|---|

**Low Public Involvement**                                                                                  **High Public Involvement**

**FIGURE 7.3**   The public involvement spectrum (Kador 2014).

## Community Archaeology in Saipan

In line with other modern conflict archaeologists who promote community-based research strategies, the Karst Defence Project was also community-based. The project was part of a long-running, community archaeology program in Saipan first developed in 2007 under Dr. Jennifer McKinnon. Research within the program has focused on submerged World War II sites in the lagoon (McKinnon & Carrell 2011; McKinnon 2014, 2015a, 2015b), Indigenous seascapes and maritime cultural landscapes (Mushynsky 2011; McKinnon et al. 2014a), World War II oral histories (Soder & McKinnon 2019) and most recently on an education program engaging with Pacific Island veterans and military families (McKinnon et al. 2019). Each project has worked to address the needs and wants of the community and collaborated with locals and organizations in research planning, fieldwork and dissemination. The Karst Defence Project, specifically, emerged from discussions with locals who were concerned about karst defence preservation, access and the desire to know more about how these sites were used during World War II.

The stakeholders and political landscapes for each project in Saipan were different. Karst defences as sites of shared heritage have a diverse group of stakeholders. The Battle of Saipan was between two colonial powers on Micronesian land. As a result, its legacy is a part of Japanese, US and Micronesian histories. While these three are the primary communities affected by the battle, it is important to note that people with various ethnic backgrounds participated in the battle, including those of Korean, Okinawan, Hispanic, Native American and African American descent (Price & Knecht 2013: 193 McKinnon 2015b: 2). There is also a range of organizations concerned with karst defences for various heritage and environmental-related reasons. Some of these organizations include the CNMI Historic Preservation Office (HPO), World War II interpretation centres and repositories such as American Memorial Park and the NMI

Museum of History and Culture, as well as environmental organizations such as the Division of Fish and Wildlife. Finally, there are tourism companies who promote visitation to karst defences and the tourists who visit them (Mushynsky 2021).

Understanding the ethical issues and sensitivities during the Karst Defence Project required an identification and analysis of the interrelationships between the above-mentioned stakeholders. There were many connections between karst defence stakeholders that we considered for the project, but it is not possible to sufficiently discuss them all here (see Mushynsky (2021) for a discussion of stakeholders and contemporary significance). To determine an appropriate level of public involvement, my strategy was to identify political, social and cultural sensitivities first then apply the public involvement spectrum to each stage of the project, including developing the research questions, field practices, data collection, analysis, storage and public dissemination. The identified sensitivities were then used to determine an appropriate level of public involvement (Figure 7.4).

The proposed approach is useful because, given the many nuances a project can have, it breaks the project down and helps identify where more engagement can be facilitated, allows for continuous discussion of ethics and ensures ethical implications are fully understood at every stage (Moshenska & González-Ruibal 2015: 14; Sturdy Colls 2015: 183). The impacts of research are not static and change

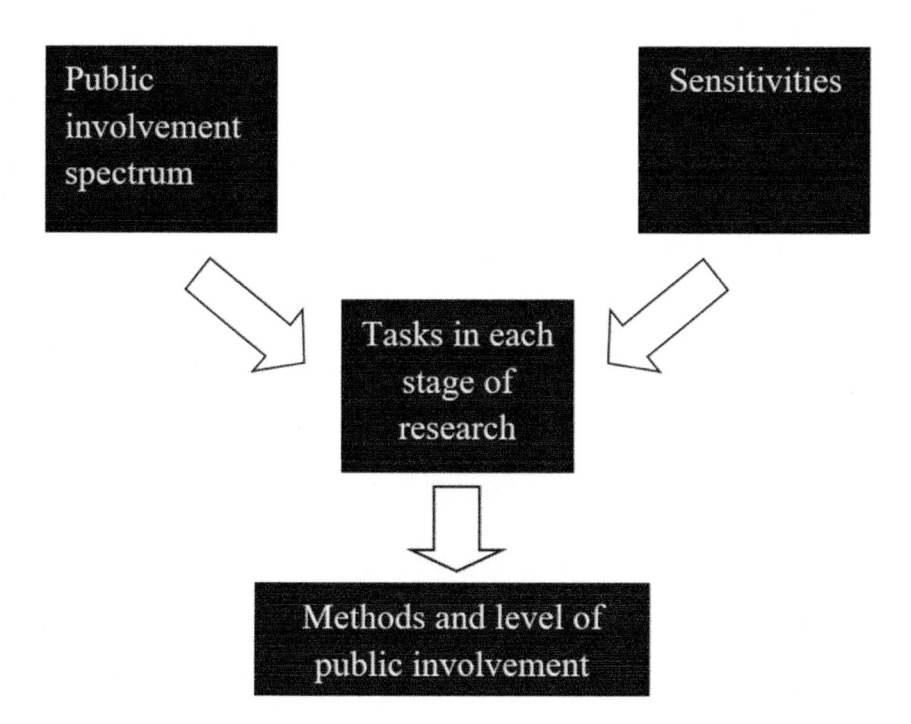

**FIGURE 7.4** Process of determining public involvement.

over time and with different age groups (McKinnon 2015b: 12), so this methodology allows analysis to occur at each stage, with new information gathered and learned from the previous stage(s). The approach also eliminates any hard dichotomy between bottom-up and top-down archaeology and allows for a more fluid understanding of how people are/can be involved in archaeological projects. Furthermore, the approach recognizes that, despite intentions, sometimes not all stages of a project are bottom-up or top-down and that what intends to be an entirely bottom-up model sometimes ends up being partially top-down with archaeologists in control. Finally, the approach also enables archaeologists to be open, honest and flexible which means that if the opportunity for involvement exists, every effort is made to include non-archaeologists in some way but is not forced.

## The Politics of World War II Human Remains in the Pacific

### *Repatriation*

Compared to other modern conflict archaeology projects on topics such as the Holocaust and the Rwandan genocide, the politics surrounding human remains from World War II in the Pacific are not as perverse. In general, there are no World War II deniers and it is well known that the US and Japanese militaries killed each other and themselves during the war and that civilians were caught in the middle. Additionally, there are no pending human rights or criminal cases. There are certainly controversies from World War II in the Pacific Theatre that are indirectly related to karst defences, including the Nanking Massacre, the Imperial Japanese Army's (IJA) Unit 731 and the use of so-called 'comfort women' (Tanaka 2002; Chang 2011; Hickey et al. 2017). However, one of the most concerning for stakeholders in the Pacific in relation to human remains is the process of repatriating fallen soldiers from various areas of the Pacific.

The ways Japan and the US repatriate the remains of those lost during World War II has evolved over the years. During the war, and several years later in some areas, the Japanese would cremate human remains in the field, then subsequently send the ashes home and place them within the Yasukuni Shrine—a Shinto Shrine in central Tokyo which holds items to commemorate Japan's war dead (Satoshi 2003: 345; Trefalt 2017: 148). In 1948, Japan's Ministry of Health and Welfare was tasked with repatriation and began organizing 'bone collecting missions' to various places in the Asia-Pacific, often in partnership with non-government organizations such as the Japan League for Bereaved Family Welfare (Satoshi 2003: 345–54; Trefalt 2017: 148). After collecting the remains, memorials were often erected in the location spots (Figal 2007: 89). Today, both Japanese government and non-government groups continue to conduct repatriation missions throughout the Pacific, including full-scale excavations of known burials.

US repatriation efforts in the Pacific centre around the Central Identification Lab (CIL) in Honolulu, Hawaii—the largest forensic laboratory in the world (Pietruszka 2015: 454). From the 1970s up until 2003, the US Secretary of the

Army relied primarily on physical anthropologists from the CIL to identify human remains (Hoshower-Leppo 2002: 80). In 2003, the CIL merged with the Joint Task Force-Full Accounting, a government agency formed in 1992 to locate Americans missing in Southeast Asia, to form the newly commissioned Joint POW/MIA Accounting Command (JPAC) under the Department of Defense (Pietruszka 2015: 455). JPAC underwent another shift in 2015 to become the Department of Defence POW/MIA Accounting Agency (DPAA) (Hoshower-Leppo 2002: 81; Pietruszka 2015: 453). Like Japan, US repatriation activities have included non-government entities through public-private partnerships and cooperative agreements (Department of Defense 2018). DPAA partners with universities, veterans' groups, consulting companies and film production teams.

Tensions exist throughout the Pacific between US and Japanese repatriation organizations, heritage organizations and local residents. For one, there have been serious concerns about the recovery practices of some Japanese and US organizations. In the Philippines, for example, locals found that Japanese bone collectors were paying Philippine locals to gather human remains for them in advance (Satoshi 2003: 363–64). In 2009, also in the Philippines, Kuentai, a private, non-profit organization was accused of hiring Filipino agents who would purchase bones from locals. These bones were suspected of being ancient remains or from more contemporary burials (Japan Times 2010, 2011). Like Japanese repatriation organizations, US organizations have also been criticized for misconduct. There are reports of fraudulent 'return ceremonies,' misidentifying remains, planting human remains in order to subsequently locate them and claim success, and accusations of organizational mismanagement (Burke 2014; Trefalt 2017: 154; Cole 2019: 181).

The desire to repatriate the remains of fallen soldiers and some of the questionable means of obtaining them has led to an active human remains trade in some countries. Satoshi (2003: 363–64) found this to be the case in the Philippines, for example. Such trade has also occurred in Papua New Guinea (PNG). In 1979, former member of the IJA, Nishimura Kokichi, who had fought in PNG during the war, returned with the goal to repatriate the remains of his fallen compatriots—a promise he made to them during the war. He spent twenty-six years collecting their remains and returning them to Japan. During his time in PNG, he found that locals were selling skeletal remains to tourists. He believes that this type of industry exists because Japanese people have paid to purchase remains they thought were those of fallen soldiers and needed to be returned home to Japan (McNeill 2008). The true extent of the trade of human remains from World War II throughout the Pacific is unclear.

Some organizations are also in conflict with heritage organizations in the Pacific. While Japanese and US repatriation groups have specific goals and methods for retrieving human remains, their wants can differ from local heritage rules and policies. In Saipan, for instance, when it comes to regulating archaeological research and development, the HPO follows US federal heritage law. The *National Historic Preservation Act* of 1966 governs heritage in the US Section 106 of the Act requires federal and private agencies to take into account the effects of their actions on historic properties and therefore they usually have to apply for a permit for any ground disturbance and artefact recovery (King 2006: 505). In terms of human remains, the HPO has a specific set of rules that were established in 1999: the CNMI 'Standards for the Treatment of Human Remains.' These standards differentiate between four different classes of remains: Ancient, Historic, World War II and Modern with different culturally appropriate ways of dealing with them (Russell 2001: 24). This means that repatriation groups must have the proper permits to recover remains, be qualified to conduct any ground disturbance or excavation to collect them and need to properly identify the ethnicity of the person to whom they belong. However, some repatriation groups have not always complied with local heritage legislation and some have even used locals and tour guides to evade the permitting process (Mushynsky 2021). Locals in Saipan who support the mission have assisted and accompanied organizations to sites with human remains.

What adds another layer of complexity to the problem is that there is conflict between some Japanese and US organizations. Kuentai, for example, has publicly criticized US practices, accusing them of downplaying the number of missing soldiers, not repatriating fast enough and for thwarting the progress of Kuentai's work (Kuentai-USA 2019). US organizations and veterans' groups from Japan and the US have questioned Kuentai's success rate and raised concerns that they were recovering and cremating non-Japanese remains (Trefalt 2017: 153–54). To speed up repatriation, Kuentai developed a US division to recover remains and have requested US financial support to follow through with their efforts. While they appear to have some support from other non-profits, citizens and local governments in the Pacific and mainland US, they are often at odds with the methods and requirements of the DPAA (Bagnol 2014).

The CNMI HPO appears to be removing the above-mentioned hurdles. In light of the politics surrounding repatriation, the HPO has begun to develop a new policy where information on human remains will be passed on to both DPAA and the Japanese Ministry of Health, Labour and Welfare (MHLW). The HPO would then allow both parties the opportunity to decide whether to conduct the recovery themselves, contract that through a third party or partnership or request the HPO to conduct the recovery. While the HPO is still working on policy language, essentially, they would require that the recovery of US remains be conducted by DPAA or their representative (currently understood to be either an organic mission or a partnership) and Japanese remains should be recovered by MHLW or their representative—the Japanese Association for Recovery and Repatriation of Wartime Casualties (JARRWC) for this region (Pruitt pers comm. 2019).

### Dark Tourism

Tourism has been a primary industry in the Pacific for several decades and in the CNMI since the early 1970s. However, since the collapse of the garment manufacturing industry, tourism has become the CNMI's only major industry (Marianas Visitors Authority 2012). Tourism reached its peak in the CNMI in 1997 when more than 700,000 people visited the islands (Marianas Visitors Authority 2012). In 2006, Japan Airlines decreased their service to the CNMI. This had significant consequences as Japan Airlines carried 29% of all tourists to the CNMI (US Senate 2007). The CNMI has been trying to recover ever since.

There are several public and private organizations involved in CNMI tourism. The government-funded, Marianas Visitors Authority (MVA) is in charge of promoting the CNMI to its key markets: Japan, Korea, China, Russia and Taiwan (Marianas Visitors Authority 2012). The MVA also provides an official tour guide certification program and publishes their tour guide list on their website (Marianas Visitors Authority 2012). Most of the tourism in the CNMI tends to surround water activities, golfing, shopping and gambling, although the MVA actively promotes visitation to well-known karst defence sites on public property as well. These include Kalabera Cave and the Last Command Post. Kalabera Cave, while used during World War II, contains rock art, which is its main attraction. The Last Command Post is likely an Imperial Japanese Navy command post, but was not actually the last command post used during the war (Mushynsky 2021). These two sites are easy to access and often part of group island tours. Other residents have also opened their own tour companies that are not affiliated with the MVA and also take tourists to these well-known karst defences.

Property owners also see the economic value of karst defences and some promote their sites to tourists themselves. Some see their karst defences as more appealing to tourists than those on public property because they are something different to see and off the beaten path. Sometimes this is difficult, however, since their location in the jungle, creates a safety issue for tourists and tour guides (Barcinas pers comm. 2014). Other property owners have attempted to make their sites more attractive to tourists by planting or 'salting' their sites with artefacts found elsewhere on the island and building railings and other infrastructure to make their sites more accessible (McKinnon et al. 2014b: 101). Some property owners charge an entrance fee for visitors to come to their sites (Mushynsky 2021). Other property owners I spoke to were willing to have tourists visit their sites as long as they could obtain some financial support to maintain the site.

While some property owners see their sites as an economic opportunity, many are also keenly aware of the shared heritage of karst defences. As a result, many property owners allow visitors to their sites for free for educational and commemorative purposes. Indeed, evidence of such visitation exists within karst defences on public and private property in the form of flowers, wreaths, stupas, candles, statues and food and beverage offerings (Figure 7.5). Of course, there are others who do not want anyone accessing the sites on their property at all.

Tourism and increased visitation are a concern in terms of the preservation of karst defences. Some tourists loot sites, move artefacts, intentionally or unintentionally damage artefacts and/or vandalize sites. There is also a concern about unauthorized visitation and several property owners explained that tourists looking

**FIGURE 7.5** Memorialization by visitors within Saipan tunnel.

to access sites on their property will do so without their consent (McKinnon et al. 2014b: 110–13). Additionally, there are visitors that publicize the locations of sites and post photographs and videos of people handling human remains on the Internet (McKinnon et al. 2014b: 15), which in turn can encourage destructive behaviour.

A primary issue with karst defence tourism is the 'darkness' of the sites. Dark tourism refers to tourism at sites associated with death, suffering, tragedy or crime as attractions (Lennon & Foley 2000: 1–12). Philip Stone (2006) developed a 'spectrum' of dark tourism, in which individual attractions may exhibit different degrees of 'darkness.' The spectrum is fluid and dark tourism can be 'lighter' or 'darker' depending on how close the site is to death and suffering. For instance, the killing fields of Cambodia would be considered the darkest types of tourism while a place like the London Dungeon attraction, with its focus on humour and theatre, would be at the 'lighter' end. The ways these sites are promoted also differ with the darkest having a more educational or commemorative focus to more fun and entertainment for the lighter sites. Despite substantial debate on the ethics of dark tourism, Light (2017: 283) argues that researchers have not provided any practical solutions on how it should be done. Furthermore, little dialogue between researchers and practitioners exists. Much of this inconclusiveness is because dark tourism and the ethics surrounding it are case-specific.

Due to the death and suffering experienced at karst defences and the continued presence of human remains, I consider karst defences to be on the darker side of Stone's (2006) spectrum. Saipan does promote some sites on the darker side of the spectrum already, particularly Banzai and Suicide Cliffs. Rather than surrender, hundreds of civilians and soldiers jumped off these cliffs during the last days of the battle. Unlike the cliffs, karst defences contain portable artefacts and remains that could be looted and might attract those with more sinister motivations. Furthermore, this could attract tour companies looking to profit off of this dark heritage. If locals and property owners wish to promote karst defences, there is no concrete plan in the CNMI to address the ethical issues of doing so.

Tourist attractions have used human remains as part of their displays. An example of this is Rwanda and the Kigali Genocide Memorial (KGM). The KGM consists of a primary centre with several sites surrounding it, many with human remains on display (Copeland 2011; Friedrich et al. 2018: 271–75). One of these sites is Murambi, a former school where 27,000 people were executed. Currently, 850 bodies preserved in lime are stacked and on display (Viebach 2014: 74–75). Similarly, in Cambodia, the Tuol Sleng and Choeung Ek, both of which the Khmer Rouge used to kill millions of people are now a genocide museum and memorial park, respectively (Copeland 2011: 43). These sites also feature human remains on display and indicators of how people died (Copeland 2011). However, as Miles (2002: 1176) argues, 'more than evoking historical knowledge, to be successful, any dark touristic 'attraction' must also engender a degree of empathy between the sightseer and the past victim.' One way to do this is to express the stories of the victims. Indeed, many successful forms of battlefield tourism refrain from trivializing or privileging any particular perspective and seek to build that understanding between tourist and victim (Frew & White 2013; McKinnon 2015b; Cullen 2017).

## Conflict and Community Archaeology

For the Karst Defence Project, I partnered with two local co-researchers: Fred Camacho, an avocational archaeologist and avid hiker, and Genevieve Cabrera, a local cultural historian. Cabrera has been a supporter of the community archaeology program since 2007 and suggested bringing Camacho on as a co-researcher. I discussed the research design with both Camacho and Cabrera prior to fieldwork and we worked through the logistics of the project. We communicated project goals to the public through public presentations, media interviews, newspaper advertisements and by distributing fliers. Together, we worked with a number of project participants. We worked with local property owners, who contacted us to record sites on their property for the project and we also conducted oral history interviews. Although some oral history professionals suggest that interviews consist of the interviewee and the interviewer only (Yow 2015: 105), due to the sensitivity of the topic and safety, myself, Cabrera and

Camacho conducted interviews and interviewees were encouraged to have family members present. We also decided that a second visit was required after the interview in order to review the interview transcript with the participant and to monitor their well-being. This was especially important if the interviewee had recounted painful memories during the interview.

In terms of recording human remains, the CNMI standards require that if the project is not a recovery mission, then archaeologists leave human skeletal remains in situ and report them to the HPO (Russell 2001: 23). If this is not possible, a professional archaeologist can recover them, perform a specialized osteological study and then release them to the HPO, who would then turn them over to the appropriate cultural group. During the Karst Defence Project, I produced a spreadsheet documenting the human remains I located during fieldwork detailing their location, a description of them and whether they were on public or private property and submitted it to the HPO.

While my policy obligations to the HPO were straightforward, the rest of the fieldwork was not. For one, opening the fieldwork to volunteers who would inevitably encounter human remains presented some challenges in light of issues already discussed. To recruit volunteers, I placed a newspaper advertisement in the local paper. Additionally, locals and potential participants learned of the project through word-of-mouth. Prior to hiring, each volunteer underwent a type of review process whereby myself and co-researchers tried to determine the underlying motivation of volunteers. We were primarily concerned with whether the person had political inclinations or whether they were interested in possibly using the site for their own economic gain. As a result, we turned down offers from two potential volunteers. In the end, we recruited all five volunteers through word-of-mouth and referral.

Volunteers assisted with fieldwork on public sites and on private sites as long as property owners consented. Volunteers recorded artefacts in the field, either electronically through FileMaker software and apps or via paper forms. In terms of human remains, I decided that I would not offer volunteers the option of recording them. At the beginning of the day, Camacho and I would brief the volunteers on the types of artefacts we would see and subsequently flag the artefacts that needed recording. Each volunteer was assigned a category of artefact to record, such as ceramics, glass or building materials. I taught them how to record specific artefact attributes which they then appeared to be interested in mastering and thus continued to record that particular artefact type for several days (Figure 7.6). None of the volunteers asked to record human remains and most appeared uninterested in them. However, if they had been interested in recording human remains, I was prepared to conduct a short workshop on recording them and allow volunteers to record human remains under my strict supervision. I believed that with some training, volunteers on the project would have been able to record human remains for the purposes of the project with a high level of competency. Furthermore, I was always in close proximity to volunteers and would have been able to monitor them closely.

Sharing the locations of caves and photographs of human remains online was another major concern for us. First, we did not want volunteers posting photographs of human remains, which could be taken out of context to be interpreted as an endorsement for handling human remains within sites, further exacerbating a key problem in Saipan. Second, we were concerned with the ethics surrounding sharing information about the dead in photographs and online environments. Scholars have debated whether using photographs of human remains infringes on the rights of the dead (Harries et al. 2018: 9; Moon 2019). Furthermore, photography, especially of marginalized peoples, has a history connected to colonial governmentality and voyeurism (Harries et al. 2018; Ulguim 2018: 10–12). Photographs of human remains are particularly sensitive in a World War II context as they are associated with another form of war souvenir collecting known as 'the trophy shot.' Such shots include photographs of soldiers holding the heads of an enemy corpse in a celebratory manner (Frederick 2011). On the other hand, many scholars support sharing human remains online. Many find that there is a significant level of public interest in death and violence and that archaeologists are in a position to contextualize this research and educate the public (Williams & Atkin 2017; Ulguim 2018: 165).

Guidelines on how to digitally represent human remains are scarce and keeping up with changing technology is a challenge (Williams & Atkin 2017; Errickson & Thompson 2019). However, some organizations are responding with their own policy documents and codes of conduct. Such guidelines require informed consent to display images of human remains. The Canadian Archaeological Association, for example, require authors to obtain documented permission from descendant community(s) to present human remains in any media or form (Canadian Archaeological Association 2019). In 2016, a Digital Bioarchaeological Ethics Panel at the World Archaeological Congress determined that while there are major benefits to creating and sharing digital data in terms of education, public outreach and preservation, they argue that the digital display of human remains needs to be determined on a case-by-case basis according to the needs of stakeholders (Hassett et al. 2018: 336; Ulguim 2018: 165).

For the Karst Defence Project, while volunteers were free to take photographs of the site and artefacts for the project, I asked them to refrain from posting locational information and photographs of artefacts related to the project online. In making this decision, I considered the sensitive nature of the human remains within karst defences. Also, since photographs and videos of visitors mishandling human remains deeply concerned locals, I chose to refrain from publicizing any photographs of human remains.

In terms of political abuses and misuses, it was possible that the project could become caught up in the politics of bone collecting and tourism. Indeed, one of the project participants told me that he was going to tell members of Kuentai that there were human remains in the cave sites we were visiting. By restricting the collection of locational data and photographs, I decreased the ability to access the sites we were visiting. As a result, anyone seeking to recover the remains from

**FIGURE 7.6** Volunteers John Fraser and Kelli Brewer recording artefacts.

these sites would need to consult the information I provided to the HPO who would then require them to follow proper permitting protocols. As for tourism, the decision to promote these sites to tourists lies with the community. My responsibility, however, is to ensure that I disseminate information to property owners who can then use the information to focus on the educational, commemorative and empathetic aspects of the sites. After the project was completed, I gave property owners individual reports detailing archaeological facts and interpretations of their sites, including whether or not someone had likely died at the site, how they died and details on who they may have been.

## Conclusion

Conflict archaeology research in the Pacific must deal with the impacts involved in re-visiting traumatic events. Researchers can turn the archaeology of 'something that is bad' into a worthwhile endeavour through collaborative methodologies. Involving locals in such research has significant benefits both to the community and to the quality of archaeological research. However, using community-based research strategies come with many challenges, especially when the work involves human remains, which conflict archaeologists working in the CNMI and any other Pacific Island, will likely encounter. Human remains in World War II contexts matter to local communities and thus such projects can be politically charged. Therefore, researchers must be prepared to take some time to evaluate the social, cultural and political environment they will be working in to ensure that the human remains they encounter and the communities they work with are given the utmost respect.

The Karst Defence Project employed a combination of bottom-up and top-down methodologies. The project was community-driven in that our decision to conduct the research was based on the concerns and wants of those we consulted with over several years. Additionally, members of the Saipan community were involved in every step of the research project, including formulating the research questions, project planning, fieldwork and the dissemination of findings. While public involvement was high, some aspects of the project were controlled to ensure that high ethical standards were maintained and to provide guidance on any potential political uses. This primarily affected our decisions on which volunteers to hire and what their level of participation would be. While this may be considered a top-down strategy, the decisions were still largely community-driven as they were based on what we understood was ethical, considering the political issues in the community.

The methods described in this chapter were developed after several years of conducting research in Saipan. However, when choosing how to ethically involve the public on conflict archaeology projects, there is no 'one-size-fits all' way of doing things. Moreover, even within the same community, what works for one project may not work for the next and circumstances may change over time. I hope that this chapter provides some insight into the dilemmas involved in working on World War II topics in Saipan, the Marianas and the Pacific and assists researchers and communities in addressing similar issues during their own conflict archaeology projects.

## Bibliography

27th Infantry Division G-2 Section. 1944. *Journal Forager Operation,* Washington, DC: United States Army.

106th Infantry. 1944. *Forager Narrative Report 15 April–5 August 1944. 'Forager' Operations Report.* Washington, DC: United States Army.

Arnold, B. 2002. 'Justifying Genocide: Archaeology and the Construction of Difference.' In: A.L. Hinton, ed. *Annihilating Difference: The Anthropology of Genocide.* Berkeley: University of California Press, 96–116.

Bagnol, R.C. 2014. *Remains of One Possible American Soldier Recovered, Kuentai-USA Digs for More.* [WWW] www.mvariety.com/cnmi/cnmi-news/local/68779-remains-of-one-possible-american-soldier-recovered-kuentai-usa-digs-for-more (accessed 23/07/2017).

Barcinas, Y. 2014. *Personal Communication.* Interview with Author. 03/11/2014.

Buchli, V. & Lucas, G. 2001a. 'The Absent Present: Archaeologies of the Contemporary Past.' In: V. Buchli and G. Lucas, eds. *Archaeologies of the Contemporary Past.* London: Routledge, 3–18.

Buchli, V. & Lucas, G., eds. 2001b. *Archaeologies of the Contemporary Past.* London: Routledge.

Burke, M.M. 2014. 'Accuracy Questioned in JPAC Identification of WWII Remains from Philippines', *Stars and Stripes*. [WWW] https://www.stripes.com/accuracy-questioned-in-jpac-identification-of-wwii-remains-from-philippines-1.318499 (accessed 05/06/2022).

Cabrera, G. 2015. 'A Historical Overview of the Battle for Saipan.' In: J.F. McKinnon and T.L. Carrell, eds. *Underwater Archaeology of a Pacific Battlefield*. New York: Springer Briefs in Archaeology, 15–26.

Castro, R. 2014. *Personal Communication*. Interview with Author. 18/12/2014.

Camp, S.L. 2018. 'Commentary: Excavating the Intimate', *Historical Archaeology*, 52 (3), 600–07.

Canadian Archaeological Association. 2019. *Presentation of Human Remains in CAA Media*. [WWW] https://canadianarchaeology.com/caa/about/ethics/presentation-human-remains-caa-media (accessed 03/06/2022).

Chang, I. 2011. *The Rape of Nanking: The Forgotten Holocaust of World War II*. New York: Basic Books.

Cole, P.M. 2019. *POW/MIA Accounting: Volume II JPAC and the Politics of Human Skeletan Idenitification*. Singapore: Springer.

Colwell-Chanthaphohn, C. & Ferguson, T.J. 2008. 'Introduction: the Collaborative Continuum.' In: C. Colwell-Chanthaphonh and T.J. Ferguson, eds. *Collaboration in Archaeological Practice: Engaging Descendant Communities*. Lanham, MD: AltaMira Press, 1–32.

Congram, D., Sterenberg, J. & Finegan, O. 2016. 'Continuing Challenges for Forensic Anthropology and Archaeology in Iraq.' In: S. Blau and D.H. Ubelaker, eds. *Handbook of Forensic Anthropology and Archaeology*. Oxford: Routledge, 563–74.

Copeland, C. 2011. 'Madness and Mayhem: the Aesthetics of Dark Tourism', *Afterimage*, 39 (1–2), 43–46.

Cullen, R. 2017. 'The Success of the Success: Negotiating Dark Tourism on an Exhibition "Convict Ship"', *Journal of Tourism History*, 9 (1), 4–26.

Denfeld, D.C. 1997. *Hold the Marianas: The Japanese Defense of the Mariana Islands*. Shippensburg, PN: White Mane Publishing.

Department of Defense. 2018. *Directive 2310.07 Past Conflict Personnel Accounting Policy. Office of the Under Secretary of Defense for Policy*. [WWW] https://www.esd.whs.mil/Portals/54/Documents/DD/issuances/dodd/231007p.pdf?ver=2018-04-23-075909-973 (accessed 05/06/2022).

Errickson, D. & Thompson, T.J.U. 2019. 'Sharing is Not Always Caring: Social Media and the Dead.' In: K. Squires, D. Errickson and N. Márquez-Grant, eds. *Ethical Approaches to Human Remains*. Switzerland: Springer Nature, 299–314.

Figal, G. 2007. 'Bones of contention: The geopolitics of "Sacred Ground" in Postwar Okinawa', *Diplomatic History*, 31 (1), 81–109.

Fowler, D.D. 1987. 'Uses of the past: Archaeology in the Service of the State', *American Antiquity*, 52 (2), 229–48.

Frederick, J. 2011. 'The Trophy Shot', *Time Magazine*. [WWW] https://time.com/3775924/the-trophy-shot/ (accessed 05/06/2022).

Frew, E. & White, L. 2013. 'Exploring Dark Heritage and Place Identity.' In: L. White and E. Frew, eds. *Dark Tourism and Place Identity: Managing and Interpreting Dark Places*. London: Routledge, 1–10.

Friedrich, M., Stone, P.R. & Rukesha, R. 2018. 'Dark Tourism, Difficult Heritage and Memorialisation: A Case of the Rwandan Genocide.' In: P.R. Stone, R. Hartmann, T. Seaton, R. Sharpley and L. White, eds. *The Palgrave Handbook of Dark Tourism Studies*. London: Palgrave Macmillan, 261–89.

Giblin, J. 2015. 'Archaeological Ethics and Violence in Post-Genocide Rwanda.' In: G. Moshenska and A. González-Ruibal, eds. *Ethics and the Archaeology of Violence.* New York: Springer, 33–50.

Giblin, J.D. 2018. *Heritage and the Use of the Past in East Africa.* Oxford: Oxford University Press.

Giblin, J., Clement, A. & Humphris, J. 2010. 'An Urewe Burial in Rwanda: Exchange, Health, Wealth and Violence c. AD 400', *Azania: Archaeological Research in Africa,* 45 (3), 276–97.

Harries, J., Fibiger, L., Smith, J., Adler, T. & Szöke, A. 2018. 'Exposure: The Ethics of Making, Sharing and Displaying Photographs of Human Remains', *Human Remains and Violence,* 4 (1), 3–24.

Harries, M. & Harries, S. 1991. *Soldiers of the Sun: The Rise and Fall of the Imperial Japanese Army.* New York: Random House Inc.

Harrison, R. & Schofield, J. 2010. *After Modernity: Archaeological Approaches to the Contemporary Past.* Oxford: Oxford University Press.

Harrison, S. 2006. 'Skull Trophies of the Pacific War: Transgressive Objects of Remembrance', *The Journal of the Royal Anthropological Institute,* 12 (4), 817–36.

Harrison, S. 2008. 'War Mementos and the Souls of Missing Soldiers: Returning Effects of the Battlefield Dead', *The Journal of the Royal Anthropological Institute,* 14 (4), 774–90.

Hassett, B.R., Rando, C., Bocaege, E., Alfonso Durruty, M., Hirst, C., Smith, S., Ferreira Ulguim, P., White, S. & Wilson, A. 2018. 'Transcript of WAC 8 Digital Bioarchaeological Ethics Panel Discussion, 29 August 2016 and Resolution on Ethical Use of Digital Bioarchaeological Data', *Archaeologies,* 14 (2), 317–37.

Henshall, K. 2013. *Historical Dictionary of Japan to 1945.* Lanham: Scarecrow Press, Inc.

Hickey, D., Li, S.S., Morrison, C., Schulz, R., Thiry, M. & Sorensen, K. 2017. 'Unit 731 and Moral Repair', *Journal of Medical Ethics,* 43 (4), 270–76.

Hoshower-Leppo, L. 2002. 'Missing in Action: Searching for America's War Dead.' In: J. Schofield, W.G. Johnson and C.M. Beck, eds. *Matériel Culture: The Archaeology of Twentieth-Century Conflict.* London: Routledge, 80–90.

Japan Times, 2010. NPO Accused over Grave Robbery. [WWW] https://www.japantimes.co.jp/news/2010/10/17/national/npo-accused-over-grave-robbery/ (accessed 05/06/2022).

Japan Times. 2011. War Remains May Contain Filipino Bones. [WWW] https://www.japantimes.co.jp/news/2011/09/26/national/war-remains-may-contain-filipino-bones/ (accessed 05/06/2022).

Johnson, M. 2011. *Archaeological Theory: An Introduction.* Malden: Wiley-Blackwell.

Kador, T. 2014. 'Public and Community Archaeology: An Irish Perspective.' In: S. Thomas and J. Lea, eds. *Public Participation in Archaeology.* Woodbridge: The Boydell Press, 35–48.

King, T. 2006. 'How Micronesia Changed the US Historic Preservation Program and the Importance of Keeping it from Changing Back', *Micronesian Journal of the Humanities and Social Sciences,* 5 (1/2), 505–16.

Krüger, K. 2010. 'The Destruction of Faces in Rwanda 1994', *L'Europe en Formation,* 357 (3), 91–105.

Kuentai-USA. 2019. *History.* [WWW] https://kuentai-usa.com/about.html (accessed 05/06/2022).

Lennon, J. & Foley, M. 2000. *Dark Tourism: The Attraction of Death and Disaster.* London: Continuum.

Light, D. 2017. 'Progress in Dark Tourism and Thanatourism Research: An Uneasy Relationship with Heritage Tourism', *Tourism Management,* 61, 275–301.

Marianas Visitors Authority. 2012. *Northern Mariana Islands Tourism Master Plan*. Saipan: Marianas Visitors Authority.

McKinnon, J.F. 2014. 'Difficult Heritage: Interpreting Underwater Battlefield Sites.' In D.A. Scott-Ireton, ed. *Meeting Challenges in the Public Interpretation of Maritime Cultural Heritage: Between the Devil and the Deep*. New York: Springer Press, 173–87.

McKinnon, J.F. 2015a. 'Memorialization, Graffiti and Artifact Movement: A Case Study of Cultural Impacts on WWII Underwater Cultural Heritage in the Commonwealth of the Northern Mariana Islands', *Journal of Maritime Archaeology*, 10 (1), 11–27.

McKinnon, J.F. 2015b. 'Underwater Archaeology of a WWII Battlefield.' In J.F. McKinnon and T.L. Carrell, eds. *Underwater Archaeology of a Pacific Battlefield: The WWII Battle of Saipan*. New York: Springer Briefs in Archaeology, 1–14.

McKinnon, J., Mushynsky, J. & Cabrera, G. 2014a. 'A Fluid Sea in the Mariana Islands: Community Archaeology and Mapping the Seascape of Saipan', *Journal of Maritime Archaeology*, 9 (1), 59–79.

McKinnon, J.F. & Carrell, T.L. 2011. *Saipan WWII Invasion Beaches Underwater Heritage Trail*. Unpublished report. Ships of Discovery, Santa Fe, NM.

McKinnon, J.F., Carrell, T.L., Burke, H., Cabrera, G., Raupp, J., Mushynsky, J. & Kimura, J. 2014b. *A Preservation Plan for the Protection of WWII-Related Caves on Saipan*. Unpublished report. Ships of Discovery, Santa Fe, NM.

McKinnon, J.F., Ticknor, A.S. & Froula, A. 2019. 'Engaging Pacific Islander Veterans and Military Families in Difficult Heritage Discussions', *Journal of Maritime Archaeology*, 14 (2), 1–15.

McNeill, D. 2008. 'Magnificent Obsession: Japan's Bone Man and the World War II Dead in the Pacific', *The Asia-Pacific Journal*, 6 (7), 1–4.

Meskell, L., ed. 1998. *Archaeology under Fire: Nationalism, Politics and Heritage in the Eastern Mediterranean and Middle East*. London: Routledge.

Miles, W.F.S. 2002. 'Auschwitz: Museum Interpretation and Darker Tourism', *Annals of Tourism Research*, 29 (4), 1175–78.

Moon, C. 2019. 'What Remains? Human Rights after Death', In: K. Squires, D. Errickson and N. Márquez-Grant, eds. *Ethical Approaches to Human Remains*. Switzerland: Springer Nature, 39–58.

Moshenska, G. 2008. Ethics and Ethical Critique in the Archaeology of Modern Conflict', *Norwegian Archaeological Review*, 41 (2), 159–75.

Moshenska, G. 2009. 'Resonant Materiality and Violent Remembering: Archaeology, Memory and Bombing', *International Journal of Heritage Studies*, 15 (1), 44–56.

Moshenska, G. 2015. 'The Ethics of Public Engagement in the Archaeology of Modern Conflict.' In: A. González-Ruibal and G. Moshenska, eds. *Ethics and the Archaeology of Violence*. New York: Springer, 167–80.

Moshenska, G. & González-Ruibal, A. 2015. 'Introduction: The Only Way is Ethics.' In: A. González-Ruibal and G. Moshenska, eds. *Ethics and the Archaeology of Violence*. New York: Springer, 1–17.

Mushynsky, J. 2021. *The Archaeology, History and Heritage of WWII Karst Defenses in the Pacific: Cultures of Conflict*. New York: Springer.

Mushynsky, J. 2019. 'Defining Karst Defenses: Construction and Features', *Historical Archaeology*, 53 (1), 193–204.

Mushynsky, J. 2011. *Sea Fluidity: Recording Indigenous Seascapes and Maritime Cultural Landscapes in Saipan, Commonwealth of the Northern Mariana Islands*. M.A. thesis, Department of Archaeology, Flinders University, Adelaide.

Mushynsky, J., McKinnon, J. & Camacho, F. 2018. 'The Archaeology of World War II Karst Defences in the Pacific', *Journal of Conflict Archaeology*, 13 (3), 198–222.

North, O.L. 2004. *War Stories II: Heroism in the Pacific*. Washington, DC: Regnery Publishing.

Pietruszka, A.T. 2015. 'Forensic Archaeology Underwater: JPAC's Inventory, Investigation and Recovery of US Casualties of War from Submerged Sites.' In W.J.M. Groen, N. Márquez-Grant and R.C. Janaway, eds. *Forensic Archaeology*. Hoboken: Wiley, 453–61.

Price, J. 2005. 'Orphan Heritage: Issues in Managing the Heritage of the Great War in Northern France and Belgium', *Journal of Conflict Archaeology*, 1 (1), 181–96.

Price, N. & Knecht, R. 2013 'After the Typhoon: Multicultural Archaeologies of World War II on Peleliu, Palau, Micronesia', *Journal of Conflict Archaeology*, 8 (3), 193–248.

Price, N., Knecht, R. & Lindsay, G. 2015. 'The Sacred and the Profane: Souvenir and Collecting Behaviours on the WWII battlefields of Peleliu Island, Palau, Micronesia.' In G. Carr and K. Reeves, eds. *Heritage and Memory of War: Responses from Small Islands*. New York: Routledge, 219–233.

Renshaw, L. 2011. *Exhuming Loss: Memory, Materiality and Mass Graves of the Spanish Civil War*. Walnut Creek, CA: Left Coast Press.

Russell, S. 2001. 'Dealing with Human Remains: An Approach from the Northern Marianas', *CRM*, 1, 23–24.

Satoshi, N. 2003. 'The Politics of Mourning.' In: I. Setsuho and L.N.Yu-Jose, eds. *Philippines-Japan Relations*. Manila: Ateneo de Manila University Press, 337–76.

Schofield, J., Johnson, W.G. & Beck, C.M. 2002. 'Introduction: Matériel Culture in the Modern World.' In: J. Schofield, W.G. Johnson and C.M. Beck, eds. *Matériel Culture: The Archaeology of Twentieth-Cenrtury Conflict*. London: Routledge, 1–8.

Sledge, E.B. 1981. *With the Old Breed, at Peleliu and Okinawa*. New York: Oxford University Press.

Soder, S. & McKinnon, J. 2019. *It Rained Fire: Oral Histories from the Battle for Saipan*. Greenville: East Carolina University Foundation.

Stone, P. 2006. 'A Dark Tourism Spectrum: Towards a Typology of Death and Macabre Related Tourist Sites, Attractions and Exhibitions', *Tourism*, 54 (2), 145–60.

Sturdy Colls, C. 2015. *Holocaust Archaeologies: Approaches and Future Directions*. Switzerland: Springer International Publishing.

Tanaka, T. 2002. *Japan's Comfort Women: Sexual Slavery and Prostitution during World War II and the US Occupation*. London: Routledge.

Thomas, S. 2014. 'Making Archaeological Heritage accessible in Great Britain: Enter Community Archaeology.' In: S. Thomas and J. Lea, eds. *Public Participation in Archaeology*. Woodbridge: The Boydell Press, 23–34.

Trefalt, B. 2017. 'Collecting Bones: Japanese Missions for the Repatriation of War Remains and the Unfinished Business of the Asia-Pacific War', *Australian Humanities Review*, 61, 145–59.

Ulguim, P. 2018. 'Digital Remains Made Public: Sharing the Dead Online and our Future Digital Mortuary Landscape', *AP: Online Journal in Public Archaeology*, 3, 153–76.

US Senate Hearing, 2007. *Conditions in the Commonwealth of the Northern Mariana Islands*. Washington: US Government Printing Office. [WWW] https://www.govinfo.gov/content/pkg/CHRG-110shrg35819/html/CHRG-110shrg35819.htm (accessed 05/06/2022).

Viebach, J. 2014. 'Alétheia and the Making of the World: Inner and Outer Dimensions of Memorials in Rwanda.' In: S. Buckley-Zistel and S. Schaefer, eds. *Memorials in Times of Transition*. Cambridge: Intersentia, 69–94.

Weingartner, J.J. 1992. 'Trophies of War: US Troops and the Mutilation of Japanese War Dead, 1941–1945', *The Pacific Historical Review*, 61 (1), 53–67.

Williams, H. & Atkin, A. 2017. 'Virtually Dead: Digital Public Mortuary Archaeology', *Internet Archaeology*, 40. [WWW] https://doi.org/10.11141/ia.40.7.4 (accessed 05/06/2022).

Yow, V.R. 2015. *Recording Oral History: A Guide for the Humanities and Social Sciences.* Lanham, MD: Rowman and Littlefield Publishers.

### *Personal Communications*

Pruitt, J. 2019. *Personal Communication. Email. Subject: Human Remains Question.* Received 05/06/2019.

# 8

# LIVES ENCODED IN LANDSCAPE

## Unlocking Lost Narratives from the World War II Battle of Peleliu

*Gavin J. Lindsay*

## Introduction

Peleliu is a small low platform reef island of 13 km$^2$ formed of uplifted coralline limestone and high limestone ridges blanketed in tropical and mangrove forest. Situated near the southern tip of the Republic of Palau on the western rim of the Caroline Islands in Micronesia (Figure 8.1), Peleliu is just one of the many islands in the Pacific to have been irrevocably transformed by the storm of war that swept across its surface in 1944. The material remains of seventy-three days of relentless, close-quarters fighting survive in such stark proliferation on Peleliu that the island represents one of the best preserved and least disturbed World War II battlefield landscapes in the Pacific. The story of how Peleliu's World War II archaeological record was formed is an epitome of the extremes that characterize the Pacific Theater of Operations (PTO) – over 16,000 lives lost on both sides plus more than 6,400 wounded in a fierce and bloody battle fought across a complex maze of steep ridges, plunging narrow valleys and rocky outcrops to secure a minor military objective. Locked within the battlefield sites, the surviving artifacts and associated landscape features reflect narratives and sub-narratives of humanity undergoing the most extreme circumstances, which archaeology can help to reveal and interpret. This chapter shares some of the incredible untold stories of this fierce battle that have survived, encoded within material and landscape, and recently brought to light through archaeological survey.

## Surveying Peleliu's Battlefield

Pacific Islands present a unique and demanding set of environmental challenges to researchers: high humidity, steep rugged terrain, dense tropical forest, minimal vehicle access and a high risk of encountering explosive remnants of war

DOI: 10.4324/9780429270468-10

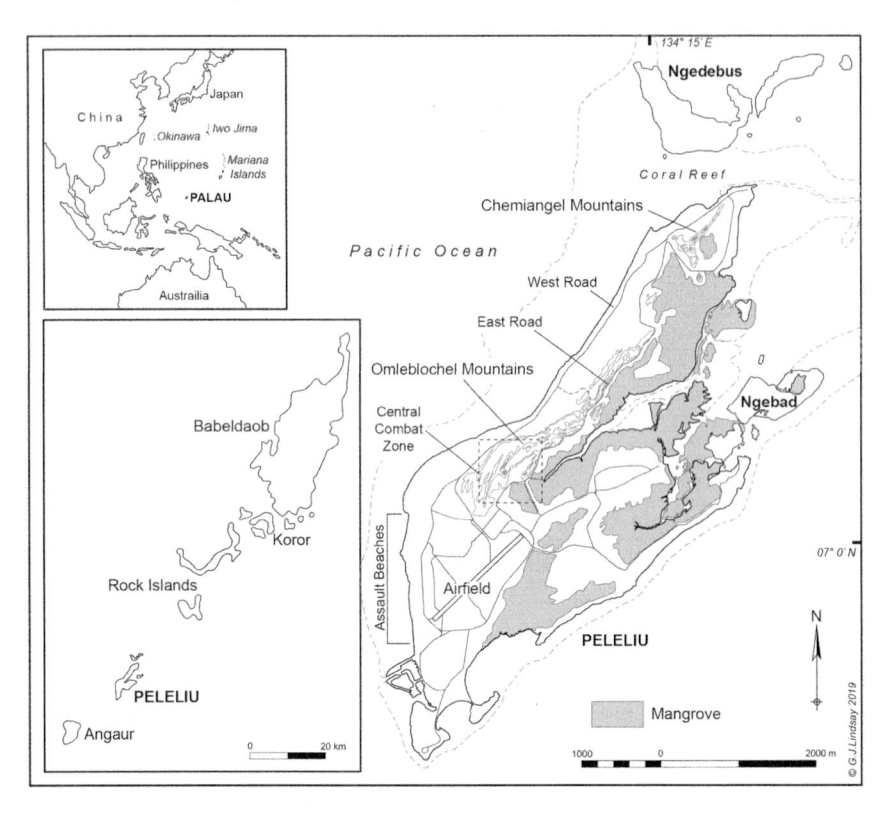

**FIGURE 8.1** Peleliu Island in the Republic of Palau, western Micronesia. Image by G.J. Lindsay.

(ERW). In late 2014, a small team of archaeologists and building conservation specialists conducted an eleven-day survey across selected areas within the Peleliu Battlefield National Historic Landmark (designated a US Historic Landmark in 1984; see Lindsay et al. 2015). The work was undertaken as part of a contract awarded to the University of Aberdeen, UK, to undertake a combined scheme of archaeological field and archive-based research for the Peleliu War Historical Society Inc. (PWHS), an American non-profit organization, and was funded by a grant from the United States Department of the Interior, National Park Service (NPS), American Battlefield Protection Program (Grant agreement no: GA-2287-13-018). The archaeological survey team, largely composed of professionals offering their expertise and time voluntarily, was accompanied in the field by Explosive Ordnance Disposal technicians and Emergency Medical Technicians contracted from Cleared Ground Demining, an indispensable team who provided forward screening of all survey areas and permitted safe working in a landscape that remains hazardous through the presence of ERW.

The 2014 survey extended the coverage of work undertaken in 2010, also under contract to PWHS and funded by an NPS grant (Knecht et al. 2012). Both non-intrusive walkover surveys have built upon the pioneering work of American social and architectural historian D. Colt Denfeld who was the first to document material remains from the battle and demonstrate the battlefield's remarkable state of preservation and archaeological potential (Denfeld 1988). Denfeld's studies across the Micronesian islands of the Western Pacific set the standard for conducting research across war-torn Pacific Island landscapes, combining textual, oral and material evidence through an effective multisource methodology (see Denfeld & Russell 1984; Denfeld 1988 for particularly good examples). The 2010 and 2014 surveys were both based on Denfeld's methodological model and extensively integrated historic aerial photographs, maps, archive documents, military field equipment manuals and published veteran accounts into both field analysis and post-fieldwork interpretation. The 2014 survey differed in that it also operated within a purpose-built community-based participatory research (CBPR) framework developed by the author (see Lindsay 2017 for specifics). CBPR is an altogether different form of methodology compared to more conventional archaeological approaches and places a greater emphasis on building capacity, reciprocity and democratizing knowledge through community-based partnering and participation (for archaeological applications of CBPR and for more on the CBPR project model see Stoecker 2005; Atalay 2012). In brief, the framework focused on nurturing relationships of trust with the local community, partnering with community-based organizations that represented the priorities and interests of multiple stakeholding groups, deploying research methods and techniques that would enable community participation, and, finally, contributing to the ongoing processes of post-conflict social recovery and reconciliation by fostering new cross-cultural/cross-community involvement in field- and archive-based research activities.

In 2010, 285 World War II sites and features (plus sixteen indigenous Palauan sites) were recorded across approximately 590 acres of the battlefield, including the principal landing beach areas, the airfield, key areas of the central combat zone (CCZ) where the fighting was most intense (such as Death Valley and Wildcat Bowl) and discrete areas in the north of the island (Knecht et al. 2012: 3). The 2010 survey and subsequent analysis not only recorded remarkable battlefield sites and artifacts but also revealed forgotten marginalized voices and multicultural narratives under-represented or indeed absent from historical accounts of the battle (Price & Knecht 2012, 2013; Price et al. 2015). The 2014 survey discussed in this chapter covered a much smaller 95-acre area of more peripheral battlefield and included the eastern CCZ, a narrow lateral corridor of the central ridge area and the northern Chemiangel Mountains. Contrary to what might be expected from a smaller survey of less intensely fought terrain, a remarkable 260 individual or clustered archaeological sites and artifacts were recorded. This included thirteen indigenous Palauan and pre-war Japanese colonial sites associated with phosphate mining activities. Such a high yield demonstrates that a very high density of truly exceptional archaeology survives, not only in the core of the battlefield but right across the island.

- Artifacts and macrofacts (large artifacts such as artillery pieces)    106
- Karst defenses (all cave types)    62
- US field fortifications    40
- IJ field fortifications    18
- Field fortifications (unknown or mixed provenance)    11
- Human remains concentrations    19
- Air crash sites    3
- Bomb craters    3
- IJ support infrastructure    3

The figures listed above illustrate the main types and quantities of battle-related archaeological material recorded during the 2014 survey and highlight the number of surviving ephemeral site classes encountered. Field fortification is one such class and includes skirmisher trenches, machine gun positions and rifle pits which are often little more than shallow depressions with low curving parapets of coral rubble boulders to their front. Owing to their temporary nature, or perhaps their innate tendency to blend into the undergrowth, field fortifications – particularly hasty positions – have rarely been documented in World War II Pacific Island surveys and certainly not in any detail or quantity (Lindsay 2017: 305). As will be evidenced more fully throughout this chapter, the ephemeral combat features recorded in 2014 can add significant value to our understanding of the battle, offering insight into momentary actions and individual experiences. The integrity of sites and assemblages proved to be generally better in more remote areas, offering enhanced levels of interpretive data. However, even sites close to population centers or in heavily frequented areas where disturbance from looting or 'intrusive exploration' was evident, enough material evidence remained to allow detailed analysis of site form and function.

## A Lost Voice from a Lost Tank Unit

D-Day on Peleliu. 08:32 on the 15th of September 1944. The first men from the US 1st Marine Division roll out over the sides of their tracked landing vehicles and onto the sands of Peleliu's south-western beaches. They are met by a hail of concentrated artillery, mortar and small arms fire that zoned in on the reef line and beaches under pre-arranged fire plans from well-concealed Imperial Japanese (IJ) positions. Aerial bombing and a heavy naval bombardment in the days and months preceding the assault had done little damage to the well-camouflaged concrete and coral positions that comprised the island's carefully planned anti-invasion defenses. From emplacements flanking the beaches and concealed caves as far inland as the ridges of the Omleblochel Mountains, the disciplined defenders of the experienced Japanese 14th Army Division exerted every effort to follow their commander Lieutenant General Sadae Inoue's order to *'annihilate the enemy landing forces on the beaches'* (USAHEC 1946a: 12). Under the intense enfilading fire at either end of the beach and accurate mortar bombardment along its extent, the US assault waves sustained heavy losses and struggled to push forward off the beach. First Sergeant Jack Ainsworth landed with C Company, 1st Battalion (Bn), 1st Marine Regiment (Regt) an hour after the first wave – *'From our position under the cliffs we can see Marines being blown to bits by mortar and artillery fire and our own tractors being blown out of the water and burning the occupants alive. This may be another TARAWA'* (Ainsworth 2012: 8). With close air support and the arrival of medium tanks, the Marines succeeded in breaching the beach defenses and by dusk (around 17:00) had established a flimsy front line along the western perimeter of the airfield, barely 180m inland.

Aside from the desperate fight of Captain Hunt's K Company (3rd Bn, 1st Marine Regt) at the western flank of the assault beaches ('The Point'), the most well-known and frequently recounted battle narrative of Peleliu's D-Day is the pre-planned counterattack across the open ground of the airfield by a combined force of Japanese light tanks and infantry (see Hough 1950 for detailed accounts of both). Although the rapid destruction of the small force by a murderous cross-fire of tank, field artillery and rocket projectiles is well documented, the location of the tank unit's operational base and maintenance area has remained unknown. Air reconnaissance observed the counterattack assembling east of the central ridges and to the north of the airfield (Hough 1950: 50), suggesting the tank force had originated somewhere up the east coast road. The 2014 archaeological survey's narrow transect across the central ridge area bisected the East Road and in a densely vegetated area adjacent to the road an unusual group of natural caves were encountered. One cave took the form of a single-chambered rock shelter with enough room to accommodate a small group of men. Another was set into the side of a roughly squared cutting with a leveled base that gave the appearance of a revetted vehicle bay. The third and shallowest shelter (Figure 8.2) was found to contain a partly buried assemblage of 270 unfired IJ 37mm high explosive pro-jectiles and 37 unfired IJ 37mm armor-piercing projectiles – the same caliber and type of ordnance used in the main armament of the Type 95 Ha-Go light tanks that equipped the 14th Division Tank Unit of the Imperial Japanese Army (IJA) (War Dept. 1944b: 245). Fragments of wooden ammunition storage crate were also found with 37mm diameter curved notches cut into the timbers for resting the projectiles. The quantity of ordnance and packing crate evidence suggests that the rock shelter had served as an ammunition store.

The recorded material evidence points favorably towards a dispersed supply and support area with sheltered hard standings that could have served the IJA 14th Division Tank Unit. Turning to historical documents, on the 16th October Superior Private Takeo Sugimura was captured in the water whilst attempting to swim from Peleliu (NARA 16/10/1944). During his interrogation, Takeo revealed that his platoon of the 2nd Infantry Regt had been attached to the Tank Unit and that their assignment was to ride on the tanks and deploy as part of a rehearsed counterattack plan (*ibid*). As a member of a grenade discharger squad, Takeo wasn't appointed to this task but was instead detailed to remain be-hind with the maintenance unit – a decision that undoubtedly saved his life. US

**FIGURE 8.2** Buried (far left) and stacked 37mm projectiles found in an ammunition store used by the IJA 14th Division Tank Unit. Visible US 30lb demolitions charges indicate ordnance disposal intentions never carried out. Photograph by G.J. Lindsay.

tactical map co-ordinates included in Takeo's prisoner of war interrogation report provide the approximate position of the tank maintenance unit. Once converted, the co-ordinates were found to match the area where the natural caves encountered during the survey were discovered. When no one returned from the counterattack, Takeo, his squad, and the maintenance personnel continued the fight. Takeo operated in a close assault team hiding in the mangrove swamp during the day and waiting by the side of the road at night to thrust wired pairs of anti-tank mines into the tracks of passing US armored vehicles (*ibid*). Without success or food, Takeo moved to a cave in the eastern CCZ where he held out for over three weeks, surviving a grenade exchange and an assault that killed 50 other defenders before eventually making the escape attempt that resulted in his capture (*ibid*). During the battle, the twenty-four-year-old chicken farmer from Osaka, Japan, came close to losing his life on at least four occasions. As the sole known survivor of the infantry platoon attached to the 14th Division Tank Unit, his account not only offers valuable context to the archaeological remains and historical insight into the disposition of the mobile counterattack force, but also reveals the untold experience of the men who supported the tank crews and infantry who counterattacked on the 15th September.

## Unlocking an Untold Story Entrenched on a Hilltop

Following the capture of the airfield and low-lying southern areas of Peleliu in the days following the invasion, the intended three-day scheme to capture the island devised by assault troop commander Major General Rupertus rapidly unraveled. The daily orders to attack concealed fortified ridge positions from the south, where they were strongest, resulted in such crippling casualties for the 1st Marine Division that, on the 23rd of September (D+8), the 321st Regimental Combat Team (RCT) of the 81st US Army Infantry Division was landed to reinforce and eventually relieve them (CARL 1944: iii–iv). The Army strategy was one of siege warfare rather than direct assault focusing instead on outflanking the strongest area of Japanese resistance in the southern Omleblochel Mountains, encircling it, and gradually reducing it from its most vulnerable points. Named after the men who secured it, the 321st Infantry Trail was a narrow prewar Palauan track that twisted through the mountainous central spine of Peleliu from coast to coast. Its capture isolated and surrounded the main IJ defense force in the CCZ and as a consequence, the seizing of the 321st Infantry Trail ranks as one of the most significant strategic maneuvers of the battle.

The role of the Army's 321st and 323rd RCT on Peleliu is in itself a relatively underrepresented narrative in battle accounts; however, recent oral historically driven works such as Blair & DeCioccio's (2014) *Victory at Peleliu* have begun to re-address this. Both official military histories and subsequent publications narrating the capture of the 321st Infantry Trail focus on the actions of E (*Easy*) Company, 2nd Btn, 321st RCT who led the eastward advance along the Trail on the 24th of September. Densely vegetated, swampy at its western extent and precipitous further east, the conditions on the Trail meant that the men of the 321st RCT received little close air or mechanized support as they advanced inland. Shortly before dusk, *Easy* Company encountered the sheer slopes of Hill 100, a summit of around 36m that dominates the center section of the Trail and which also commands the northern approach ridges into the CCZ. Using improvised ladders, the men of *Easy* Company climbed and crawled up the slopes of the hill exchanging hand grenades with the defenders above (*ibid*: 131) and taking fire from the escarpment to their south (81WDHC 1948: 141). The strategic hilltop position was strongly defended and fiercely contested with the short, sharp action best summarized as one of '*independent exploits of individuals as they battled their way upward hand over hand*' (*ibid*: 142).

Although at the center of this pivotal action, *Easy* Company didn't operate in isolation and their achievement wouldn't have been possible without the support of F *(Fox)* Company to the immediate north and I (*Item*) Company of the 3rd Bn to the south. *Item* was particularly important as Hill 100 presented very steep slopes on all sides except to the south where it connected to the rest of the ridge system by a narrow escarpment. Beyond general references to their position and movements on *Easy's* right flank, very little detail of *Item's* combat experience along the 321st Infantry Trail is recorded in historical narratives. From the 81st

Infantry Division's official World War II history, we know that as *Easy* assaulted Hill 100, *Item* employed alpine assault techniques to scale the precipitous western rim of the 30m high escarpment and that after securing the top, prepared defensive fighting positions (*ibid*). In a reversal to the common relationship between sources, it is the archaeological evidence on the escarpment that offers the finer detail and a glimpse into *Item* Company's otherwise untold story of the 24th–25th September.

A total of twenty mutually supporting defensive fighting positions were recorded on a summit plateau at the north end of the escarpment during the 2014 survey. These formed three groupings aligned roughly with the western and eastern crests and the narrowest southern neck where the plateau connects to the rest of the escarpment and ridges beyond. The size, quantity and layout of the positions conform to contemporary US Army infantry field manual guidelines for a platoon defense area (War Dept 1944a: 246). This suggests that the plateau was occupied by one of *Item's* three rifle platoons with supporting light machine guns and mortars from the weapon platoon. Field fortifications on Peleliu – and defensive fighting positions in particular – are a fascinating site type that demonstrates the adaptability and ingenuity of US Army and Marine personnel whilst under fire. As early as D-Day the Marines discovered that the shallow soil and hard bedrock prevented them from digging defensive earthworks. Instead, published memoirs describe how Marines built upwards rather than down by piling loose coral rocks around where they lay (McEnery 2013: 212).

On the escarpment, the men of *Item* Company encountered the same issue. Having received their basic, unit and combined arms instruction prior to 1944 (US Army field manuals were revised and reissued in early 1944), soldiers would have been trained to dig a hasty fortification type known as the skirmisher trench whilst in contact with the enemy (War Dept. 1940: 63–64). Hasty positions could be expanded into the ubiquitous foxhole if terrain and circumstances allowed and provided a position to fire from whilst also offering a degree of concealment and protection from flat trajectory small arms and artillery fire (*ibid*). The morphology of *Item's* positions appears to be an adaptation of the skirmisher trench (a form omitted from the 1944 field manual) with low coral rock parapets curving around a roughly rectangular shallow depression. Many were found to be twice the size of the 'textbook' skirmisher trench, more oval in plan and with fully encircling coral rubble parapets (Figure 8.3). These closely resemble the open shallow pit layout of the Horseshoe type infantry weapon emplacement, a type advised for the Caliber .30 (Light) Machine Gun in the US Army's 1944 Rifle Company Field Manual (War Dept. 1944a: 247–51). What we see evidenced on the escarpment is field-inspired fortification development combining pre-1944 entrenching dogma with the latest concepts from field manuals likely issued whilst enroute to Theater. The result was a flexible and original form of defensive fighting position suited to the terrain and combat conditions of Peleliu that provided all-round protection for pairs of riflemen or automatic weapons teams.

**FIGURE 8.3** An oval, field-inspired defensive fighting position with encircling coral rubble parapet built by Item Company on the Hill 100 escarpment plateau. Photograph by G.J. Lindsay.

In selected areas of the battlefield, an artifact survey (involving GPS log, a photographic record and object identification) was carried out to record the extensive artifact and macrofact horizon that remains visible amongst the leaf litter but has previously proven difficult to record and interpret in a methodical and meaningful way (Lindsay et al. 2015: 25–26). This survey technique was used to record an extensive assemblage of US military equipment and ordnance found in close association with the defensive fighting positions on the Hill 100 escarpment. Lengths of communications wire and cable drums indicated platoon signals posts. Ration cans lay individually and in heaps where the contents had been consumed and the cans thrown out of the way. Fragments of corrugated iron sheet were found in five fighting positions signifying where overhead protection had been improvised to protect against falling hostile and friendly shrapnel – *Item's* twenty-two-year-old radio operator Private Corwin Berry recalled: '*our Company came back down from the ridge after Marine artillery zoned in within [30m] of us […] but we went back up after our [Commanding Officer] was wounded*' (Blair and DeCioccio 2014: 137).

From unit reports and division histories, we know that the men of *Item* didn't have long to wait before their hasty fortifications were tested. '*At 1700 an enemy counterattack stuck forward elements of the 2nd Btn*' (CARL 1944: 19). As

*Fox* Company reeled back several hundred meters under the attack, IJ troops made a bid to retake *Easy's* positions on Hill 100. The eastern group of *Item's* defensive fighting positions on the plateau faced IJ-held territory to the west and covered the saddle connecting the escarpment to Hill 100. The artifact assemblage recorded amongst these positions indicates that at least part of the counterattacking IJ force advanced up the saddle and engaged *Item* Company. Empty Thompson machine gun magazines lay discarded around the positions and single unfired .30 cal. cartridges indicated where rifles had jammed in the heat of action and the offending cartridges ejected to free stoppages.

'*During night combat the hand grenade was the principle weapon of the infantrymen in the outpost*' – Major General Paul Mueller, 81st Infantry Division commander (*ibid:* iv). All along the eastern crest, unused hand grenades and clips of small arms ammunition were found carefully stashed in niches or on ledges in the coral parapets of the positions, ready for immediate use. An unexploded IJ Type 99 hand grenade lay on the slope below one fighting position, resting where it had rolled after being thrown short or cast back by a defender. A fully loaded US M1 Carbine magazine was nearby, lost over the edge of the crest as a squad leader reloaded in a hurry, or perhaps thrown at a rapidly approaching assailant following a weapon malfunction – a common trait of the M1: '*all this time the [Japanese soldier] was getting closer to the lieutenant, "click" went the carbine again, [...] he finally*

FIGURE 8.4 Artifact assemblage showing sabre cut to US water canteen, associated rifle clips and large caliber shrapnel. Photograph by G.J. Lindsay.

*threw the carbine at the [soldier] who was less than [three meters] from him'* (Ainsworth 2012: 70). Evidence that the IJ troops reached the crest and engaged the defenders in hand-to-hand combat was observed through discarded equipment such as a US bayonet – and most poignantly – an assemblage containing US .30 cal. M1 Garand rifle clips and a US water canteen arranged as they would be if attached to a now disintegrated rifleman's belt. The canteen bore the unmistakable linear dent of an IJ sabre blade (Figure 8.4). Private First Class Joseph A. Notarianni was one of the Company's aid men and earned the Bronze Star on the escarpment:

> *With utter disregard for his own safety, this intrepid soldier exposed himself to the hostile fire in order to care for the wounded and dying. […] He rendered exemplary service in this difficult situation until he himself was struck down and wounded by a shell fragment.*
>
> *(USAHEC 1946b: Vol1 Pt J: 21)*

Together, the sites and artifacts tell a vivid story of the action that unfolded on the Hill 100 escarpment, representing one of the most intact and best-preserved examples of a US Army infantry platoon defense area thus far encountered and documented in the Peleliu Battlefield National Historic Landmark.

## Living and Fighting from the Chemiangel Caves

In addition to the 2nd IJA Infantry Regt's considerable combat experience, the key to Peleliu's resolute defense was the new IJ strategic policy of defense-in-depth: '*I issued strict orders that the BANZAI attack was not to be employed because it wasted manpower. […] I ordered that the men fight a delaying action from prepared positions, causing as many casualties as possible*' – Lieutenant General Sadao Inoue, 14th IJA Division commander (USAHEC 1947a: 8). Colonel Kunio Nakagawa and the men of the 2nd IJA Infantry Regt and Peleliu sector defense units under his command strictly followed Inoue's orders, employing insurgent tactics to defend concealed fortified positions by day and raiding US positions in close-quarters combat pairs by night (USAHEC 1946a: 80). In a post-war interview, Inoue's second in command Colonel Tokechi Tada explained the principles more metaphorically:

> *The situation closely resembled a contest between a large man armed with a long spear and a small man armed with a short sword. The man armed with the short sword must crowd into the large man so that his spear is useless. We had to attempt to infiltrate into the American lines to render American air attacks, naval bombardments and tank attacks ineffective. We did not believe that this method of attack could defeat air and sea power, but we believed that the great number of American losses would cause them to think that the price was not commensurate with the value of Palau and therefore withdraw.*
>
> *(USAHEC 1947b: 3)*

From his command post deep in the CCZ, Nakagawa reported by radio to Inoue on the island of Koror that his northern units had engaged advancing US troops and armor in a fierce battle (USAHEC 1946a: 111). It was the 26th of September (D+11) and by implementing Inoue's strategy, the men of the IJ Northern Defense Sector – a mixed force of around 1,000 Army and Navy personnel occupying some of Peleliu's most sophisticated cave and tunnel systems – had briefly succeeded in stalling the US advance up the low-lying west coast of the Chemiangel Mountains. This inverted T-shape range exhibits similar topographic characteristics to the Omleblochel with exposed hilltops and knife edge ridges linked by plunging saddles. Although lacking the multi-ridge depth that turned the southern mountains into a deadly zone of interlocking fields of fire (Gayle 1996: 29), the Chemiangel was honeycombed with natural caves and fissures which were exploited by both the IJ Army and Navy to create concealed combat positions, protected personnel shelters and subterranean storage facilities. The IJ Navy's principle refuge area lay in the central spine of this ridge and predominantly comprised shelter-type caves (Phelan 1945: 3–4). Twenty-seven-year-old Corporal Ko Takahashi (6th Company, 2nd Bn, 2nd IJA Infantry Regt) described the shelter caves as places of rest from which combat troops were regularly rotated to dispersed frontline positions (NARA 15/10/1944: 1). The area didn't sustain much damage from the pre-invasion bombardments which left the jungle vegetation largely intact, concealing the jagged terrain and cave positions.

As the main US force attempted to break through a well-defended choke point near the pre-war phosphate drying plant, E Company (2nd Bn, 5th Marine Regt) turned off the West Road and up the precipitous western face of the Chemiangel to begin a northward push along the narrow ridge top (Hough 1950: 121). Observing these movements below, IJ troops on the upper slopes prepared for close-quarters defense of both their fighting positions and hastily fortified shelter caves. The official US Marine battle account describes how little opposition was encountered along the exposed crests but that persistent confrontations occurred with IJ troops entrenched in unreachable caves deep within the ridge (*ibid*). Well prepared, well concealed and reinforced by troops landed from the northern Palau islands, the Japanese defenders resisted tenaciously against the reduced ranks of the advancing 5th Marine Regt.

Peleliu's caves are an incredible yet chilling archaeological resource, artifactually rich and fundamentally complicated. They form part of what could be described as an IJ vernacular architecture of defense, recently defined collectively as 'karst defenses' (Mushynsky et al. 2018: 198). Whether utilizing wholly natural caves, employing enlisted and forced labor to enhance natural caves or constructing entirely artificial tunnel systems, the sophisticated tactical use of karst topography was undeniably central to the formidable resistance of island garrisons and the severity of casualties inflicted across the PTO. Carved into the upper core of the narrow northern ridgeline and extending through it from east to west is an improved natural cave, as inaccessible in 2014 as it was in 1944. Within it remains the telltale evidence of frequent troop movements from a shelter cave hastily adapted to resist the approaching Marines. Weaving through the hillside like a labyrinth, the complex cave system is best described illustratively in Figure 8.5 and consists of four discrete zones linked by passages. Zone 1 is the largest space, formed by a natural cavity along a fissure in the rock. The interior zones lead off from this and exhibit architecture consistent with IJ Navy

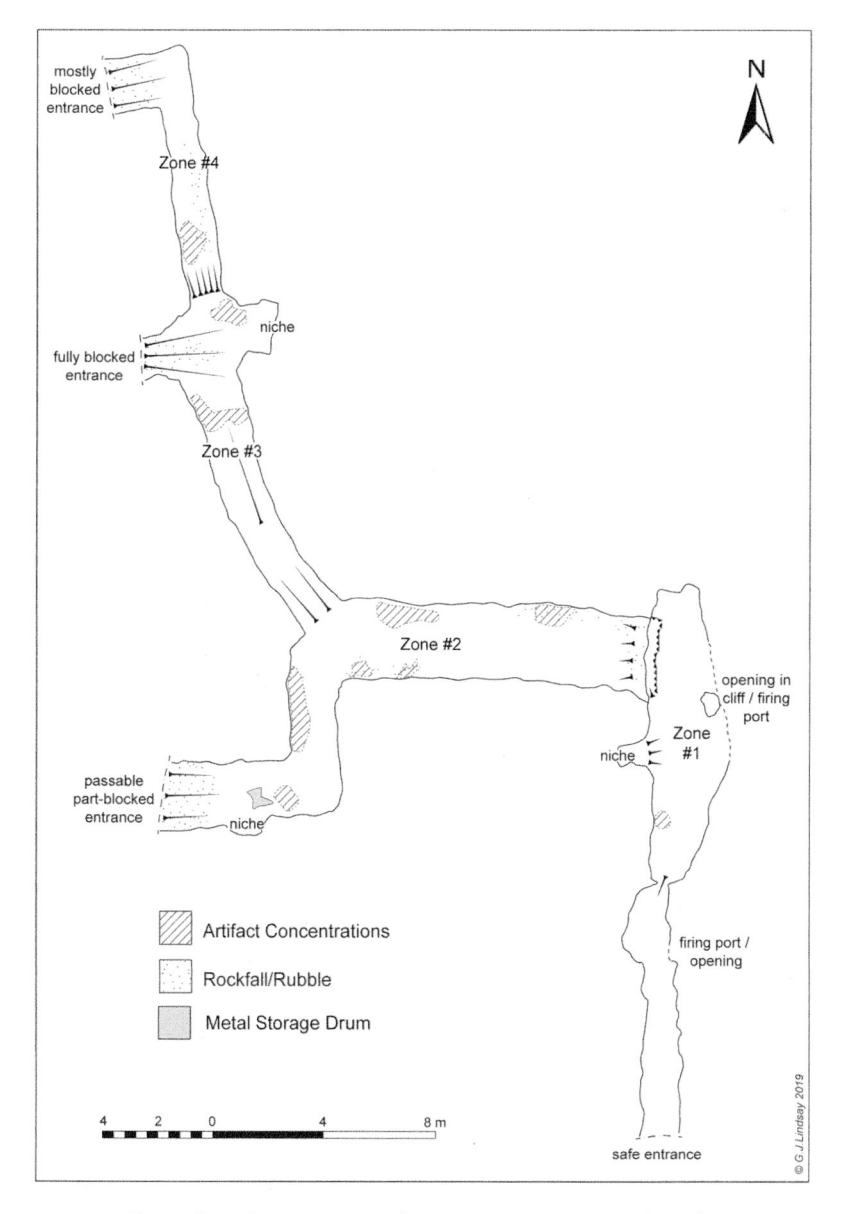

**FIGURE 8.5**  Floor plan of cave interior depicting main zones and artifact concentrations. Image by G.J. Lindsay.

construction techniques (smoothly hewn walls and ceilings with sizeable niches at strategic intervals). The quality and complexity of these zones suggest the natural cavity was exploited and then enhanced by the IJ Navy's expert 214th Naval Construction Bn. Substantial wooden planks and nails driven into the smooth walls of Zone #2 indicate interior furnishings and possibly wall cladding existed. Rougher workmanship, narrower passages and discarded mining chisels in Zones 3 and 4 evidence the efforts to hastily modify the cave for defense. Fire ports and exits cut into the sides of the hill would have provided ideal vantage points from which to observe and fire on the Marines below. A large number of personal IJ equipment items such as water canteens, mess kits, leather ammunition pouches and combat boot fragments reveal that many men once lived in the deeper areas of the cave. Personal hygiene items commonly associated with officers and a broad range of weapon accoutrement (artillery ranging ruler fragments, rifle ammunition, hand grenades, heavy machine gun strip-clips) point to a cave occupied by a mixed, active and transient military community. Ko Takahashi's experiences exemplify the diversity and fluidity of the cave garrisons; his Army unit shared a cave with a Navy detachment for fifteen days before moving on to another position (NARA 11/10/1944: 1).

Personal water canteens perforated by shrapnel and bullets, human remains, cot bed supports and a high number of small aqua-blue and amber glass medical bottles are a potent sign that the cave also served as an aid station. Medical supplies issued in individually carried first aid kits were found in caches suggesting that medical treatment was improvised with the limited provisions pooled together. Three empty cans of decontaminant were identified amidst an assemblage containing medical bottles, gas mask fragments, personal equipment and cot bed brackets (Figure 8.6). Issued singly to personnel, decontaminant was designed to neutralize the effects of liquid blister gases such as sulfur mustard (more commonly known as mustard gas) (War Dept. 1944b: 263). Although officially recognized chemical weapons such as sulfur mustard were not used by US forces on Peleliu, similar physical symptoms of skin and lung blistering were caused by white phosphorous (WP). Produced in aerial bomb, artillery, mortar and hand grenade variants, WP generated an impenetrable white plume of smoke and was liberally employed defensively across all theaters in World War II to obstruct enemy visibility on the battlefield. WP is rich in phosphorus pentoxide which, although thirty times less potent than sulfur mustard, can still cause serious injury and death through inhalation and direct contact. It was used prolifically on Peleliu in defensive roles but also offensively against caves where it was delivered by M15 smoke grenade or by the mortars of the 88th Chemical Weapons Btn. Combined with the high frequency of IJ gas masks identified in cave assemblages during both the 2010 and 2014 surveys, the additional evidence of used decontaminant indicates how the IJ forces on Peleliu were responding to what they perceived as US chemical weapons attacks. As the M15 hand grenades rolled into their caves and emitted plumes of white smoke, the occupants grabbed their gas masks to try and protect their respiratory systems. Those who

| | |
|---|---|
| 1. IJ Ammunition Pouch Fragments | 4. IJ Type 99 Hand Grenades |
| 2. IJ Decontaminant Cans | 5. Medical-Type Glass Bottles |
| 3. IJ Gas Mask Tissot Tube | 6. Metal Cot Support Bracket |

© G.J.Lindsay 2019

**FIGURE 8.6**  Zone 4 artifact assemblage. Photograph by G.J. Lindsay.

survived the excruciating burning effects of the WP were treated by their comrades as sulfur mustard casualties. Takajiro Kumaki was a thirty-two-year-old non-combatant laborer in the IJ Naval Construction Force who hid for about a week in a cave with a large group of unarmed fellow laborers. In his prisoner of war report, Takajiro's interrogator 2nd Lieutenant Harry Foote wrote '*he said he surrendered when US troops gassed the cave, evidentially referring to white phosphorous grenades*' (NARA 27/09/1944). All the men who surrendered were either wounded or suffering from burns to the skin following the attack on their shelter (*ibid*).

## Discussion

From complex cave shelters unlocking a largely overlooked chemical weapons story to lost tales of tenacity encoded in platoon positions high on the ridge tops, non-intrusive survey has been revealing areas of Peleliu's battlefield at a finer resolution than has previously been achieved. Every site and object has its own story to tell. Applying a multi-source methodology drawing on a range of survey techniques and historical archive sources, the ongoing interpretation of Peleliu's remarkable World War II material remains is offering uniquely detailed and often personal insights into the actions, experiences and narratives of a battle that irrevocably transformed the island landscape and the lives of those who fought over it. For stakeholding and resident communities, the material legacy of the battle continues to wield influence in the present and looms over the island's future. The community-based participatory approach taken for the 2014 Peleliu Archaeological Survey proved effective for engaging with and working alongside a range of community representatives. Such a framework has wider application potential across war-affected islands in the Pacific and beyond, offering an effective research project model for better understanding the long-term sociocultural impacts of recent, material-rich conflicts on small communities and the world we live in today (Lindsay 2017: 307). The Peleliu survey has also demonstrated that contracted work of this nature can be successfully co-designed and undertaken to ensure relevance and provide positive assistance to community-based organizations as they seek to understand, manage, renegotiate and reconcile a violent past as heritage within a complex and powerfully charged post-conflict environment. In some ways, Peleliu's story is typical of the dehumanizing scale of escalating barbarity (Strachan 2005: 49) that sets the PTO apart from all others in World War II (Weinberg 2005: 26). However, what distinguishes Peleliu is the unique contribution that its substantially well-preserved archaeological record can provide to our understanding of the conflict in this region. The detailed narratives that can be extrapolated from surviving objects and sites, interpreted in conjunction with a rich assemblage of historical records, provide an exceptionally high-resolution lens through which we can view, and try to better understand, the transformative typhoon of war that swept across the Pacific region in World War II.

## Acknowledgments

This chapter has drawn from research undertaken for my PhD in archaeology at the University of Aberdeen, UK. I'd like to extend my thanks to the teaching, technical and administrative staff at the university as well as fellow researchers in the Archaeology Department for their support, advice and guidance throughout my studies. Most notably, I wish to thank my supervisors Rick Knecht, Neil Price and Keith Dobney, and my examiners Gordon Noble and Tony Pollard. The Peleliu Archeological Survey 2014 was directed by Rick and Neil the co-principal investigators. I am sincerely grateful to both the PWHS (the client) and the US NPS American Battlefield Protection Program (the grantor) for their financial assistance and to Rick and Neil for entrusting me with so many lead elements of the project. I'd also like to thank Steve Cypra of PWHS for his unwavering support throughout. The project volunteers, Ben Raffield, Phillip Ashlock, Charles Bello, David McQuillen and Rob Raney deserve liberal acknowledgment for donating their time, energy and expertise and for assisting in the field, with archive research, and contributing to the final report; thank you. Also, my thanks to John Currie who fortuitously joined us on Peleliu where we benefited from his skilled photography, enthusiasm and shared discoveries from his personal research.

The Project team has been greatly honored by the hereditary chiefs of Peleliu for granting permission to work on their lands and by the *chad ra Beliliou* (people of Peleliu) for allowing us to explore their island's past and share a part of their story with the global community. Fieldwork on Peleliu would not have been possible without the support of the Palauan government, namely Governor Temmy Schmull and the State Legislature of Peleliu. At the Palauan Bureau of Arts and Culture, I'd like to thank Sunny Ochob Ngirmang and Calvin Emesiochel for their encouragement, expertise and trust. In the US, I'm grateful to the staff at the United States Army Heritage and Education Centre in Carlisle, Pennsylvania and the United States National Archives and Records Administration in College Park, Maryland. Finally, I would like to pay a special tribute to Steve and Cassandra Ballinger and their exceptional team of EOD technicians at Cleared Ground Demining. This group of remarkable experts often went above and beyond the call of duty to keep us safe in the field.

## Bibliography

81st Wildcat Division Historical Committee (81WDHC). 1948. *The 81st Infantry Wildcat Division in World War II.* Washington, DC: Infantry Journal Press.

Ainsworth, J.R. 2012. *Among Heroes: A Marine Corps Rifle Company on Peleliu.* Quantico: Marine Corps University Press.

Atalay, S. 2012. *Community-based Archaeology: Research With, By and For Indigenous and Local Communities.* Berkeley, Los Angeles and London: University of California Press.

Blair, B. & DeCioccio, P. 2014. *Victory at Peleliu: The 81st Infantry Division's Pacific Campaign.* Norman: University of Oklahoma Press.

Combined Arms Research Library (CARL). 1944. *Operation Report 81st Infantry Division: Operation on Peleliu Island, 23 Sept – 27 Nov 1944.* Call No: N8100.2. Unpublished archive document. Fort Leavenworth, Kansas, KS.

Denfeld, D.C. 1988. *Peleliu Revisited: An Historical and Archaeological Survey of World War II Sites on Peleliu Island.* Micronesian Archaeological Survey, Report No.24. Saipan: Division of Historic Preservation.

Denfeld, D.C. & Russell, S. 1984. *Home of the Superfort: An Historical and Archaeological Survey of Isely Field.* Micronesian Archaeological Survey, Report No.21. Saipan: Division of Historic Preservation.

Gayle, G.D. 1996. *Bloody Beaches: The Marines at Peleliu.* Marines in World War II Commemorative Series. Washington, DC: Marine Corps Historical Centre.

Hough, F.O. 1950. *The Assault on Peleliu.* USMC Historical Monograph. Historical Branch, G-3 Division. Washington, DC: Headquarters, United States Marine Corps.

Knecht, R., Price, N. & Lindsay, G.J. 2012. *WWII Battlefield Report of Peleliu Island, Peleliu State, Republic of Palau.* Unpublished Report: National Park Service American Battlefield Protection Program. [WWW] www.peleliuhistorical.org/Uploads/Peleliu_Report_2012.pdf.

Lindsay, G.J. 2017. *Legacies of Conflict: A Community-Based Approach to World War II Archaeology on Small Islands.* Unpublished PhD thesis in Archaeology. Aberdeen: University of Aberdeen. [WWW] https://ethos.bl.uk/OrderDetails.do?uin=uk.bl.ethos.720590 (accessed 13/04/2022).

Lindsay, G.J., Knecht, R., Price, N., Raffield, B. & Ashlock, P. 2015. *Peleliu Archaeological Survey 2014: WWII Battlefield Survey of Peleliu Island, Peleliu State, Republic of*

*Palau*. Unpublished Report: National Park Service American Battlefield Protection Program. [WWW] www.peleliuhistorical.org/Uploads/Peleliu_Report_2014.pdf (accessed 13/04/2022).

McEnery, J. with Sloan, B. 2013. *Hell in the Pacific: A Marine Rifleman's Journey from Guadalcanal to Peleliu*. New York & London: Simon & Schuster Paperbacks.

Mushynsky, J., Mckinnon, J. & Camacho, F. 2018. 'The archaeology of World War II karst defences in the Pacific', *Journal of Conflict Archaeology*, 13 (3), 198–222.

National Archives and Records Administration (NARA). 27/09/1944. *Preliminary Interrogation Report, Prisoner No. 16*. Record Group 127, Box 307, Folder C1-3. National Archives at College Park, MD.

National Archives and Records Administration (NARA). 11/10/1944. *Preliminary Interrogation Report, Prisoner No. 232*. Record Group 127, Box 307, Folder C1-3. National Archives at College Park, MD.

National Archives and Records Administration (NARA). 15/10/1944. *Supplementary Interrogation Report, Prisoner No. 232*. Record Group 127, Box 307, Folder C1-3. National Archives at College Park, MD.

National Archives and Records Administration (NARA). 16/10/1944. *Preliminary Interrogation Report, Prisoner No. 299*. Record Group 127, Box 307, Folder C1-3. National Archives at College Park, MD.

Phelan, W.C. 1945. *Japanese Military Caves on Peleliu: "Know Your Enemy!"*. Bulletin 173-45. CinC Pac – CinCPOA.

Price, N. & Knecht, R. 2012. 'Peleliu 1944: The Archaeology of a South Pacific D-day', *Journal of Conflict Archaeology*, 7 (1), 5–48.

Price, N. & Knecht, R. 2013. 'After the Typhoon: Multicultural Archaeologies of World War II on Peleliu, Palau, Micronesia', *Journal of Conflict Archaeology*, 8 (3), 193–248.

Price, N., Knecht, R. & Lindsay, G. 2015. 'The Sacred and the Profane: Souvenir and Collecting Behaviours on the WWII Battlefield of Peleliu Island, Palau, Micronesia.' In: G. Carr and K. Reeves, eds. *Heritage and Memory of War: Responses from Small Islands*. Oxon: Routledge, 219–34.

Stoecker, R. 2005. *Research Methods for Community Change: A Project-Based Approach*. London: Sage Publications.

Strachan, H. 2005. 'Total War: The Conduct of War, 1939–1945.' In: Chickering, R., Förster, S. and Geriner, B., eds. *A World at Total War: Global Conflict and the Politics of Destruction*. Cambridge: Cambridge University Press, 33–52.

US Army Heritage & Education Centre (USAHEC). 1946a. *Central Pacific Area Operation Record – Vol I*. Japanese Monographs Reel 4 No.49. Unpublished Microfilm Archive Document.

US Army Heritage & Education Centre (USAHEC). 1946b. *Unit History – 321st Infantry: Operation against the Japanese on Peleliu Island, Palau Group*. Call No: 603-321 1945/4. Unpublished Archive Document.

US Army Heritage & Education Centre (USAHEC). 1947a. *Interrogation of Lieutenant General Sadae Inoue*. Rex W Beasley Papers, Call No: ARCH COLL Bay 5 Row 190 Face B Shelf 4 Box 59 Folder 10. Unpublished archive document. United States Army Military History Institute, Carlisle, PA.

US Army Heritage & Education Centre (USAHEC). 1947b. *Interrogation of Colonel Tokechi Tada*. Rex W Beasley Papers, Call No: ARCH COLL Bay 5 Row 190 Face B Shelf 4 Box 59 Folder 10. Unpublished archive document. United States Army Military History Institute, Carlisle, PA.

War Department. 1940. *FM 5-15: Engineer Field Manual, Field Fortifications*. Washington, DC: United States Government Printing Office.

War Department. 1944a. *FM 7-10: Infantry Field Manual, Rifle Company, Infantry Regiment.* Washington, DC: United States Government Printing Office.

War Department. 1944b. *TM-E 30-480: Handbook on Japanese Military Forces.* Washington, DC: United States Government Printing Office.

Weinberg, G.L. 2005. 'Total War: The Global Dimensions of Conflict.' In: Chickering, R., Förster, S. and Greiner, B., eds. *A World at Total War: Global Conflict and the Politics of Destruction.* Cambridge: Cambridge University Press, 19–31.

# PART 3
# 1945

# 9

# THE CURRENT SITUATION OF THE BATTLEFIELD ARCHAEOLOGICAL SITE SURVEY IN OKINAWA PREFECTURE

*Tetsuya Seto*

## Introduction: The Current Situation of Battlefield Archaeological Sites in Okinawa Prefecture

At around the time of Okinawa's reversion to Japan in 1972, the research and preservation of battlefield archaeological sites on Okinawa was primarily associated with peace education, which aimed to 'never again repeat the tragedy of the Battle of Okinawa.' In 1984, Shinichi Touma suggested that 'war site archaeology' would reveal the reality of the Battle of Okinawa through the archaeological study of battlefield sites and artifacts. This idea received national attention (Touma 1984). Touma excavated position caves in his hometown of Nishihara as a part of the Nishihara Town History compilation project (Touma 1996). Despite this, such attitudes toward the preservation of war-related sites did not become the standard policy of prefectural cultural property administration for some time. While the prefecture hesitated to treat war-related sites as cultural property, Shinobu Yoshihama's interview research project, which collected wartime experiences from the local residents of Haebaru Town, led to the registration of Okinawa Army Hospital Haebaru Cave as the first registered battlefield site in Japan. Haebaru Town initiated the excavation of the hospital cave in collaboration with Yoshifumi Ikeda and the Archaeology Department of Ryukyu University. The town has attempted to maintain the cave, which has been open to the public since 2007, in its original condition (Yoshihama et al. 2010; see also Hokumori, this volume).

During the 1990s, Okinawa Prefecture started to consider the preservation and utilization of battlefield sites such as the 32nd Army HQ cave, located under Shuri Castle, which had been the initial site of the Japanese Army HQ during the Battle of Okinawa. This was as a result of increasing interest in battlefield sites, in addition to the inauguration of Masahide Ota (who had served in the

DOI: 10.4324/9780429270468-12

student corps during the war) as the governor of Okinawa. The plan, however, has not been implemented because of serious structural damage, the huge costs associated with the maintenance of the site, and changes in the political situation.

From 1998 to 2005, Okinawa Prefecture Board of Education and later Okinawa Prefecture Archaeology Center conducted battlefield site distribution surveys across Okinawa Prefecture in order to confirm the location and current condition of archaeological sites. As a result, by 2006, 979 battlefield site locations had been identified and described in six reports (Okinawa Prefecture Archaeology Center 2001, 2002, 2003, 2004, 2005, 2006). Despite this, there was still no clear policy for battlefield site research and preservation. Individual research excavations gradually increased in number.

From 2010 to 2014, Okinawa Prefecture Archaeology Center selected important battlefield sites based on the last survey for inclusion in a future cultural property resister. By 2016, the number of confirmed battlefield sites in Okinawa had risen to 1,077 (Okinawa Prefecture Archaeology Center 2015). Despite this, it was not until 2018 that any of the battlefield sites were designated as cultural property of the Okinawa Prefecture. The main reason for this was the high costs associated with preservation and utilization efforts, in addition to the fact that many of the sites are located on private land. At a municipal level, however, a few rescue excavations undertaken with the aim of protecting sites from developmental construction have been conducted annually. Therefore, while not all of the battlefield sites on Okinawa are protected by the prefectural government, their locations and current condition are gradually being confirmed, and the number of rescue excavations is increasing. The problems of budgeting and cooperation with land owners excepting, the significance and necessity of battlefield site research are becoming increasingly recognized. As the number of individuals with lived experience of the war is decreasing, battlefield sites are becoming the most important medium for conveying the history and realities of the Battle of Okinawa. It is therefore important to designate them as cultural properties in order to maintain and preserve their current condition.

The author joined the 'Battlefield Sites Details Confirmation Survey' and 'Excavation Research of Confiscated Village by US Military Bases' survey, which was conducted by Okinawa Prefecture Archaeology Center, as a Site Manager in order to report on the current condition of battlefield sites in Okinawa Prefecture (Seto 2017). Based on these projects and personal experiences, in this chapter, the author briefly summarizes the battlefield sites on Okinawa, reports the result of excavations at the confiscated village, and introduces the current utilization project for battlefield sites. As a conclusion, a future plan for battlefield site research will be discussed.

## General Overview of Battlefield Archaeological Sites in Okinawa

The survey report published by Okinawa Prefecture Archaeology Center divides the battlefield sites in Okinawa into those which existed before and after the Battle of Okinawa (Okinawa Prefecture Archaeology Center 2015). The criteria for inclusion are that sites must postdate March 22nd 1944, when the Japanese Army established the 32nd Army to defend the Nansei Island Chain. This idea was suggested by Shinobu Yoshihama, who joined the report editing (Yoshihama 2017). The descriptions in this section, with a few exceptions, are based on the report produced by the Okinawa Prefecture Archaeology Center (2015).

## Battlefield Sites before the Battle of Okinawa

In 1879 (Meiji 12), the Meiji government conducted the so-called Disposition of Ryukyu, in which the government sent the military and police to abolish the Ryukyu Han and to establish Okinawa Prefecture. Okinawa was a strategic location and various military-related facilities were built there after the Sino-Japanese War of 1894–95 (Meiji 27) and Japan's subsequent occupation of Taiwan. A submarine line landing house (located at Sakieda, Ishigaki City), which was used for pulling submarine cable on the ground and connecting the ground power network, in addition to a water reservoir at Nakagusuku Supply Branch Warehouse (in Sashiki, Nanjo City), were used to supply vessels.

After the Russo-Japanese War of 1904–05 (Meiji 37), Naval observatories were built in Iriomote (Taketomi Town) and Kyan (Itoman City) in order to enhance surveillance of the coast (see also Nakahodo, this volume). Parts of these structures survive today. At the same time, monuments to the loyal dead (Figure 9.1) and Hoan-den, which were used to house the photograph of the Emperor and the Empress (Figure 9.2), were built everywhere in Okinawa Prefecture. These are not military facilities but nevertheless reflect the patriotism and fighting spirit of the local citizens. As such, the author regards them as a type of battlefield archaeological site.

Shortly before the outbreak of the Pacific War in 1941 (Showa 18), temporary forts were constructed in Nakagusuku Bay and Funauki on Iriomote Island (see Nakahodo, this volume). These were the first military bases in Okinawa that were intentionally constructed as combat fortifications. The temporary forts were small-scale military bases which housed batteries for guarding the coast and air defense in important bay areas. Batteries remain on the Katsuren and Sashiki peninsulas in Nakagusuku Bay and along western Iriomote Island. Currently, confirmed batteries have mound-like gun floors. According to the military documents and features, the batteries possibly housed Type 38 Field Guns. Another – Heshikiya Battery in Nakagusuku Bay – was likely designed to house a Type 88 7 cm anti-aircraft gun. Documentary and interview evidence, however, does not support the installation of this type of gun at the temporary fort. This discrepancy between archaeological, documentary, and oral evidence indicates that the history of the Battle of Okinawa is complex.

The presence of US military air forces around Japan following the beginning of the Pacific War prompted the establishment of Air Guard Units all over Japan. These units were tasked with the early detection of aircraft, and eleven Air Defense Guards were deployed in Okinawa Prefecture in 1943 (Showa 18). These facilities were controlled by police and operated by local students and

FIGURE 9.1 Memorial Statue at Misato (Naha City). Photograph by Okinawa Predecture Archaeology Center 2015.

FIGURE 9.2 Ho-an-den at Tonoshiro Elementary School (Ishigaki City). Photograph by the author.

city hall staff commanded by reservists. Surveillance information was reported through local police departments. Air Defense Guard sites remain in Yonashiro in Uruma City, Motobu Town, and Itoman City.

## Battlefield Sites from the Battle of Okinawa

The Battle of Okinawa is generally considered to have lasted from the US military landings on the Kerama Islands on May 26th 1945, until the Japanese signing of the Instrument of Surrender at Kadena airfield on September 7th of the same year. The battle can also be considered to have begun, however, on March 22nd 1944, when the Japanese military established the 32nd Army for the defense of Nansei Island Chain. Battlefield sites in the Battle of Okinawa are therefore considered to have been constructed or used after that date, and it should be noted that internment camps and confiscated village sites built after the US military landing are also associated with the battle.

In this section, representative battlefield sites dating from the Battle of Okinawa are described from four perspectives: (1) battle preparation by the Japanese military, (2) air-defense sites manned by local residents and city halls, (3) sites relating to the US landings on Okinawa, and (4) internment camps and later US military base constructions.

## The Japanese Army's Preparations for Battle

Following the sudden US attack on the Japanese military base in the Truk Islands in February 1944, the Japanese Army HQ was urged to strengthen the defenses of mainland Japan, the Nansei Islands, and Taiwan. On March 22nd, the 32nd Army was established in order to prepare air operations for the defense of the Nansei Islands. Airfields were quickly constructed and coastal positions were built in order to counter enemy shipping. However, due to the serious damage caused by the US invasion of the Mariana Islands in June, the Japanese military increased their defense forces in anticipation of a future ground battle. In consequence, Japan sent the 9th, 24th, and 62nd Battalions to Okinawa Island, and the 28th Battalion to Miyako Island from July to September in order to support the 32nd Army. The redeployment of the 9th Battalion to Taiwan in December, however, greatly impacted the strength of the 32nd Army.

With the looming threat of a ground battle, individual units constructed not only airfields and coastal positions but also HQ caves and tunnel complexes inland, in addition to many batteries with heavy guns and hidden caves to house suicide boats. Army battalion hospitals were moved to underground caves as the situation worsened and the prospect of a ground battle became inevitable. Students were mobilized to help construct defensive caves in addition to their own evacuation caves. Studying at school was the out of the question. In the discussion below, the author introduces currently confirmed remains of these facilities by category.

## *Airfields*

In addition to those already constructed at Oroku, North Ishigaki Island (Hekina), and on Minami Daitou Island before 1944, eighteen airfields were built prior to the Battle of Okinawa. This includes those on Ie Island and North Okinawa (Yomitan). The majority of the confirmed sites are bunkers such as those at Zakimi in Yomitan Village and Ohama in Ishigaki City. The Naha City Board of Education unearthed part of a landing strip at Oroku Air Field site (Naha City), which was paved with pebbles and powder stones.

## *Headquarters Caves*

The 32nd Army HQ cave was first built at Tsukazan (Haebaru Town), where a well-constructed gallery with supporting timbers has been excavated (Haebaru Town Board of Education 2008). However, its strength was questioned after an air raid on October 10th 1944 due to it being built into a layer of soft mudstone (Kucha layer). The HQ was therefore moved to a series of caves and tunnel caves beneath Shuri Castle. A detailed survey of these caves has not been conducted because of heavy collapse inside. When the retreat of the HQ was ordered in late May of 1945 (Showa 20), it was moved to Mabuni 89 High Land Position Cave in Naha City. Following the air raid, the first Navy HQ was also moved from the concrete caves in Kyosui (Naha) to the more rigid Navy HQ cave in Tomigusuku city.

## *Coastal Positions*

The basic defensive strategy of the Japanese military was to annihilate attacking enemies on the beach. As such, many positions with artillery guns and batteries were constructed along coasts of the Nansei Islands. In the Daitou Islands, especially, positions were located all along the coast, and three of these have been recorded as archaeological sites. There is enough surviving Japanese military archival material to provide a good knowledge of the function of these positions.

Cannon units were a major force in the Battle of Okinawa, so a large number of battery positions were constructed. The navy tended to build concrete bunkers for battery structures. Toma Naval Battery (Naha City), currently located in a Japan Self-Defense Force base, is the only remaining battery which has a possible battleship main cannon as the battery gun (see Nakahodo, this volume). In contrast, the majority of army positions used underground limestone cave entrances as embrasures. Examples can be seen at Shinkawa-Kubougusuku Position on Tsukenjima Island (Uruma City) and Ufugusuku Position (Nanjo City), which were constructed by the Heavy Artillery 7th Regiment, formerly the Nakagusuku Temporal Fort Unit described above. In addition, simple structures for use by small mortar units were constructed and manned by the Independent Mortar Company, which was deployed on the main island of Okinawa. The unit composition comprised twelve mortars with a bunker for the mortars. The bunkers at Zaha Mortar Position can still be seen today. One of the bunkers has square gun floor measuring 3 m$^2$ and 2 m in depth, with an evacuation cave to one side. The spatial interval between the bunkers was about 15 m. A similar position has also been confirmed at Mukaiyama Mortar Position in Kochi prefecture (Kouchi Prefecture Archaeological Center 2012) on the Japanese mainland island of Shikoku, which tells us that the military expected the conflict on Okinawa to eventually extend to the mainland.

## Suicide Boat Caves

Suicide attacks using small boats against enemy battleships were a tactic developed during the Pacific War. On Okinawa and the mainland, a large number of caves were constructed to hide the suicide attack boats. The artificial cave was usually 10–20 m in length and 2–3 m in width and height, and they were mostly built about every 10 m along the coastline. On Okinawa, these caves were located along west coast of Okinawa Island, the Kerama Islands, Miyako Island, and Ishigaki Island. The cave of Karimata in Miyakojima City has a complex structure comprising six interconnected caves.

## Air Defense Plans by Local Residents and City Halls

In Okinawa Prefecture, local residents built private evacuation caves in their yards by order of local police departments at around the time of the 32nd Army's deployment. However, the construction of evacuation caves and planning for the use of natural caves as evacuation shelters intensified after the large air raid on October 10, 1944, which targeted the Nansei Islands and Naha City, the prefectural capital. Every prefecture and city hall additionally had caves built in order to store documents and photographs of the Emperor and Empress.

## Evacuation Caves

Evacuation caves in private properties are confirmed by excavations at the Former Kamiyama Village, which was confiscated when the US established Futenma Air Base. Many of these caves are less than 5 m in length and have a single entrance. There are also examples of more complex evacuation caves that were made by large families and villages along river banks or hills. These include the caves in Nerome (Ogimi Village) and Maekawa and Yamakawa (Yaese Town, Nanjo City), which are built on valley or riverbank slopes. Many of them are around 10 m in length and have two entrances. In some cases, multiple caves are connected internally. These complex caves have supporting timbers or shelves, which are similarly found in Japanese military caves. A military use is therefore also possible. There is also large evacuation cave complex in Nago City, location of the Airakuen (a facility for leprosy patients). This was constructed by the patients on the orders of the director of facility, and the construction work was terribly hard. The width and height of the gallery are close to 2 m, and it features supporting timbers and large iron nails on the wall. Military technologies and supplies were provided.

## Government Office Caves

Plans were made to construct a prefecture hall and police department cave near Shuri Castle, where the 32nd Army HQ was deployed, and in 1945 this was established at Shippoujinu Gama Cave on the Hantagawa River. The cave consists of a natural cave and connected artificial gallery with a water reservoir. It was still under construction even after the ground battle had started. Therefore, while the actual date when the governor settled there is thought to be April 25th, it is difficult to think that the cave was complete enough to actively support the evacuation of the residents. City hall caves can also be found in other places. The Former Nishihara Village Hall Cave is significant because it was the first battlefield site in Okinawa Prefecture to be archaeologically excavated in 1985.

## Emperor and Empress Photograph Protection Caves

After the October 10th air raid, the photographs of the Emperor and Empress stored in every schools Ho-an-den were to be moved to safer places. The prefecture constructed protection caves in the wetland areas of northern Okinawa, and photographs from various places were gathered there from January 1945.

## The US Landings on Okinawa

A US landing and battle on Okinawa became inevitable after the Japanese defeat at Iwotou (Iwo Jima) in February 1945. Air raids on the Nansei Islands intensified from March, and naval bombardment started on around March 23rd. Local residents evacuated not only to evacuation caves but also natural caves and the mountains. In order to slow the US advance, the Japanese military blew up bridges in various places. Remains of exploded bridge piers can be seen today at Okukubi Bridge (Kin Town), Tengan Bridge (Uruma City), and Sakae Bridge (Kadena, Yomitan Town).

The US military occupied the islands sequentially after their landing on the Kerama Islands on March 26th. After landing on the west coast of central Okinawa on April 1st, US military forces separated and advanced toward the north and south of the island. Motobu Peninsula and Ie Island in the north were conquered, while intensive battles in Ginowan, Urazoe, and Nishihara continued into late April. The failure of a counter-attack by Japanese forces in May precipitated the retreat of the 32nd Army HQ to Mabuni at the end of that month. This served to displace and bring together both military and civilian populations, thereby generating a tremendous number of victims, especially at the military hospitals in the south (see Hokumori and Koga, this volume). This included the Okinawa Army Hospital Hebaru Caves, where wounded soldiers were poisoned, abandoned, or killed by artillery fire.

In June, naval units in Oroku were destroyed. The 32nd Army continued its retreat to Kyan, the southernmost point of Okinawa, and fought on. The Commander and Chief of Staff killed themselves on June 23rd, bringing organized Japanese resistance on Okinawa to an end. The mopping-up campaign by the US, however, continued, causing damage and hardship everywhere. Local residents were slaughtered and assaulted by Japanese soldiers, and they also suffered from starvation and malaria.

## Evidence of Air Raids and Naval Bombardment

Bullet holes remain on the Kohatsu Family House Stone Wall (Nishihara Town), a water reservoir tank at Airakuen (Nago City). Seifa-utaki – a sacred altar dating from the Ryukyu dynasty and a World Heritage monument – features a cannon impact mark from an air raid or navy bombardment called the 'Bomb Hole.' Bullet holes on the concrete wall (a material that was rarely used in construction at this time) of a public pawn shop tell of an intensive battle on Ie Island (Figure 9.3).

## Japanese Military and Local Residents on Tokashiki Island

The 3rd Marine Volunteer Squadron, trained to use suicidal attack boats, was deployed on Tokashiki Island. Instead of dispatching with the boats when the

**FIGURE 9.3** Bullet holes on a public pawn shop (Ie Village). Photograph by the author.

US military landed on March 26th, they moved to a mountainous area called Kitayama, located in the northern part of Tokashiki Island, and hurriedly constructed positions. Because of this, the Kitayama Position Caves site contains numerous small artificial caves dug into valley slopes. That one of these caves contained a cooking oven indicated that they were intended to be used as part of a long, drawn-out battle. The military did not allow local islanders to enter the position and the latter had to move another part of the valley, about 1 km north of the position. After the move, family 'group suicides' are thought to have occurred as the will to 'never be allowed to be taken prisoner' hardened. While surviving residents suffered from starvation, majority of Japanese soldiers went down the mountain on August 24th when they accepted the disarmament order.

### The Evacuation of Local Residents in Various Places

Although many of the locals fled into natural caves, people on northern Okinawa Island and Ishigaki Island evacuated into the mountains. Parts of huts and ovens still remain at Ishikawadake Mt. (Onna Village) and Nagura Shiramizu (Ishigaki City). In addition to food shortages, many residents suffered from malaria. More tragic still, some participated in 'group suicides' or were slaughtered by Japanese soldiers. The fate of civilians varied greatly. For example, while mass suicides took place at Chibichiri Gama cave in Namihira, Yomitan Village, those residents taking shelter at Shimuku Gama cave all survived. There are several potential reasons to explain this difference. The former cave, for example, was relatively small, about 600 m$^2$, and had only one entrance. The latter had multiple entrances, a running stream inside of the cave, and a 2.5 km long gallery.

### Internment Camps and US Military Base Construction

The US military placed the Nansei Islands under the control of the military government on March 26th when they landed on Kerama Islands. From April, they had constructed internment camps in central and northern Okinawa in order to house locals and Japanese POWs. Structural foundations and pathways between these were confirmed at the Ourasaki Internment Camp site, which is located in Camp Schwab of Nago City. Interned peoples at this camp were primarily from Nakijin, Motobu, and Ie Island.

As the US military continued the landings on Okinawa, they repaired the former Japanese airfields in conquered places such as Ie Island and Kadena. US forces also constructed new airfields such as that in Futenma in order to prepare for operations against mainland Japan. The mopping-up campaigns had almost finished in August. On September 7th, representatives from both the Japanese and US militaries signed the Instrument of Surrender at Kadena Air Field. Below, the author will discuss Former Kamiyama Village, which lay within the boundary of the airfield and represents an example of the villages confiscated during US military base construction.

Even though more than seventy-five years have now passed since the end of the war, US military bases including airfields built during the Battle of Okinawa still remain. About 70% of all US military facilities stationed in Japan are concentrated in Okinawa Prefecture, and these forces occupy about 10% of land within the prefecture.

## Excavation at a Village Confiscated by the US Military: Former Kamiyama Village, Ginowan City

Okinawa Prefecture Archaeology Center has conducted rescue archaeology inside of the US military base in preparation for construction of the US military and Japanese Self-Defense Force shared facilities. It is common to find artifacts and features of the villages before base construction. The author led excavations at the Former Kamiyama Village site in Futenma Air Field in 2016–17 (Okinawa Prefecture Archaeology Center 2019a).

### *Background to the Excavation*

Futenma Airfield, the US Marine Corps' air base in Okinawa, measures some 480 ha in area and features a 2,800 m airstrip. It is located in the central part of Ginowan City and occupies 25% (it becomes 33% if the other bases are included) of the city. It symbolizes many of the problems associated with US military base construction on Okinawa, mainly because of the US military helicopter crash incident on the Okinawa International University campus in 2004, in addition to other accidents and noise pollution. Based on the final report of SACO in December 1996, Japan and the US agreed to return the Futenma Base to Okinawa. In July 2002, the 'Camp Schwab Water Area of Henoko Coast in Nago City' was decided as the site for the relocated base (Department of Military Base Policy, Ginowan City 2012; Office for Military Base Counterplan, Okinawa Prefecture Governor's Office 2019). Because Camp Schwab is currently an active base, rescue excavation was conducted through consultancy with the Okinawan Defense Bureau, a part of the Ministry of Defence, which takes place when there is planned and unavoidable destruction of archaeological sites. The Former Kamiyama Village excavation, conducted by the Okinawa Prefecture Archaeology Center, was planned in advance of the construction of a water reservoir system.

### *The History of Kamiyama Village*

The oldest documented record of Kamiyama Village is a 17th-century historical map (Anonymous 1646). The map shows the village spread along a major road (Ginowan Street), with Ginowan Village lying to the south of Kamiyama. The village population in 1944 was 467. Sugarcane farming was the primary means of subsistence before World War II, with the farmers producing homemade sugars.

There were rice paddy fields before the Showa period, but these had already been turned into dry farms before the Battle of Okinawa. The village was designed along a grid-like pattern and, according to US military aerial photographs, each house was covered by windbreak forests. The excavation area is located at the northeast end of village; an area with relatively large houses including the village founder's house as revealed by village folklore (Figure 9.4).

Some Japanese military units were stationed in the village houses after June 1944, and vacant houses were used as resting places. A field warehouse (renamed as a depot in February) to store supplies (such as food and fuel) was also established in the village. About ten members of the local population were mobilized every day for airfield and position construction, while others were required to deliver potatoes and vegetables to the military. There was no schoolchild evacuation to other prefectures, and evacuation to northern Okinawa was not organized. Therefore, a large portion of the residents fled to five different natural caves in late March 1945 (Ginowan City Board of Education 1998). During the night of April 1st, when the US military landed on the shores of Kadena and Yomitan, rice and other food supplies at the Kamiyama Depot were moved and partially burned. On April 4th, the soldiers stationed there (the Independent Infantry, 13th Battalion, 5th Company) deployed to two positions located at the north end of Kamiyama Village and fought against US forces. Although the US forces comprised about 10 tanks and 300 infantry, they were forced to retreated to Tomiyama (Urazoe City) for the night (Office of War History, National Institute for Defense Studies, Ministry of Defense 1968; The 32nd Army Liquidation Department 1947).

The construction of Futenma Airfield by the US military was already underway by June 1945. The majority of the houses in the west half of the former village were destroyed, and a long airstrip and accompanying facilities were under construction (Figure 9.5). Local villagers who had evacuated to natural caves were put into the internment camp in August. A large part of the village was already confiscated when the villagers were released in November 1947. As such, they could not return to their homes. The villagers cultivated the eastern part of the former village and settled into the area – now a part of Aichi area which is next to Kamiyama (Ginowan City Board of Education 2012). They could continue farming within the confiscated area of Futenma Air Field until the 1960s. However, farming stopped after an additional facility was constructed in the 1970s. The area returned to wilderness in the 1990s.

### Kamiyama Village Revealed through Excavation

The presence of chinaware dating from the Gusuku Period (15th and 16th centuries CE) and cultivation remains indicates that the village area was used as fields at that time. Although Japanese porcelain such as Bizen and Qing dynasty 'blue and white' dating from the Modern Period (17th and 18th century CE) has been

**FIGURE 9.4** Aerial photograph of Former Kamiyama Village before the battle and excavated localities (January 1945) (Okinawa Prefecture Archaeology Center 2019a).

found, only a few building features belonging to the same period were found. It was determined, therefore, that the main function of the site had been a farm.

Because tremendous quantities of 19th- and 20th-century porcelain wares were unearthed, it seems that the village site was primarily formed during the Modern Period. Twelve houses and a connecting alleyway were confirmed through excavation, and these can be seen on aerial photographs dating from before the battle. These houses could have been used by the time of the Battle of Okinawa, but it was impossible to identify which sub-period of the Modern Period the features belong to. It was possible, however, to establish the chronological order of the Modern Period features during the excavation. This tells that there were few changes in the function of the site during the Modern Period.

The housing area was defined by ditches and evident disparities in the intensity of occupation, which spoke to the existence of windbreak forests around the houses. The traditional stone walls usually seen in Okinawan villages were not detected. The large amount of stone material recovered during the excavations, however, indicates that these may have been present. These finds correspond with what has been seen in Futenma Old Village in Ginowan City – another confiscated village within the US military base (Okinawa Prefecture Archaeology Center 2015). Furthermore, post holes, stone wells, a stone pavement around buildings, and stone- or concrete-lined pits (which could be a reservoir), were found within the housing area (Figure 9.6).

### Features Relating to the Battle of Okinawa

Large numbers of features associated with the Battle of Okinawa were identified, the most obvious examples being transportation trenches, so-called foxholes, and air-raid evacuation caves. The transportation trench is a ditch-like feature built alongside the village alleyway. It measures 0.6 m in width at the bottom, 0.5–1.2 m depth, and more than 40 m in length within the excavation area. These are usually defined as 'trenches.' According to 'Field Battle Fortification Textbook,' a Japanese Army position construction manual, the trench can be classified as a transportation trench and bunker (Ministry of Army 1943). The ditch-like feature is relatively straight and consistent in its width. The uneven bottom surface tells that the feature is obviously different from ordinary street drains. Moreover, there is a larger area which could have served as a resting place for soldiers. These transportation trenches can be seen outside of the village in aerial photographs taken before the battle. These probably functioned as inter-village transportation trenches. Thus, the presence of an intra-village transportation trench means that the position construction plan expected a battle inside the village itself. If this was the case, then these confirmed transportation trenches were likely built after the local villagers had evacuated to caves in the surrounding area in March. Ironically, these rare features remained intact because of the confiscation of the village and rapid infilling by the US military.

**FIGURE 9.5**  Aerial photograph of Former Kamiyama Village taken during the construction of Futenma Air Field. This is the same location as Figure 9.4 (August 1945) (Okinawa Prefecture Archaeology Center 2019a).

**FIGURE 9.6** Excavated housing area of Former Kamiyama Village site (Okinawa Prefecture Archaeology Center 2019a).

Footholds dug into the sides of foxhole features were identified, and these comply with information obtained from the 'Field Battle Fortification Textbook.' Excavators need to pay attention to indentations on pit walls in future excavation of modern period village sites. Although it is difficult to identify the details of soldiers' behaviors only from excavated military boots and empty cans, the indentations give us an image of the battlefield at that time. Some other large pits, each measuring several meters in diameter, are connected to the transportation trench. These pits could have served as tank shelters or soldiers' workshops.

It is also important to consider evacuation caves. Many of these were located at the edge of house yards. Based on aerial photographs, these were built near the windbreak forests which surrounded houses. While it is evident that these were civilian evacuation caves, it is worth noting that there are caves with multiple rooms, measuring up to 16 m in length, which were connected to the transportation trenches. As such, some of these caves could have been built or repaired by the Japanese military. In addition to this, large numbers of soy beans, multiple large Okinawan jars for storing water, seasonings, and 1.8 liter bottles and Tokkuri Sake bottles were excavated from different caves. While all of these products would have been consumed by civilians, a military association is expected because given that the village became a strongpoint. Other possible military-related artifacts include a copper plate with a lined star figure (a symbol of the army), a tripod for survey instruments, a bronze cap possibly for a military iodine tincture bottle, and a Seto or Mino porcelain hot water bottle. Moreover, fragments of US white phosphorus cartridges and hand grenades were excavated. Although it is not certain that these were used inside the position, they were at the least surely used in the nearby area.

Based on the village's historical background, described above, we can expect that the Japanese soldiers prepared for a ground battle while they were hiding in the trenches found by the excavation. It is important to note, however, that this interpretation is based only on the study of contextual evidence. A more-certain and rich history of this area will be revealed through further research of pre-war village sites on Okinawa. The excavated well feature was relocated to the community house yard for the former Kamiyama Villagers who had been forced to move because of the airbase construction. The results of excavation will be handed down to the village descendants and others in the future.

## Conclusion: Site Conservation and Utilization Based on the Results of Battlefield Site Excavations

While the number of the war survivors is decreasing, battlefield archaeological sites on Okinawa offer significant potential to convey the realities of the Battle of Okinawa and to learn about peace. In the past, schools in Okinawa Prefecture annually pursued peace learning curriculums before or after June 23rd, which is a memorial day. Also, students from other prefectures routinely visit Okinawa Prefectural Peace Memorial Museum and the caves in southern Okinawa that represent the last sites of Japanese resistance during the battle. Students learn of the tragedy of the Battle of Okinawa through survivors' storytelling and experiencing the hospital cave. Indeed, the sense of tragedy gained during these experiences moves the heart. People who do not know the war, including the students and the author, are reminded of the importance of peace and the foolishness of war. However, these tragic and terrible stories of war are not enough to encourage people to think about why the Battle of Okinawa occurred, and what it must have been like to experience it. As such, the author considers that the archaeological and historical study of battlefield sites is important for the future.

It is of course important to emphasize that the stories of survivors are important. What the author emphasizes, however, is the need for researchers to consider how we can study battlefield sites as material culture, using ordinary archaeological methods, and to what extent we should take a critical perspective on documentary and oral sources. The majority of scholars have never experienced war. Therefore, they themselves can learn much from the study of battlefield sites. It is from this perspective that Okinawa Prefecture Archaeology Center, to which the author belongs, planned and opened 'The Battlefield Archaeological Sites in Okinawa Prefecture: Learn Together with Students' exhibition in 2019, which shared the experiences of students who attended battlefield site visits with the center staff (Okinawa Prefecture Archaeology Center 2019b). The author feels that even though students in Okinawa have heard numerous stories about the Battle of Okinawa, many of them never been to the nearby battlefield sites. Although we have never experienced and do not know war, it is important to experience and learn from these sites. In the future, the author considers it important for both the public and national defense personnel to visit and conduct further research on the battlefield sites, and to encourage the sharing of information in order to facilitate international cooperation and communication.

## Bibliography

Department of Military Base Policy, Ginowan City. 2012. Bei Kaiheitai Futenma Hikoujou [*Marine Corps Air Station, Futenma*]. [WWW] http://www.city.ginowan.okinawa.jp/organization/kichiatochitaisakuka/archives/2008.html (accessed 28/02/2020).

Ginowan City Board of Education. 1998. *Ginowan Shi no Senseki [Battlefield Sites in Ginowan City]*. Ginowan: Ginowan City Board of Education. (In Japanese).

Ginowan City Board of Education. 2012. *Ginowan no Chimei: Nairikubu Hen [Place Names in Ginowan: Inland Area]*. Ginowan: Ginowan City Board of Education. (In Japanese).

Haebaru Town Board of Education. 2008. *Dai 32 Gun Shireibu Tsukazangougun Tsukazankitachiku Kyu Nihongungougun: Kokudou 507 Gou (Tsukazanchiku) Kairyou kouji to Tsukazan Kitachiku Kukakuseirijigyou Ni Tomonau Maizoubunkazai Hakkutsu Chousa Houkokusho [The 32nd Army Head Quarter Tsukazan Caves, Tsukazan North Area Former Japanese Army Caves: Buried Cultural Property Excavation Report Accompanied with National Road 507 (Tsukazan Area) Construction and City-lots Adjustment]*. Haebaru Chou Bunkazai Chousa Houkokusho Dai 7 Shu [Haebaru Town Cultural Property Excavation Report Vol. 7]. Haebaru: Haebaru Town Board of Education. (In Japanese).

Kouchi Prefecture Archaeological Center. 2012. *Mukouyama Sensou Iseki [Mukouyama Battlefield Site], Kouchiken Maizou Bunkazai Center Hakkutsu Chousa Houkokusho 126 [Kouchi Prefecture Archaeological Center Excavation Report No. 126]*. Nankoku: Kouchi Prefecture Archaeological Center. (In Japanese).

Ministry of Army. 1943. *Yasen Chikujyou Kyouhan [A Manual for Building Field Fortification]*. Tokyo: Buyoudou.

Office for Military Base Counterplan, Okinawa Prefecture Governor's Office. 2019. *FAC6051 Futenma Air Field*. Okinawa Prefecture Official Website. [WWW] https://www.pref.okinawa.jp/site/chijiko/kichitai/1224.html (accessed June 17/06/2019).

Office of War History, National Institute for Defense Studies, Ministry of Defense. 1968. *Senshi Sousho: Okinawa Houmen Rikugun Sakusen*. Tokyo: Asagumo Shinbunsha.

Okinawa Prefecture Archaeology Center. 2001. *Okinawaken Sensouiseki Shousai Bunpu Chousa (I) Nanbu Hen [Distribution Survey of Battle Field Sites in Okinawa Prefecture (I) South]*. Naha: Okinawa Prefecture Archaeology Center.

Okinawa Prefecture Archaeology Center. 2002. *Okinawaken Sensouiseki Shousai Bunpu Chousa (II) Chubu Hen [Distribution Survey of Battle Field Sites in Okinawa Prefecture (II) Central]*. Naha: Okinawa Prefecture Archaeology Center.

Okinawa Prefecture Archaeology Center. 2003. *Okinawaken Sensouiseki Shousai Bunpu Chousa (III) Hokubu Hen [Distribution Survey of Battle Field Sites in Okinawa Prefecture (III) North]*. Naha: Okinawa Prefecture Archaeology Center.

Okinawa Prefecture Archaeology Center. 2004. *Okinawaken Sensouiseki Shousai Bunpu Chousa (IV) Hontou Shuuhen Ritou Oyobi Nahashi Hen [Distribution Survey of Battlefield*

*Sites in Okinawa Prefecture (IV): Remote Islands around the Main Island and Naha City]*. Naha: Okinawa Prefecture Archaeology Center.

Okinawa Prefecture Archaeology Center. 2005. *Okinawaken Sensouiseki Shousai Bunpu Chousa (V) Miyako Shotou Hen [Distribution Survey of Battlefield Sites in Okinawa Prefecture (V): Miyako Islands]*. Naha: Okinawa Prefecture Archaeology Center.

Okinawa Prefecture Archaeology Center 2006. *Okinawaken Sensouiseki Shousai Bunpu Chousa (VI) Yaeyama Shotou Hen [Distribution Survey of Battlefield Sites in Okinawa Prefecture (VI): Yaeyama Islands]*. Naha: Okinawa Prefecture Archaeology Center.

Okinawa Prefecture Archaeology Center. 2015. *Okinawaken no Sensouiseki: Heisei 22-26 Nendo Sensouiseki Shousai Kakunin Chousa Houkokusho [Battlefield Sites in Okinawa Prefecutre: 2010-2014 Report of the Distribution Survey of Battlefield Sites in Okinawa Prefecture]*. Naha: Okinawa Prefecture Archaeology Center.

Okinawa Prefecture Archaeology Center. 2019a. *Kyu Kamiyama Shuraku [Former Kamiyama Village]*. Naha: Okinawa Prefecture Archaeology Center.

Okinawa Prefecture Archaeology Center. 2019b. *Okinawaken no Sensouiseki: Seito Gakusei to Tomoni Manabu [Battlefield Sites in Okinawa Prefecture: Learning with Students]*. Naha: Okinawa Prefecture Archaeology Center.

Seto, T. 2017. 'Okinawaken no Sensouiseki Chousa no Genjyou' [Current researches on Battlefield sites in Okinawa Prefecture], *Koukogaku Kenkyu*, 63 (4), 23–27.

The 32nd Army Liquidation Department. 1947. *Dai 62 Shidan Shireibu Sentou Keika Gaiyou [The 62nd Division Headquarters Combat Progress Summary]*. Japan Center for Asian Historical Records, National Archives of Japan. Ref.C11110333700, C1111005510.

Touma, S. 1984. 'Senseki Koukogaku no Susume' [Recommendations for Battlefield Archaeology], *Nantou Kouko Dayori*, 30, 2.

Touma, S. 1996. 'Senseki Koukogaku' [Battlefield Archaeology], In: Nishihara Town Hall, ed. *Nishihara Chou Shi Dai 5 Kan: Nishihara no Kouko [Nishihara Town History Volume 5: Archaeology of Nishihara]*. Nishihara: Nishihara Town Hall, 487–542.

Yoshihama, S. 2017. *Okinawa no Sensouiseki <Kioku> wo Mirai ni Tsunageru [Battlefield Sites in Okinawa: Inheriting "memories" to the Future]*. Tokyo: Yoshikawa Koubunkan.

Yoshihama, S., Ooshiro, K., Ikeda, Y., Uechi, K. & Koga, N. 2010. *Okinawa Rikugun Byouin Haebarugou: Sensou Iseki Bunkazai Shitei Zenkoku Dai 1 Gou [Okinawa Army Hospital Haebaru Caves: The First Registered War Related Site as Cultural Property in Japan]*. Tokyo: Koubunken Co., Ltd (In Japanese).

# 10

# RESEARCH, CONSERVATION, AND UTILIZATION OF WAR-RELATED SITES IN HAEBARU TOWN, OKINAWA

*Akira Hokumori*

## Introduction

Haebaru Town has been working to preserve war-related sites through the excavation of hospital caves that were used by the Japanese military and evacuated citizens during the Battle of Okinawa. In 1990, the town registered the Okinawa Army Hospital Haebaru Clinic caves as a cultural property of Haebaru Town. The site was classified as war-related, and it was the first of its kind in Japan. Following the registration of the site, the town proceeded to research ways to conserve the site while utilizing its potential as a visitor destination. Based on this research, the town renovated the 20th Clinic cave and it has been open to the public since 2007. About 10,000 people visit to the site annually, which presents problems for the conservation and utilization of the hospital clinic caves.

In this chapter, the author focuses on the problems encountered during the process of research prior to the public opening of Okinawa Army Hospital Haebaru Clinic caves, which is an historic case study for the conservation and utilization of a war-related site in Okinawa and Japan. From this case study, the author considers the most effective methods for the conservation and use of war-related sites.

## Background of Haebaru Town

Haebaru Town is located in the south-central interior of Okinawa Island and it is the only municipality that does not face the ocean. Because the town is located next to Naha City – the prefectural capital, it has been developing as a commuter town. As of April 2019, the population was 39,427 and still growing.

Haebaru sits at an important crossroads in the interior of Okinawa and possesses transport links to Shuri (the capital of Ryukyu Kingdom until 1872), the

DOI: 10.4324/9780429270468-13

port towns of Naha and Yonabaru, and also the southern portion of the island. Although the administrative unit changed to Haebaru Village after the dissolution of the Ryukyu kingdom, its function remained the same until the Battle of Okinawa. Two of three light railway lines, the Naha-Itoman line and Yonabaru line operated by Okinawa Prefectural Railway, run through the village. The geographical environment of the town is reflected in the nature of the corps that were assigned to it during the Battle of Okinawa.

## The Battle of Okinawa in Haebaru

### Assigned Corps to Haebaru

Japanese troops were stationed at Haebaru following the establishment of the 32nd Army in March 1944. From here, they commanded the defense of Okinawa. Because Haebaru was an important transportation hub, logistical support corps were primarily assigned to the area (Haebaru Town History Editorial Board 1999). The foremost of these logistical support corps was the Okinawa Army Hospital, which was under the direct control of the 32nd Army, 62nd Division Field Hospital, 32nd Army Field Armory, a cargo depot supplying clothing and provisions, and the Accounting and Military Medicine Department of the 32nd Army HQ. Of course, combat units were also assigned. These included the 27th Tank Regiment (the only troops who operated tanks on Okinawa Island), the Individual Anti-Aircraft Gun 27th Battalion, and the 4th Company of the Field Heavy Gun 23rd Regiment. Only a small number of the assigned troops were combat infantry.

The deployment of the 27th Tank Regiment to the area may reflect Japanese predictions that US forces would land in south or central Okinawa, and as such Haebaru was the best location to utilize the high mobility and firepower of the tanks. The Japanese Army troops deployed in Haebaru built up positions using community halls and houses as barracks and a depot. Military supplies, including artillery shells, were piled up outdoors. Thus, the deployment of the Japanese Army would have dramatically changed the landscape of the village. Local residents had been forced to provide shelter for soldiers, to deliver and produce increased amounts of food, and to act as a labor force working with troops in the construction of defensive positions.

### War Damage in Haebaru

Air raids against the Nansei Islands[1] on October 10th 1944 by the US Army Air Force caused extreme damage to Naha and its surrounding areas. Yonaha Village in Haebaru was also burned down during the air raids. Seventy-two out of eighty-two houses in the village were destroyed by fire. A few people were injured or killed by US aerial machine gun attacks in other villages.

In late March 1945, when the US Army started to violently bombard Okinawa Island before the landing operation, the amount of damage in Haebaru increased. US forces landed on central Okinawa on April 1st. On April 9th, the Haebaru Village government ordered villagers to evacuate to Oyakebaru in the former Tamashiro village area. However, because the order did not reach the villagers who were under bombardment, only a small number received message. Although the 32nd Army mounted a counterattack against the US invasion on May 4th, this proved to be a failure. US forces then began to surround Shuri, where the 32nd Army CIC was located. With the encirclement of Shuri almost completed on May 22nd, the 32nd Army HQ decided to retreat from Shuri to the south of Okinawa. Japanese soldiers and local residents passed through Haebaru as they moved south. Intense battles started to emerge around Haebaru, with US troops attacking both soldiers and refugees. As the casualties mounted and corpses began to pile up in the area, Kaneshiro Crossroad in Haebaru became known as 'Death Crossroad,' and Yamakawa Bridge was called 'Death Bridge'. Many Haebaru refugees lost their lives in early June, when the soldiers and local residents were pushed toward the south. Further incidents can be confirmed even after June 23rd, following the end of the organized combat as a result of the death of the 32nd Army Commander, Ushijima, and Chief of Staff Osa.

In total, 3,505 out of 8,023 people in Haebaru died during the Battle of Okinawa. The mortality rate was about 44%, meaning that almost one in two people lost their priceless lives.

## War-Related Sites in Haebaru

During the years 1983–96, Haebaru Town conducted a comprehensive survey of all households in order to research the impacts of the war within the town. Because those conducting the interviews were local high-school students and housewives who had no experience of war, this survey functions to transmit the memory of the Battle of Okinawa. One hundred and thirty people were involved to the project.

The survey revealed not only the details of war damage, but also where the Japanese Army was stationed and built their positions. It also identified the location of the evacuation cave for locals. During this survey, the Okinawa Army Hospital Haebaru Clinic caves attracted strong attention, and a research excavation was later conducted by Haebaru Town Cultural Protection Council. Following the excavation, Haebaru Town proactively registered the clinic caves as a cultural property. As a result of this, the town started to regard war-related sites as cultural property and has since been conducting investigations of other sites in the area (Haebaru Town Board of Education 2008b).

In 1998, the deputy chief of Agency of Cultural Affairs notified the superintendents of education in all municipal Boards of Education in Japan of 'Buried Cultural Property Conservation and Smoothing of Archaeological Excavation.' This notice was created for balancing the conservation of Buried Cultural Property with developmental construction, with the aim of expediting archaeological (rescue) excavations. The range of Buried Cultural Property is described as follows:

i  Archaeological sites dated from the medieval period should be included.
ii  Archaeological sites dated as early modern can be included if it is needed locally.
iii  Late modern and recent sites can be included if it is especially important to the local community.

Given that late modern war-related sites including those related to the Battle of Okinawa fit into 'category iii,' decisions regarding the conducting of excavations are more dependent on local governments. Because of this, unfortunately, attitudes to the conservation of war-related sites differ among each local government. Below, I will briefly describe the outcome of excavations that have been conducted at war-related sites in Haebaru Town.

## Okinawa Army Hospital Haebaru Clinic Caves

Okinawa Army Hospital Haebaru Clinic caves are the clinic caves that belonged to the 32nd Army, the main Japanese corps engaged in the Battle of Okinawa. The site consists of about thirty clinic caves built within Koganemori Hill. Before describing the details of the Okinawa Army Hospital and the conservation and utilization project, I will outline the archaeological research (including excavations) that has taken place to date.

Archaeological excavations have previously taken place as part of a project directed by the Haebaru Army Hospital Clinic Caves Conservation and Utilization Research Council, which was established to ensure the protection and utilization of the hospital clinic cave in 1993. The excavation took place in cooperation with Professor Yoshifumi Ikeda of the Archaeology Department of Ryukyu University, who was also one of the council members. Four stages of research took place (Yoshihama *et al.* 2010). The first stage was to collect interview and historical data for the Okinawa Army Hospital Haebaru Clinic caves. The second stage was to create a topographic map of known clinic caves to be used alongside the data collected during Stage One. The third stage saw an attempt to create an archaeological database and to conduct test-pit excavations in order to confirm the location and taphonomy of clinic caves and associated archaeological features. The fourth stage, where necessary, was to undertake large-scale excavations in order to study the archaeological features more comprehensively.

The four stages were set as aims of the project and followed general archaeological methods. As a consequence of the research, sixteen clinic caves have been located. Survey and excavation were conducted at the 20th clinic cave, the main clinic cave of the 2nd Surgical Department (Haebaru Town Board of Education 2000, 2008a). A survey of the 24th clinic cave, occupied by the 1st Surgical Department, was also conducted.

The 20th clinic cave excavations yielded many interesting results (Figure 10.1). The width and height of the clinic cave was 1.8–2.0 m, and the length about 70 m. Holes for roof-bearing posts lined up along both sides of the cave at c.90cm intervals. Although they were decayed, surviving horizontal beams connected these vertical posts. Some part of the roofs and walls are burned by US flame throwers. Medicines and hypodermic needles were unearthed in the 'surgical room,' which matched data provided by interviewees. Interestingly, a kanji letter '姜' (ginger) or '菱'(water chestnut) was found carved into the roof where bunk beds for patients were located. After the finding, the research team re-interviewed a person who worked for the hospital and found that a soldier originally from the Korean Peninsula had occupied the top of the bunk beds.

As described above, modern war-related site excavations allow investigators to match up excavation data to that collected during interviews. However, interviews and written records provide only a partial account of the whole event. Therefore, in this case, the effectiveness of archaeological excavation was ensured by the comprehensive nature of the accompanying research.

Currently, only the 20th clinic cave is open to public, an information board has been set up in front of the 24th clinic cave. Thus, new efforts for the utilization of the clinic cave site are urged. This will be discussed in more detail below.

## Excavation of the 32nd Army Tsukazan HQ Clinic Caves

Tsukazan HQ Clinic caves were the largest facilities built by the Japanese Army in Haebaru. The clinic caves were built on 'Chikashimo' hill and Takatsukazan hill, which are located north of Tsukazan Village in Haebaru town. The man-made clinic caves are 1,500–2,000 m in total length, and feature many sub-clinic caves (measuring about 100m in length), which connect to the main clinic cave (which measures c. 400m in length) at right angles.

Construction of the clinic caves started in the summer of 1944, and a private company was contracted to build portions of these. Because the majority of the walls were boarded and lights were installed, the clinic cave interior was of much better quality than others. Kikuko Miyagi of the Himeyuri Student Corps, who moved from the Army Hospital clinic caves to the HQ Clinic cave, says '…what surprised me was its better construction and large area. The light bulbs lit, and we almost lost our words because we came from the dark hospital clinic caves….' (Miyagi 1990: 87).

Although the HQ Clinic cave was well-constructed, the mudstone geology surrounding the cave caused concerns regarding its durability to be raised after the air raid of October 10th 1944. Also, because the visibility from the hills was limited, the battle command post and other major departments of the HQ moved to Shuri in December of 1944. Other logistics support departments such as accounting and medicine remained at the Tsukazan HQ Clinic caves.

On May 27th 1945, while the Japanese Army was retreating from Shuri to the south of the island, the Commander Ushijima and other HQ officers stopped by

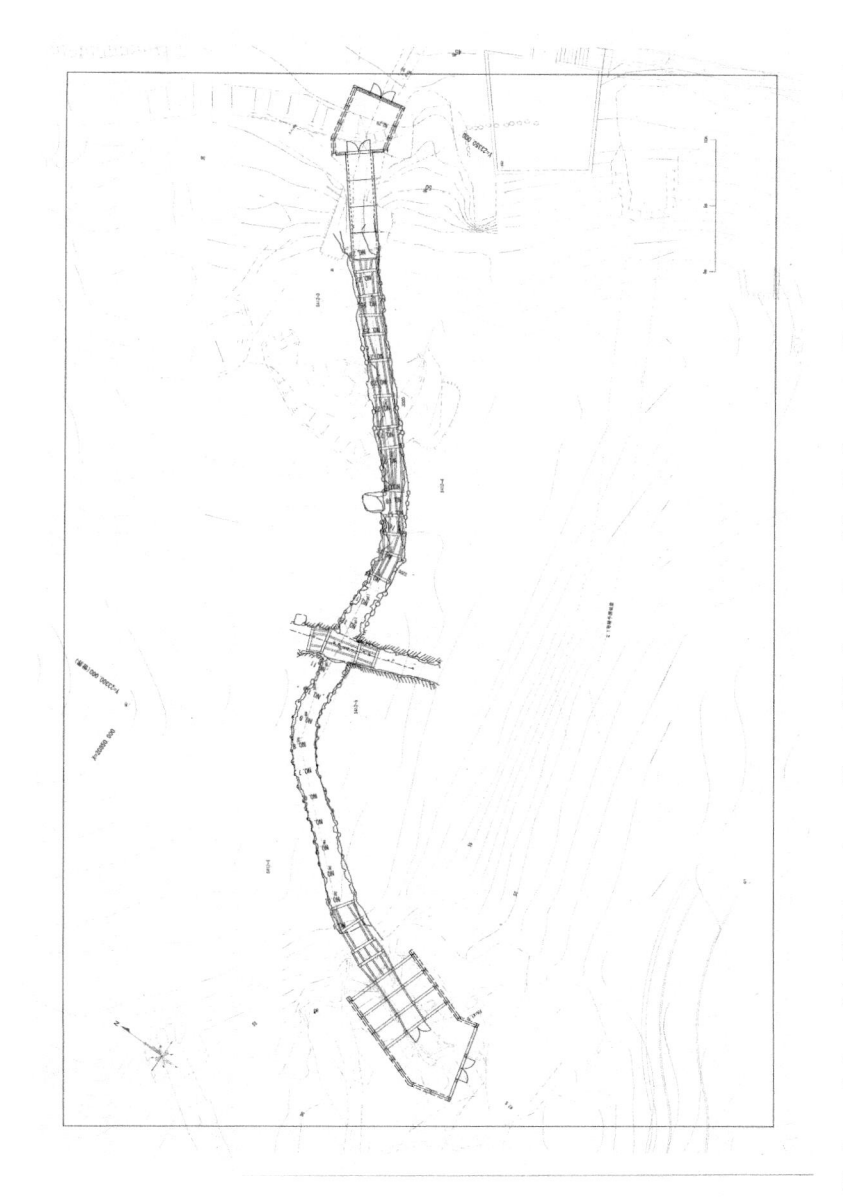

**FIGURE 10.1**  Horizontal plan of the Okinawa Army Hospital Haebaru Cave No. 20. Image by Haebaru Town Board of Education.

the Tsukazan HQ Clinic caves. After this, the Tsukazan HQ area functioned as a transit camp for the Japanese Army. Troops were deployed to support the retreat from Shuri, and battles began to take place in the surrounding area.

The 32nd Army Tsukazan HQ Clinic caves were found during a rescue excavation undertaken prior to road construction in 2006 (Haebaru Town Board of Education. 2008b; see Figure 10.2). Because there was a risk of ceiling collapse, the excavation took an 'open cut' method, exposing the remaining floors and walls after a topographic survey. The dimensions of the excavated clinic cave were 2m in height and 2–2.2 m in width. The measured length of the clinic cave was 34m; however, the clinic cave entrance had been removed by previous development. The clinic cave slightly curves from its entrance to the rear. Two small, square rooms were situated about 10m and 13m from the entrance. A similar curvature of a clinic cave has been confirmed at the Okinawa Army Hospital Haebaru Clinic caves. This was intended offset damage from attacks or explosions, and to hide the occupants from the enemy.

The cave incorporated a drainage system, comprising floor drains and a 3-degree downward slope in the floor toward the entrance. The floor was partly paved with red roof tiles, which were used by soldiers in an attempt to drain water to the outside and to provide a more secure footing on the muddy floor.

**FIGURE 10.2** Photograph of excavated Tsukazan HQ Caves. Photograph from Haebaru Town Board of Education 2008b.

The clinic cave was reinforced by many post holes inserted into the floor, but it is worth noting that the presence of crossbars, which supported the posts, was also confirmed. Weak spots were reinforced with square-shaped posts. Other objects found within included a diverse array of tools, medical supplies, and weapons. These various artifacts might have been brought into the clinic cave, which was located far behind the frontline, because different troops came and went based on the shifting nature of the battle.

Only a small part of the 32nd Army Tsukazan HQ Clinic caves were revealed by the rescue excavation. If further excavation and research takes place, more archaeological evidence will be recovered from the large unexcavated area.

### Tsukazan Northern Block Former Japanese Army Clinic caves

The Tsukazan Northern Block Former Japanese Army Clinic caves were excavated during road construction and the adjustment of city lots. Individual excavated clinic caves were named in alphabetical order from A to K. The function of the caves and details of related troops were ascertained from the excavated materials and interviews conducted with local residents (Haebaru Town Board of Education 2008b, 2010).

Clinic cave A: related to the Field Operations and Well Drilling 14th Company, which was assigned to depot and transport missions.

Clinic cave B: associated with depot and transport troops, as evidenced by many medicine and boxes with calligraphic labels.

Clinic cave C: a set square with curved letters and other artifacts indicate that this cave was related to soldiers of the army air corps.

Clinic cave D (Figure 10.3): this was the only penetrated clinic cave with more than two entrances. Medicine and fishing gear reveal that the clinic cave was associated with depot and transport troops, who also engaged in fishing to supplement provisions.

Clinic cave E: a fastener, horseshoes, and medicine revealed a relationship with the transport corps, which used army horses.

Clinic caves F and G: the clinic caves may be related with 'clinic cave I' or a defensive cave, although the clinic cave was disturbed by later land modification.

Clinic cave H: heavy machine gun ammunition contained within an ammunition box tells of a relationship with an infantry or machine gun unit.

Clinic cave I: numerous finds of medicine and interview data indicate that this cave was a hospital or store for the transport corps.

Clinic cave J: a possible defensive, anti-tank clinic cave. Interview data reveals that the area surrounding clinic cave J was used as a defensive position by machine gun and anti-aircraft troops.

Clinic cave K: interviewees have revealed that the clinic cave was originally used for the evacuation of local residents. But, because of the nearby anti-aircraft gun corps, it was also used as a defensive clinic cave. Anti-aircraft gun ammunition was excavated.

As such, the function of the clinic caves and their related corps have been reconstructed from the excavation and interview data. Only the D clinic cave had more than one entrance. Generally, large structures such as clinic caves should have more than two different entrances. It is possible that the clinic cave builders could not complete the other clinic caves because of time and labor shortages.

### Okinawa Army Hospital Haebaru Clinic Cave

The Okinawa Army Hospital Haebaru Clinic cave was used by the Okinawa Army Hospital (KYU 18803) and directly controlled by the 32nd Army and comprises a number of clinic caves located on the Koganemori Hills in Haebaru (Figure 10.4).

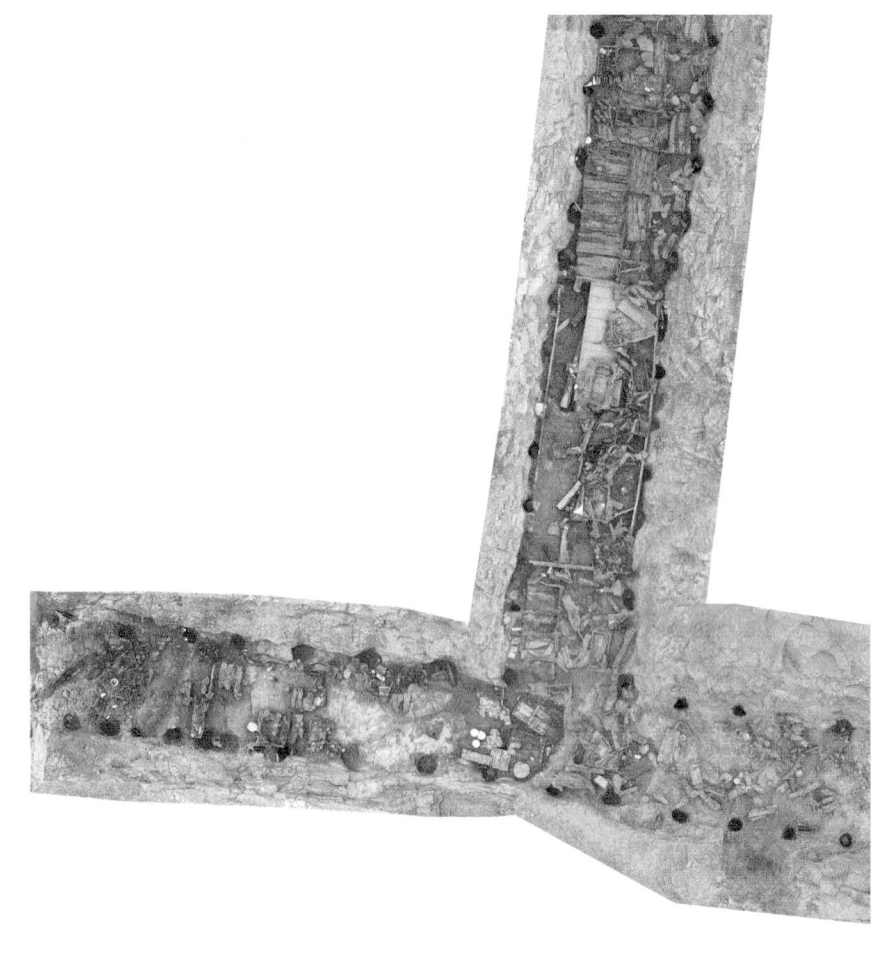

**FIGURE 10.3** Orthographic photograph of Cave D and D-1 at the Tsukazan Northern Block Former Japanese Army Clinic caves. Photograph from Haebaru Town Board of Education 2008b.

The Okinawa Army Hospital was first established in Kumamoto in May 1944. From June, the hospital HQ was located at Kainan Junior High School in Naha. From September 3rd, the Second Field Battle Castle Corps First Company and other troops started to construct clinic caves at the Koganemori Hill near Haebaru in order to counter the forthcoming US landings. After the medical facilities were largely damaged by the air raid on October 10th 1944, the hospital function was moved to Haebaru Citizen's School (now Haebaru Elementary School) during the night of the same day.

As heavy guns had been placed on the school playground during the summer of the same year, teachers and students were already prohibited from entering. Classes were taught at a community center or vacant houses, but older students were forced to work as laborers on the construction of positions. With the commencement of fierce pre-landing attacks on March 23rd 1945, the hospital functions were moved to clinic caves in Koganemori. However, many of the clinic caves were not completed. At that time, the progress of the construction 'of horizontal clinic caves reached only less than 30% of scheduled plan' (The 32nd Army Liquidation Department 1947).

Surgical, internal medicine, and infectious disease departments were located on the south, east, and northwest sides of the hills. Because the number of patients with bullet wounds would increase later, the departments were renamed as the 1st to 3rd Surgical Department Clinic caves. The total number of constructed clinic caves is about 30. At the Army Hospital, 222 students from Okinawa Female Normal School and Okinawa First Girl's High School, led by eighteen teachers, were mobilized as nurses to assist about 350 army surgeons, nurses, and combat medics. Since World War II, these students and teachers have been referred to as the Himeyuri Student Corps (see Koga, this volume). Although hospital practices in the clinic caves started at the end of March, the hospital lost a large quantity of medicines during the air raid of October 10th 1944. The number of patients increased day by day, but there were no medical supply deliveries. Under these circumstances, many amputation surgeries were conducted as treatment for wounded patients to prevent infections. Because of the medical supply shortage, bandage-changing intervals were gradually extended and gauze was also reused after washing with boiled water. The clinic cave was without lights, and it would have been filled by the smell of blood, sweat, pus, death, feces, and medicine. In addition, the grievous groans or shouts of patients echoed through the cave.

With the US invasion, the Army Hospital started to retreat south on around May 25th. Cyanide was provided or administered to serious case patients who could not walk. According to Mr. Okajo, the only survivor who was administered the cyanide, combat medics returned to the cave on May 28th and provided the patients milk mixed with cyanide. However, some army surgeons and medics refused the order to poison their patients. After the retreat, the hospital HQ was established in Yamashiro, Itoman. The 1st Surgical Department was set up in Namihira and Ihara. The 2nd Surgical Department was located in Itosu. The 3rd Surgical Department was established in Ihara. By this time, however, hospital practice had effectively

**FIGURE 10.4** Distribution map of Okinawa Army Hospital Haebaru caves. Image from Haebaru Town Board of Education 2013, modified by the author.

ceased, and non-officer army surgeons and combat medics were deployed with other troops fighting at the frontline. The Okinawa Army Hospital finally dismissed the troops on June 19. Consequently, fifty-four out of eighty army surgeons and combat medics, fifty-five out of ninety nurses, twenty out of forty-five women who worked as copyists, cooks, and doing odd jobs, and 136 students and teachers of the 240-strong Himeyuri Student Corps lost their valuable lives.

## Conservation of Okinawa Army Hospital Haebaru Caves

After World War II, the collection of skeletal remains of the victims from the Battle of Okinawa has increased in Okinawa prefecture. According to a farmer who lived near the Army Hospital Caves right after the war ended, human remains were found every time they plowed their field. Throughout the 1970s and 1980s, the collection of human remains at the Army Hospital Caves was actively conducted by the Ministry of Health and Welfare (currently the Ministry of Health, Labor and Welfare) and people working at the present-day hospitals. The Ministry of Health and Welfare used power shovels and dug up all possible locations. Little care was given to the local topography and cave entrances, and only a tiny part of this process was recorded. The next collection project, which was undertaken by the Ministry of Health, Labor and Welfare in 1987, was also large. Members of Haebaru Cultural Property Conservation Board who oversaw this collection process were consulted in order to ensure the recording and conservation of the caves while also conducting rescue mapping surveys and interviews.

War-related site protection is important for effective peace education. The caves have been described as follows '…Koganemori is a 'treasure' of Haebaru's history and 'living textbook to know the war' for the generation who has not experienced it. If the caves are destroyed eternally, it will create a grudge to future generations' (Yoshihama 1987: 70).

In 1990, Haebaru Town registered the Army Hospital site as the first war-related cultural property (Historical Sites) in Japan. The reason for the registration is written as:

> handing down the stories of the Battle of Okinawa becomes more difficult year by year because survivors of the war are now less than half. It will become almost impossible to interview a survivor in the 21st century. Under these circumstances, the caves are the only storyteller of the battle. If we preserve the caves then they will continue to tell stories to future generations in order to allow them to relive the experience of conflict. Haebaru Army Hospital Cave is a living witness of the battle and the common property of local citizens.
>
> *(Haebaru Town Board of Education 1991: 22–23)*

When the board had consultations with the national and prefectural government, it was revealed that the site was not suitable as cultural property because it is too recent. At that time, there was no provision to recognize modern war-related sites in national Cultural Property Protection law. Therefore, Haebaru Town, by their own decision, added a provision 'archaeological site related to the Battle of Okinawa' into the criteria for registering cultural property (Historical Site). After this, and in taking advantage of the movement to register the Atomic Bomb Dome in Hiroshima as a UNESCO World Heritage site, National Cultural Property Protection Law was amended in 1995 with the addition of 'war and other political related archaeological site' to its criteria. This case proves that the amendment of the local regulation criteria for war-related sites in Haebaru Town was a pioneering achievement.

In 1993, the Haebaru Army Hospital Cave Preservation and Utilization Research Board was established to ensure site conservation and utilization. As a result of this, not only were archaeological mapping surveys and excavations conducted, but also geological surveys. The board also discussed how to utilize the eroding cave and whether to open the cave for visitors or only let them see inside from the entrance (Haebaru Army Hospital Cave Preservation and Utilization Research Board 1996). Because of safety issues and budget limitations, in 1996 the board submitted a report stating that visitors should be kept outside of the cave. However, Town Mayor Kaneshiro Yoshio decided to keep the cave open to public in keeping with his principle that 'the most important thing is walking through the cave.' In 1997, the Haebaru Army Hospital Caves Maintenance and Consideration Board (HAHCMCB) was established, and in 2003, it submitted a report that considered practical preservation and opening methods (Haebaru Town History Editorial Board 2013). The 20th Cave was maintained according to three plans: (1) keeping the original part if it well-preserved, (2) to shore up dangerous parts and to reconstruct them like the original, and (3) to cover the most collapsed entrance with concrete. In addition to maintaining the 20th Cave in accordance with these plans, the board also suggested maintenance and public opening plans for the 24th Cave, which is located near the 20th (Haebaru Army Hospital Cave Maintenains Review Committee 2003). The plan includes reconstructing the entrance and providing a reliving experience through looking inside from the entrance. However, because the 24th Cave entrance roof collapsed during the 20th Cave maintenance, the project on the 24th Cave is now in a frozen state. This incident highlights the difficulties associated with the management of erosion and weathering.

## Utilization of Okinawa Army Hospital Haebaru Caves

Maintenance construction in advance of the public opening of the 20th Cave was conducted in 2006. The construction was initiated with two aims: (1) to preserve the original features and (2) to provide the most accurate cave reconstruction based on archaeological data.

The construction was proceeded with the creation of a blueprint based on archaeological survey. Obviously, the surveyed map provides two dimensional horizontal and vertical plans, but the actual construction was undertaken in three dimensions. Therefore, the construction effort had to counter many problems such as a lack of reinforcement material. Because of the narrow cave space, work could be conducted only by hand. Safety equipment was installed both inside and outside of the cave. This included a pipe strain meter for measuring landslides around the site, a load meter on the roof to measure movement in the cave ceiling, and a displacement gauge inside of the wall to observe the movement of the walls.

The opening of the 20th Cave took place on June 17th 2007 (Figure 10.5). At the time of opening, ensuring the safety and preservation of the site were issues because of the narrow confines of the cave, as well as its sand and mudstone composition. In response to this, several rules were set. These included limiting visitor groups to less than ten people at a time, ensuring that visitor guides must finish a Haebaru Town guide training course, and the securing of permission prior to visits by large groups (Haebaru Town History Editorial Board 2013). Based on these rules, Haebaru Town had conducted guide training courses on ten occasions by April, 2019. Qualified guides established the Haebaru Peace Guide Association, and its members stay at the site and guide visitors. There are about 60 guides aged from their 20s to their 80s. These guides take on a role of disseminating accurate information of the Okinawa Army Hospital Haebaru Cave site and also the maintenance of a safe environment for both the site and visitors. Haebaru Town runs these utilization projects not only with support from the government but also from the local residents. The annual number of visitors to the 20th Cave is about 10,000, and the total visitor number has reached more

**FIGURE 10.5** Publicly exhibited Cave No. 20 at the Okinawa Army Hospital Haebaru cave. Photograph by Haebaru Town Board of Education.

than 100,000. From January 2015 to March 2018, visitors could participate in an experiential activity whereby the smell of the caves was reconstructed. Until this attempt, the visitor's experience had been limited to 'sight' and 'hearing.' Adding the reconstructed smell provided a more realistic image of the hospital environment and the experience of those who inhabited it. The purposes of the smelling experience was to provide a realistic wartime experience, to encourage the consideration of peace and rejection of warfare, and to more accurately maintain the inheritance of war-related sites and testimonies. However, because of budget measures the smelling experience was stopped in 2019 and restarted in 2021. Realistically, although it is not easy to continue this activity, Haebaru Town regards it as a globally unique activity associated with a World War II hospital cave site and hope to provide the experience for future visitors.

## Conservation and Utilization Issues of Okinawa Army Hospital Haebaru Caves

The author has primarily described past research, preservation efforts, and the utilization of the Okinawa Army Hospital Haebaru Caves. In this section, current problems of conservation and utilization are described.

Over seventy years have passed since construction of the cave, and more than ten years since the public opening. During this time, cracks and peeling on the roof and walls have been observed, and annual visits by 10,000 people have accelerated this process. Under these circumstances, the eroding conditions within the cave and potential solutions for this are major priorities. In terms of the site utilization, the biggest problem is that only the 20th cave is open to the public. In past excavations, sixteen caves, a 'transportation cave' that connected the caves and positions, a 'rice delivery road' used to transport rice from cooking locations, and a number of artillery holes have been found. In Koganemori, there is also folklore and natural heritage besides the hospital-related features to consider. As folklore material, *Utaki*, used by local residents for worship, and *Kyan-shiji*, a celebration place used during the Ryukyu Dynasty when villagers completed their tax payment, are also known (Haebaru Town History Editorial Board 2003). With regards to the natural heritage, about 44% of all animal populations in Haebaru reside at Koganemori (Haebaru Town History Editorial Board 2000). Although such valuable heritage resources are confirmed around the caves, we are still far away from productive utilization. These factors currently exist individually. Therefore, we need to consider maintenance and trial plans that connect those individual archaeological sites to create a historic area.

## Future Conservation and Utilization Plan of Okinawa Army Hospital Haebaru Caves

Haebaru Town established the Haebaru Town Cultural Property Conservation Board (HTCPCB) for research and to review the conservation and utilization of cultural properties. The director of Haebaru Town Board of Education inquired 'about the utilization of the 20th Cave, Okinawa Army Hospital Haebaru Cave site, and other war-related sites around Koganemori Hills' to the board (Okinawa Prefecture Haebaru Town Cultural Property Conservation Board 2019). The inquiry is designed to check the utilization of the sites in Koganemori and the condition of the 20th Cave in the 10th year of its opening. In response to this, Okinawa Army Hospital Haebaru Cave and Koganemori Area War Related Site Utilization Consideration Working Group (Koganemori Area War Related Site Utilization Working Group, KAWRSUWG) and the 20th Cave of Okinawa Army Hospital Haebaru Cave Research and Review Working Group (Research and Review Working Group, RRWG) were established to begin research and discussion.

KAWRSUWG evaluated the progress of the utilization plan submitted by HAHCMCB in 1993 and discussed the new utilization plan in light of the current situation. During this process, the working group interviewed Peace Guides in Okinawa, the former curator of Haebaru Town Museum, elementary school teachers, and local housewives about the new utilization approach. Also, one of the group members suggested that the author consult with the 'Local Field Museum (*Chiiki-Marugoto-Hakubutsukan*),' a project which is run in Tateyama City, Chiba prefecture, to utilize the entire local area as a field for learning through a collaboration with the local community. The knowledge gained from this project was applied to the Haebaru case study by the author. At the same time, RRWG started their research with a survey of the erosion within the 20th Cave. The survey included a review of the data from multiple pieces of safety equipment. This was the first intensive survey since 1995, and it coordinated records of fallen walls and roofs with the cave map created at that time. The survey found that the wall and roof were not degraded in terms of their integrity, but it nevertheless confirmed the seriousness of the surface erosion. Based on this, the working group considered how to handle the eroding surfaces. Because there are no prior preservation cases of caves consisting of eroding sand and mudstone, a new construction method was discussed and applied experimentally. After several tests, the board confirmed that putting glue between the wall and peel was the most effective preservation method (Figure 10.6).

A report of the inquiry including two and half years of research and discussion results was submitted from HTCPCB to Haebaru town. The report suggests continuous observation of eroding surfaces, repair with glue, and further consideration of conservation methods. In addition, the necessity of the 'Local Field Museum,' the maintenance of the park path and installation of guide plates were emphasized. The report also considered the creation of new trail routes, the creation and continued application of experiential activities including the 'smell experience,' and the holding of family workshop events in order to ensure the utilization of the whole Koganemori area. Based on the report, Haebaru Town is considering whether to make further efforts for the preservation and utilization of the Okinawa Army Hospital Haebaru Cave site.

**FIGURE 10.6** Filling cracks in the cave with glue. Photograph by Haebaru Town Board of Education.

## Conclusion

In this chapter, the author has described the researching, preservation, and utilization of war-related sites in Haebaru Town through the efforts applied to the Okinawa Army Hospital Haebaru Cave. The author has confronted many large obstacles while conducting these projects. Foremost of these is the damage to the 20th Cave from 10,000 annual visitors, but this is somewhat unavoidable. Therefore, the maintenance of a balance between preservation and utilization is an unsolvable issue for the author. However, utilization is just as significant for war-related sites as their preservation. There are strong messages that can be only told by the war-related sites, which were created as a result of tragic experiences. With seventy-seven years having passed since the last war in Japan, it has become much more difficult to ask war survivors about their experiences. Under these circumstances, the importance of war-related sites increases every day. To avoid the unforgettable mistakes of conflict and to prevent the creation of new war-related sites, it is important to learn from those which already exist, and to ensure that the next generation inherits their history.

## Note

1 The island chain extending from southwestern Kyushu to northern Taiwan.

# Bibliography

Haebaru Army Hospital Cave Maintenance Review Committee. 2003. *Haebaru Rikugun Byouingou: Seibi/Koukai Ni Tuite No Toushinsho [Haebaru Army Hospital Cave: Report on the Maintenance and Opening to the Public]*. Haebaru: Haebaru Town Board of Education (In Japanese).

Haebaru Army Hospital Cave Preservation and Utilization Research Board. 1996. *Haebaru Rikugun Byouingou: Hozon/Katsuyou Ni Tuite No Toushinsho [Haebaru Army Hospital Caves: Report for the Inquiry about Utilization and Opening to Public]*. Haebaru: Haebaru Town Board of Education (In Japanese).

Haebaru Town Board of Education. 1991. *Haebaru no Bunkazai [Cultural Properties in Haebaru]*. Bunkazai Youran Dai 3 Shu [Cultural Properties in Haebaru. Cultural Property Catalogue No.3]. Haebaru: Haebaru Town Board of Education (In Japanese).

Haebaru Town Board of Education. 2000. *Haebaru Rikugun Byouingou I [Haebaru Army Hospital Cave I]*. Haebaru Chou Bunkazai Hakkutsuchousa Houkokusyo Dai 3 Shu [Haebaru Town Cultural Property Excavation Report Vol. 3]. Haebaru: Haebaru Town Board of Education (In Japanese).

Haebaru Town Board of Education. 2008a. *Haebaru Rikugun Byouingou I [Haebaru Army Hospital Cave II]*. Haebaru Chou Bunkazai Hakkutsuchousa Houkokusyo Dai 6 Shu [Haebaru Town Cultural Property Excavation Report Vol. 6]. Haebaru: Haebaru Town Board of Education (In Japanese).

Haebaru Town Board of Education. 2008b. *Dai 32 Gun Shireibu Tsukazangougun Tsukazankitachiku Kyu Nihongungougun: Kokudou 507 Gou (Tsukazanchiku) Kairyou kouji to Tsukazan Kitachiku Kukakuseirijigyou Ni Tomonau Maizoubunkazai Hakkutsu Chousa Houkokusho [The 32nd Army Head Quarter Tsukazan Caves, Tsukazan North Area Former Japanese Army Caves: Buried Cultural Property Excavation Report Accompanied with National Road 507 (Tsukazan Area) Construction and City-lots Adjustment]*. Haebaru Chou Bunkazai Chousa Houkokusho Dai 7 Shu [Haebaru Town Cultural Property Excavation Report Vol. 7]. Haebaru: Haebaru Town Board of Education (In Japanese).

Haebaru Town Board of Education. 2010. *Tsukazankitachiku Kyu Nihongungougun II: Tsukazan Kitachiku Kukakuseirijigyou Ni Tomonau Maizoubunkazai Hakkutsu Chousa Houkokusho [Tsukazan North Area Former Japanese Army Caves II: Buried Cultural Property Excavation Report Accompanied with City-Lots Adjustment Project in Tsukazan North Area]*. Haebaru Chou Bunkazai Chousa Houkokusho Dai 8 Shu [Haebaru Town Cultural Property Excavation Report Vol. 8]. Haebaru: Haebaru Town Board of Education (In Japanese).

Haebaru Town History Editorial Board. 1999. *Haebaru Ga Kataru Okinawa Sen [The Battle of Okinawa Told by Haebaru]*. Haebaru Choushi Dai 3 Kan Sensouhen Daijesuto Ban [Haebaru Town History Vol.3]. Haebaru: Haebaru Town (In Japanese).

Haebaru Town History Editorial Board. 2000. *Haebaru No Shizen To Chiri [Nature and Geography in Haebaru]*. Haebaru Choushi Dai 4 Kan Shizen/Chiri Honpen [Haebaru Town History Vol.4]. Haebaru: Haebaru Town (In Japanese).

Haebaru Town History Editorial Board. 2003. *Haebaru: Shima No Minzoku [Haebaru: Folklore of the Island]*. Haebaru Choushi Dai 6 Kan Minzoku Shiryou Hen [Haebaru Town History Vol.6]. Haebaru: Haebaru Town (In Japanese).

Haebaru Town History Editorial Board. 2013. *Ikusayu No Haebaru: Kataru Nokosu Tsunagu [War Period of Haebaru: Tell, Preserve, and Inherit]*. Haebaru Choushi Dai 9 Kan Sensou Hen Honpen [Haebaru Town History Vol. 9]. Haebaru: Haebaru Town (In Japanese).

Miyagi, K. 1990. 'Tsukazan Gun Shireibu Keiribugou' ['Tsukazan Head Quarter Financial Section Cave.'] In: S. Yoshihama, ed. *Tsukazan Ga Kataru Okinawasen [The*

*Battle of Okinawa Told by Tsukazan].* Haebaru Town War Damage Research in Okinawa 4. Haebaru: Haebaru Town Board of Education, 87–90 (In Japanese).

Okinawa Prefecture Haebaru Town Cultural Property Conservation Board. 2019. *Okinawa Rikugun Byouin Haebarugougun Oyobi Koganemori Shuhen Senseki katsuyou Ni Tsuite, Okinawa Rikugun Byouin Haebarugougun 20 Gou Genkyou Chousa Ni Tsuite Toushinsho [A Report for Inquiry: About the Okinawa Army Hospital Haebaru Cave and Koganemori Area War Related Site Utilization and The 20th Cave of Okinawa Army Hospital Haebaru Cave Research and Review].* Haebaru: Haebaru Town Board of Education, Okinawa, Japan (In Japanese).

The 32nd Army Liquidation Department. 1947. *Dai 32 Gun Gunchoku Butai Shijitsu Shiryou (4) [The Okinawa Army Hospital. The 32nd Millitary Direct Unit Historical Fact Materials (4)].* Unpublished military document stored in Japan Center for Asian Historical Records, National Archives of Japan, Online Archive. Ref. C1111016700 (In Japanese).

Yoshihama, S. 1987. *Haebaru Rikugun Byouin [Haebaru Army Hospital].* Haebaru: Haebaru Town Board of Education (In Japanese).

Yoshihama, S., Ikeda, E., Kamiji, K., Koga, N., & Daijo, K. 2010. *Okinawa Rikugun Byouin Haebarugou: Sensou Iseki Bunkazai Shitei Zenkoku Dai 1 Gou [Okinawa Army Hospital Haebaru Caves: The First Registered War Related Site as Cultural Property in Japan].* Tokyo: Koubunken Co., Ltd (In Japanese).

# 11

# THE TRANSITION OF BATTERY POSITIONS ON OKINAWA ISLAND

*Katsuya Nakahodo*

## Introduction

Many Japanese army and navy forces were deployed to different locations in the Ryukyu Islands from 1944. On the island of Okinawa, where the military forces were concentrated, military facilities including batteries were constructed and expanded. The 1998–2005 Okinawa Prefecture Battlefield Sites Distribution Survey (Okinawa Prefecture Archeology Center 2001, 2002, 2003, 2004, 2005, 2006) and the 2010–14 Okinawa Prefecture Battlefield Sites Details Confirmation Survey (Okinawa Prefecture Archeology Center 2015), both of which were conducted by the Okinawa Prefecture Board of Education, have confirmed the identification of battery remains and other related features built by the army and navy. In addition to these, there are a number of as-yet unlocated batteries that are known from historical literature such as staff diaries. This chapter, based on the results of the Okinawa Prefecture Battlefield Sites Details Confirmation Survey and the author's own research, will discuss the historical context surrounding the construction and operation of batteries on Okinawa during the Pacific War.

## Definition of a Battery

Before continuing, it is necessary to define the term 'battery' as it is used in this chapter. Although battery is a term which indicates a position to set artillery, many different forms of artillery (such as a 'fixed' and 'traction' type) exist. The battery structures also vary from robust, permanent fortifications to temporary structures. Throughout this discussion, the author will use the terms 'gun platform,' 'battery (only targeting enemy forces on the ocean),' and 'fort (only targeting enemies on the ground)' to describe 'batteries,' although some

DOI: 10.4324/9780429270468-14

historical documents separate these terms. Machine gun, tank, self-propelled artillery positions, and floating batteries are not included in the discussion due to their functional differences.

## History of Modern Military Facilities on Okinawa

Although modern military facilities have been built on Okinawa since the 19th century, the batteries were not constructed at the same time. A battery construction plan, which was never carried out, will be discussed below.

## Military Facilities on Okinawa during the Late 19th- and Early 20th Centuries

From the end of the 19th to the early 20th century, modern Japanese military facilities were installed on Okinawa. Details of these circumstances can be seen in a study by Yoshihama (2011a). The author summarizes and categorizes the results of this study below.

### Security Unit Facilities

The earliest modern military forces that served on Okinawa were army forces deployed there in 1876 and 1879. The deployment was associated with the Disposition of the Ryukyus, which was a forced assimilation of the Ryukyus into the Japanese nation. The units were first stationed at Shuri, with barracks and shooting ranges being later built in Mawashi Village (now Naha city). This unit was abolished in 1896. There are no known archaeological sites associated with the unit.

### Facilities for Supplying Naval Vessels

Nakagusuku Supply Branch Warehouse was constructed in Tsuhako and Shinzato in Sashiki on Okinawa in 1896, primarily as a facility to supply fuel and other provisions to naval vessels. Torpedo motorboat coal and water warehouses were built at Hunauki on Iriomote Island in 1902, and at the Unten Port of Nakijin Village on Okinawa Island in 1904. Archaeological remains of the Nakagusuku Supply Branch Warehouse remain in Nanjou City.

### Coastal Defense and Weather Observation Facilities

Naval observation towers were built in Kyan, Itoman, and Sakiyama on Iriomote Island. These facilities allowed surveillance of the ocean, radio transmission with vessels, and the taking of weather observations. Some parts of the tower at Sakiyama can still be seen today.

## *Okinawa Garrison District Headquarters (Okinawa Regiment Headquarters)*

Associated with enforcement conscription orders in 1898, the Okinawa Garrison District Headquarters (renamed the Okinawa Regiment Headquarters in 1926) was built in Naha City, Okinawa. While an office for conscription and inspection work had existed beforehand, no large military posts of the types seen in mainland Japan were present.

## Battery Installation in the Region Surrounding Okinawa during the Late 19th to Early 20th Centuries

### *Keelung and Penghu Island Forts (Taiwan)*

After the Sino-Japanese war and the conclusion of the 1895 Shimonoseki Convention, Japan maintained forts and built batteries on Taiwan for the protection of bays and borders. Headquarters were established there in 1901, and strong batteries with 28 cm howitzers were built at the Keelung and Penghu Island Forts (Ministry of Army 1907a, 1907b).

### *Amami Oshima Fort (Amami Oshima)*

In Amami Oshima, battery construction lasted from July to November of 1921. Although the 1922 Washington Naval Disarmament Treaty forced the construction to stop, the headquarters were nonetheless established in 1923 (Printing Bureau 1923).

### Plans to Install Batteries on Okinawa

The first battery construction on Okinawa took place in 1919. The purpose of the battery was to protect the port in Nakagusuku Bay from enemies (Ministry of Army 1919). In 1922, there were plans to build forts in various parts of Japan, which included forts designed for emergency use at Nakagusuku Bay on Okinawa Island, Karimata on Miyako Island, and Funauki on Iriomote Island. However, because of the Washington Naval Disarmament Treaty, headquarters were not established in the same way as at Amami Oshima Fort (Yoshihama 2011b).

### Batteries after the Lapse of Washington Naval Disarmament Treaty

Following the lapse of the Washing Naval Disarmament Treaty in 1937, Japanese naval forces started to construct air fields and port facilities in Micronesia, as well as batteries to protect them. Both army and naval forces planned and constructed batteries on Okinawa in 1941. Many of these batteries had an artillery emplacement at the center of round battlements, with a 360-degree field of fire and associated ammunition depots. However, the installed artillery comprised only 75–120 mm caliber field guns or anti-aircraft guns. They did not have enough firepower to protect against battleships. As such, when the Pacific War started in late 1941, the batteries were scaled down and some artillery pieces were removed. Okinawa was not considered as an important location for national protection at that time.

## Cape Chinen Air Defense Battery (Navy)

This was the first naval battery in Okinawa Island. According to *Chinen Village History Vol. 3: War Experience Diary* (Chinen Village Board of Education 1994), two naval anti-aircraft guns, batteries, and barracks were constructed there in October, 1941. Soldiers were then deployed. At the outset of the Pacific War in December, the soldiers operating the battery moved south with the guns in order to support the intensification of the southern frontline. The Cape Chinen air defense battery was not considered as an important defense facility, and the defensive capabilities of Nansei Island were reduced by the redeployment of troops in January 1942 (Nakahodo 2015). Based on army documents and interviews with local residents, the battery was never used during the Battle of Okinawa (Nakahodo 2015).

## Nakagusuku Bay Emergency Fort and Funauki Emergency Fort (Army)

The Nakagusuku Emergency Fort (NEF) and the Funauki Emergency Fort (FEF) were the first forts to be constructed for use by army combat troops in the defense of Okinawa. Their armament composition varies according to the available historical documents, but it seems that two 120 mm guns and eight-to-ten 75 mm guns were installed. According to The 32nd Army Liquidation Department (1947) and The 8th Heavy Artillery Regiment (1946), the fort garrisons were organized in July 1941. Various types of batteries were maintained when the NEF troops were deployed for the defense of the Nakagusuku Bay area on Okinawa Island. The FEF was constructed in order to protect the surrounding area. The troops were reorganized, however, in September and October 1942. The forts were then scaled down, and some artillery pieces and soldiers were sent to the frontline (The 8th Heavy Artillery Regiment 1946). Although a construction plan for Karimata Fort was discussed, there is no evidence to suggest that a fort was constructed here (Yoshihama 2011b).

## Other Batteries on Okinawa and within the Surrounding Region

Archaeological features of the other batteries on Okinawa and the surrounding area are described below.

## *Ikei Battery Site*

The Ikei Battery site is located at the North end of Ikei Island, which lies in the northern part of the Katsuren Peninsula on Okinawa. The battery was constructed on a flat area of cliff about 20 m above sea level. Although the site is now covered by heavy vegetation, a 60 m trench connecting two 6 m–wide batteries was found by an Okinawa Prefecture survey in December 2013 (Okinawa Prefecture Archeology Center 2015: 61). The two battery battlements are made of concrete, and drainage ditches were installed in the floor. The central part of the battery floor was built up using conical-shaped cobbles and earth. The upper part has a flat surface measuring c.1.6 m in diameter, and its center has holes without bolts that were used to fix artillery pieces to the floor. From these features and the documented armament record of NEF, there is a possibility that 75 mm Type 38 Field Guns (a traction-type piece with wheels) were used here.

Although a battery was built on Ikei Island when the 2nd Company of NEF was deployed there in 1941, the company was moved to the Chinen Peninsula during the unit reorganization of September 1942 (The 32nd Army Liquidation Department 1947). The battery might not have functioned as an artillery emplacement after this time. However, an interviewee revealed that a dummy

FIGURE 11.1   Aerial photograph of Ikei Island Battery taken by US military forces in 1945 (Okinawa Prefectural Archives Collection, collection code 0000026728).

artillery piece constructed of soil and pine wood was built on military orders in 1945, and only the first reserve unit remained in the area when US forces landed (Okinawa Prefecture Archeology Center 2015: 61). Four batteries along the edge of the cliff, a possible command post to the rear, and a trench connecting the two facilities (but not artillery pieces) can be seen in US Army aerial photographs that are currently stored in the Okinawa Prefectural Archives (see Figure 11.1).

## Heshikiya Battery Site (Uruma City)

This site is located at the eastern end of the Katsuren Peninsula. Four batteries with associated features remain on a hill about 80 m above sea level, to the west of Heshikiya Village (Okinawa Prefecture Archeology Center 2015). Although the site is not lined by fences, it is in the area of the US military's White Beach facility today.

The 3rd Company of NEF was deployed in order to maintain the battery in October 1941. However, the company was moved to Oroku after the unit reorganization of September 1942 (The 32nd Army Liquidation Department 1947). No other artillery unit was deployed here. The 5th Company Inoue Squad of Independent Infantry, 12th Battalion, was organized locally with the purpose of keeping watch for enemy units (Independent Infantry 12th Battalion 5th Company 1945). No record of a ground battle or conflict in the Heshikiya area can be found in either Japanese or US documents.

Four batteries remain today, and three of them share a similar form. The interior of the batteries measure around 6 m in diameter, with battlements made of cut stones and modified base rocks. An entry-way measuring 3 m in width was constructed (Okinawa Prefecture Archeology Center 2015: 55–56). A few ammunition stores, measuring $1 \times 1 \times 0.8$ m were installed inside the battlement. A drain runs along the floor. The battery floor was mostly made of soil, but a 3.7 m-wide ring-shaped concrete pedestal, surrounding a 1.5 m-wide circular area covered with pebbles and earth, is present. Five shallow ditches spread radially from the center (see Figures 11.2 and 11.3). The concrete pedestal has remains of black paint indicating a camouflage pattern. Although the last battery is the same as the others in terms of its dimensions, the battlement and floor are constructed of earth. Around the battery, a transportation trench and concrete buildings remain (Okinawa Prefecture Archeology Center 2015). Historical documents do not allow us to identify which type of artillery which was installed at the Heshikiya Battery. Given the battery pedestal form with five radial ditches, however, the battery could have been designed for installing the Type 88, 70 mm Field Battle Anti-Aircraft Gun. The location of soil-covered areas on the pedestal matches the positions where stakes would usually have been installed in order to secure the gun.

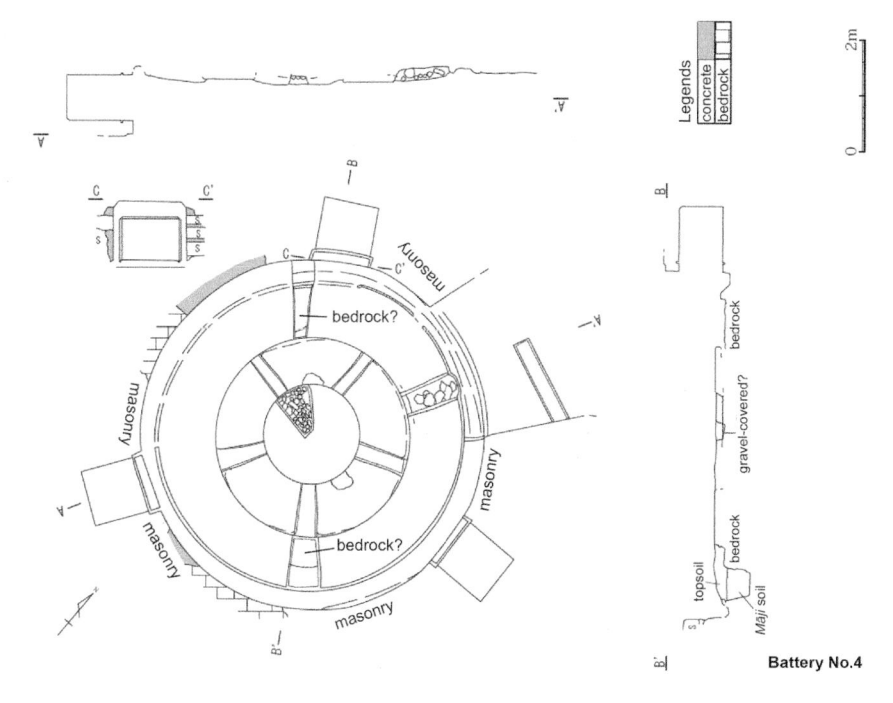

**FIGURE 11.2**  Battery No.4 plan at the Heshikiya Battery site (Okinawa Prefecture Archaeology Center 2015: 57).

**FIGURE 11.3**  Photograph of Battery No.4 at the Heshikiya Battery site (Okinawa Prefecture Archaeology Center 2015: 59).

## Uroker Battery Site (Nanjo City)

The battery site is located at the middle of a seawards-facing hill, which is on the eastern side of *Seefaa Utaki* (a sacred worshipping place), located on the Chinen Peninsula in southern Okinawa. Although the original name is ambiguous, the site was named as 'Uroker Battery Site' because of its close proximity to the worshipping place. When the 2nd Company of NEF moved to the Chinen Peninsula from Ikei Island in around September 1942, the battery was constructed as a part of a larger position. The battery was made of concrete, rocks, and earth. Based on research by Nanjo City in 2013, two battery features measuring 6 m in diameter are known. A path connecting the batteries and the location of an armory were also confirmed (Okinawa Prefecture Archeology Center 2015: 64). No artillery remains, but given its similarities with the Ikei Island Battery, it is possible that the Type 38 field gun was used at the site. Because the landscape to the west of the battery site is more open than on its east side, it is reasonable to suggest that it was used for defense against enemy vessels approaching Okinawa from the east. The two confirmed batteries lie about 60 m from each other and are connected by a path with concrete flooring. The battery structures have an artillery platform measuring 1.6 m in diameter, and there are drainage holes with a diameter of 6 m. Like the other batteries already described, the battery floor was painted black. These structures are therefore of the same type as those at Ikei Battery, with the main difference between them being that that the artillery platform of Uroker Battery was constructed using only heaped earth. Heavy destruction of the battlement and armory indicates that the site may have been reused by the local residents for construction materials during the post-war period. There is no evidence to suggest that the battery was used during the battle of Okinawa.

## Batteries During the Latter Phases of the Pacific War

As the tide of the war turned against Japan from late 1942, air field enlargement and construction intensified at several locations on Okinawa. In April and May 1944, the Navy Okinawa Base Corps and the 32nd Army were formed in order to prepare for a large battle. An unprecedented number of soldiers were deployed to Okinawa, and construction began on both open-air and underground batteries. The former type of battery has a 360-degree field of fire as seen at Heshikiya and Ikei Batteries. This type of battery allowed air-defense gunners a wide field of view in order to track moving targets, but it was vulnerable to aerial attack. Because underground batteries were constructed inside of covered trenches or tunnels, artillery emplaced in such locations had high defensive ability but only limited visibility. Almost all of the open-air type air-defense batteries were destroyed due to their low defensive power (see Figure 11.4). As such, the batteries discussed in this section are all of the underground type. These remain today because of their highly durable structures.

**FIGURE 11.4**  Aerial photograph of Oroku Air Field (current Naha Airport) taken by US military forces in 1945 (Okinawa Prefectural Archives Collection, collection code KS00000095, ON27836 [Photo No. 26]).

## Ukamajii Navy Battery Site

The battery site at Hamakawa (currently US Military base Kadena), Kitaya Machi, in Central Okinawa is located on the east slope of Ukamajii Hill and faces the ocean to its west. The battery site consists of a reinforced concrete bunker and features an artillery room measuring 5 × 4.2 m, with a path extending to the west (Okinawa Prefecture Archeology Center 2015: 136). The profile of the bunker and artillery room is arch-shaped with an earthen covering. The northern wall of the artillery room has a large, flared opening, measuring c.1.3 m in width at its interior and 2 m in width at its exterior. Although the artillery does not remain, sixteen reinforcing steel rods are exposed concentrically with a 1 m-wide circular depression at the back of the northern opening. There is a bolt for a fixed-type, ship-based cannon with a cylindrical base. The exposed bolt could have been used to fix the artillery piece, with the opening representing an embrasure for the gun barrel. On the southern wall, there is an entrance measuring 1.7 m in height and 0.5 m in width, and two 40 cm-wide square ventilation or cable holes. The western wall is attached to the trench, which was constructed by digging into the Ryukyu Limestone bedrock. The trench measures 3 m in width, and its roof has collapsed c.20 m from the battery. There is a natural cave on the steep slope on the other side of the hills, which would be connected to the battery by the trench. This gallery might have functioned as an armory and a refreshment room for soldiers. Other remaining features include two concrete buildings on top of the Ukamajii Hills. Although the structures are different from each other, their north-facing windows, like that of the battery embrasure, indicate that the buildings were used for running observation equipment such as collimators or rangefinders. Because the embrasure provides a viewshed over the coastlines of Kadena and Yomitan, the battery could have been used to attack landing forces. Additionally, because the battery stands on the eastern side of the hills, enemy vessels would find it difficult to locate and attack it from an offshore position to the west. As the battery armament was fixed only by a bolt on its bottom, it is likely that this was a rapid-fire, light-vessel cannon, perhaps equivalent to a destroyer main cannon or a battleship sub-cannon with a 12–15 cm inner diameter (Nakahodo 2015).

The battery's operation during the Battle of Okinawa can be described as follows. Historical records show that the Ukamajii Battery site was called 'Navy 11th Battery' or 'Henzan Battery.' The battery was commanded by army troops rather than the Navy Okinawa Base Corps. In January 1945, it was under the command of the Independent Hybrid 44th Brigade, Independent Hybrid 15th Regiment (Nakahodo 2015). After the regiment reformed and moved to south, the battery was operated by the 62nd Infantry Division, 63rd Brigade Independent Infantry, 12th Battalion (Nakahodo 2015). When the US military landed on April 1st, the battery fought with other navy batteries commanded by army troops, and Warrant Officer Nishikawa and thirty soldiers died during the battle (Office of War History, National Institute for Defense Studies, Ministry of Defense 1968b). Because there is no record of the battery being used before April 1st 1945 in historical documents, it likely functioned as a coastal defense position against enemy landing forces. It is also interesting to note, given that the Warrant Officer military rank only existed in the Japanese Navy during the Pacific War, that the battery appears to have been under the command of the army but operated by navy troops.

## Touma Navy Battery Site (Naha City)

The site is located on top of Mēmatamō Hill within the current Naha Base of the Air Self-Defense Force, formerly Oroku Navy Air Field. This is the only battery on Okinawa that features complete artillery remains. Although there is no historical record to confirm the battery's construction date, a sign in front of the battery states that it was built by the navy in June-September 1943. The reinforced concrete bunker battery is about 12 m in length and 11 m in width, with an artillery room and a nearly complete cannon (Okinawa Prefecture Archeology Center 2015: 139; see Figure 11.5). The top of the bunker was covered in earth. The exterior of the extant wall is damaged by bullets, especially on its west side. The central part of its interior plan is constructed like a constricted drum. Its depth is about 9 m, with a width of about 6.4 m toward the rear and about 4.5 m inside the embrasure. The embrasure opening provides a 90-degree field of fire and runs almost parallel with the southern coastline. The cannon's barrel is partially exposed outside of the battery. At the back of the north and east sides of the artillery room, two paths measuring about 1.0 m and 1.1 m in width are present. The eastern part is depressed by roof-collapse, but the northern path continues to the outside. Details of the artillery room floor are unknown because of soil accumulation. Although the entrance is now gone, there is a space which allows a person to walk through. This space might have functioned as an ammunition chamber or as a generator room. There is a step plank and an iron cylindrical base (measuring around 4.5 m in diameter), which served as the cannon emplacement. A gun carriage is installed above the step, and there is a riveted shield to protect the gunner. The gun barrel passes through the riveted shield and today remains pointing upwards. The breechblock, which can be confirmed as a screw-type, is also extant. Because of corrosion, the inner diameter of the barrel is not known. A sign that stands in front of the battery indicates that the barrel diameter was 12 cm or 14 cm (though it could be 20 cm). Although the exact barrel length is also not known, it is evidently a long barrel measuring more than 7 m. Based on this data, the gun was equivalent to a light- or heavy-cruiser class main canon, and the gun carriage was solidly built. Other parts, however, are poorly made with iron panels attached by rivets and welding. This indicates that the artillery gun was not directly transplanted into the battery from a ship. Rather, it was hastily built using a mix of existing parts (Nakahodo 2015).

The battery was built on top of the hill in order to avoid harming aircraft on nearby taxiways with shock waves from gunfire. The artillery gun is suited to counter vessels approaching the west coast of southern Okinawa. With a 90-degree field of fire, and an assumed range of more than 20 km, it could attack battleships patrolling offshore. It is uncertain, however, whether the artillery gun could handle heavily armored battle ships and aircraft. Because it could fight against a destroyer squadron comprising destroyers and light cruisers, the battery took on multiple roles for the defense of the air field.

As noted above, the sign in front of the battery states that Touma navy battery was built between June and September of 1943 by Navy Facility Yamane Unit for the defense of Oroku Air Field. The battery was operated by navy troops under the command of a guard unit that was arranged at the 951 Navy Air Corps Mission (Office of War History, National Institute for Defense Studies, Ministry of Defense 1968a, 1968b). A navy telegram tells us that the Touma naval battery did not fire during air raids after October 1944 or against approaching US battleships at the end of March, 1945. Navy 3rd battery, which was commanded by Sergeant Chief Nomura, attacked and sank a stranded destroyer, an oil tanker, and a cargo ship on May 18th (Historical Document Archive Unit of Cultural Properties Office of Okinawa Prefecture Board of Education 2012). While the

**FIGURE 11.5** Touma Navy Battery site (photograph by the author).

location and context of the battery is very different from that at the Ukamaji Battery, it fulfilled a similar function as a coastal defense position that was used to attack nearby stranded enemy ships. The reason that the battery did not fire during the air raid is because the troops may have wanted to avoid revealing the battery's location. This decision reflects the worsening war situation, the Japanese loss air superiority, and the loss of its ability to defend the nearby air field. All operators belonged to the navy and there no evidence to suggest that the army was involved. As with the Touma naval battery and other navy-commanded batteries such as Kyosui Naval Battery that were constructed on the Oroku Peninsula and its surrounding area, this was the territory of the Navy Okinawa Base Corps (Nakahodo 2015).

## Sobe Beach Battery Remains (Yomitan Village)

The battery was located in a rock shelter on the limestone cliff above Sobe Beach, on the west coast of central Okinawa, with embrasures facing south along the coastline (Figure 11.6). Because Sobe Beach is close to Yomitan Air Field, it is uncertain whether the battery was constructed by the Field Artillery 81st Battalion or the Machine Gun 105th Battalion. From its locational context, the battery might have been intended to attack the flanks of enemy landing forces. However, there is no record of the battery being used in either

**FIGURE 11.6**   Sobe Beach Battery remains (photograph by the author).

Japanese or US archives. Therefore, the battery was likely abandoned before the US landing operation.

## Gushikami Village Battery Remains (Yaese Town)

This battery is located in Gushikami Village in Yaese Town. It was built on a steep slope near the eastern coast in southern Okinawa. The embrasure looks out along the coastline and faces toward the north. Because the battery rooftop is now used as a road, with an asphalt cover and curve mirror, it looks like a drainage inlet.

The battery chamber is made of concrete and is connected to a natural cave at the rear. However, because the cave roof has collapsed, the inner part is not accessible. Dirt and debris fill the inside of the battery and cover the artillery gun platform. It is therefore difficult to identify the artillery gun type used. Because the wall and roof construction style is similar to that at the Touma Naval Battery, this battery could have been built by the navy. During the Battle of Okinawa, both the army and navy built batteries, so which unit built the battery is uncertain. Since local residents indicate that the battery 'was built in 1944,' 'soldiers carried bullets by rail,' and that the 'US military pulled the artillery gun out with a tank,' it is almost certain that the battery was established in preparation for the Battle of Okinawa, but more detailed research on its operational status and armament is required.

## Battery Operational Status in Other Areas

While both army and navy operated batteries and fought against enemy units and the US fleet during and after the landing, they had not fought before the invasion in 1945. Is this a unique case only seen in Okinawa? Batteries were built and operated in other regions during the Pacific War. In this section, the author briefly summarizes the operation of batteries on Iwotou,[1] where both army and naval units were stationed together in the same manner as those on Okinawa.

## Naval Batteries on Iwotou

Both naval and army units, including the 109th Division, the Mixed 2nd Division, the Ogasawara Corps, and the Iwotou Guard Corps were deployed on Iwotou. The command system of the Ogasawara area, which included Iwotou, was designed as a cooperative system as part of 'The Central Agreement of Army and Navy on Commandment System between Army and Navy on Ogasawara Islands' on August 27th 1944. The chief commander on each island controlled both army and naval corps during ground battles. They did not control air force units. On September 19th, the 'Ogasawara Corps Iwotou Battle Plan' was decided. This plan stated that the naval artillery guns should be commanded when the enemy landed (Office of War History, National Institute for Defense Studies, Ministry of Defense 1968b). The US fleets approached and started firing on Iwotou on February 16th. The army and navy batteries planned to attack only when the US units were landing. However on the 17th, a Japanese battery revealed its position by firing its gun on a patrolling US ship. Twenty-seven naval batteries were destroyed during the US fleet counterattacks which continued until February 19th (Office of War History, National Institute for Defense Studies, Ministry of Defense 1968b).

## Conclusion

The location and operation of batteries on the Okinawa islands was heavily influenced by prevailing political and military strategies. Even though military facilities had been constructed on Okinawa since the end of the 19th century, larger batteries were built on Taiwan (which was incorporated into the Japanese Empire after the Sino-Japanese War) because it was more significant both defensively and as a base for advancing overseas. After 1919, a plan of fortification construction on Okinawa was considered, but it was abandoned as a result of the 1922 Washington Naval Disarmament Treaty. After the treaty lapsed, battery construction plans on Okinawa were reconsidered. In 1941, both the army and navy built batteries that could operate against small enemy units. However, after the Pacific War started in December of that year, the number of artillery guns and operators was reduced and some batteries were abandoned. This reduction in troop numbers was because Okinawa was located far from the frontline and not considered significant at that particular time. As Japan's position became more tenuous during 1943, Okinawa's significance gradually increased, and large numbers of army and naval batteries and air fields were built.

The construction of the batteries is also interesting. In addition to the standard open-air type, underground batteries were constructed. The artillery guns' shooting line is often parallel to the coastline, indicating that the batteries were intended to attack landing enemies while remaining hidden from enemy ships.

In terms of the batteries' operation, many of the naval batteries on the Oroku Peninsula, where main the force of the Okinawa Navy Base Corps was deployed, were under the command of the navy. Some of the naval batteries in other areas were commanded by the army. The main reason for this was the treaty between local army and naval units. This system for the batteries that were situated in remote locations away from the naval HQ was expected to be more effective in allowing them to target enemies and ensure smoother cooperation during amphibious landings (Nakahodo 2015).

In the future, when the battery remains are regarded as war-related sites, it is necessary to not only collect information from site surveys, but also to also analyze both army and navy records, as well as documentation from adjoining facilities such as observatories. The development of more comprehensive research methods has the potential to reveal not only information about the artillery itself, but also the wider structure and operational status of the batteries from a strategic point of view, including the communicative networks that existed between army and naval units. This is an important point that deserves further consideration.

## Note

1 Although the island is known as 'Iwo Jima' in the US Army archives and other oversea documents, the correct pronunciation is 'Ioutou' in Japanese. Therefore, the author uses 'Iwotou' when referring to the island.

## Bibliography

Chinen Village Board of Education. 1994. *Chinen Sonshi Dai 3 Kan: Sensou Taikenki [Chinen Village History Vol.3: War Experience Diary]*. Chinen: Chinen Village Town Hall.

Historical Document Archive Unit of Cultural Properties Office of Okinawa Prefecture Board of Education. 2012. '525 Jyushin 0155 Kimitsu Dai 241640 Banden 2 Bunno 1, 2.' In: Okinawa Prefecture Board of Education, ed. *Okinawaken Shi Shiryouhen 23: Okinawasen Nihongun Shiryou Okinawasen 6* [Okinawa Prefecture History Appendix 23: Japanese Army Historical Records of the Battle of Okinawa, the Battle of Okinawa 6]. Naha: Okinawa Prefecture Board of Education, 577.

Independent Infantry 12th Battalion 5th Company. 1945. *Ishi125 Chuu Saku Mei Dai 3 Gou Dai 5 Chuutai Meirei [Ishi 125 Chuu Saku Mei No. 3: the 5th Company orders]*. Unpublished Military Record Stored in Japan Center for Asian Historical Records, National Archives of Japan. JACAR.C11110078200.

Ministry of Army. 1907a. *Keelung Yousai Kahou Suetsuke no Ken [Issue of Installation of Artillery at the Keelung Fort]*. Unpublished Military Record Stored in Japan Center for Asian Historical Records, National Archives of Japan. JACAR.C02030337800.

Ministry of Army. 1907b. *Houkotou Yousai Kahou Suetsuke no Ken* [Issue of Installation of Artillery at the Penghu Islands Fort]. Unpublished Military Record Stored in Japan Center for Asian Historical Records, National Archives of Japan. JACAR. C0203032470.

Ministry of Army. 1919. *Taisho 9 Nendo Nihon Teikoku Rikugun Sakusen Youryou Sonota ni Kansuru Ken [Issue of Imperial Japanese Army Operational Procedures and Others in Taisho 9]*. Unpublished Military Record Stored in Japan Center for Asian Historical Records, National Archives of Japan. JACAR. C02030151200.

Nakahodo, K. 2015. 'Shishiryou kara mita Okinawa tou no kaigunhoudai no unnyou keitai' [Operational Patterns of Naval Gun Batteries on Okinawa Island from Historical Documents]. *Nantou Kouko* 34: 77–86.

Office of War History, National Institute for Defense Studies, Ministry of Defense. 1968a. *Senshi Sousho: Okinawa Houmen Kaigun Sakusen [Millitary History Series: Naval Operations in Okinawa]*. Asagumo Shinbunsha: Tokyo.

Office of War History, National Institute for Defense Studies, Ministry of Defense. 1968b. *Senshi Sousho: Chubu Taiheiyou Rikugun Sakusen (2) – Peleliu, Angaur, Ioutou [Military History Series: Central Pacific Army Operations (2): Peleliu, Angaur, Ioutou]*. Tokyo: Asagumo Shinbunsha.

Okinawa Prefecture Archeology Center. 2001. *Okinawaken Sensouiseki Shousai Bunpu Chousa (I) Nanbu Hen [Distribution Survey of Battle Field Sites in Okinawa Prefecture (I) South]*. Naha: Okinawa Prefecture Archeology Center.

Okinawa Prefecture Archeology Center. 2002. *Okinawaken Sensouiseki Shousai Bunpu Chousa (II) Chubu Hen [Distribution Survey of Battle Field Sites in Okinawa Prefecture (II) Central]*. Naha: Okinawa Prefecture Archeology Center.

Okinawa Prefecture Archeology Center. 2003. *Okinawaken Sensouiseki Shousai Bunpu Chousa (III) Hokubu Hen [Distribution Survey of Battle Field Sites in Okinawa Prefecture (III) North]*. Naha: Okinawa Prefecture Archeology Center.

Okinawa Prefecture Archeology Center. 2004. *Okinawaken Sensouiseki Shousai Bunpu Chousa (IV) Hontou Shuuhen Ritou Oyobi Nahashi Hen [Distribution Survey of Battlefield Sites in Okinawa Prefecture (IV): Remote Islands around the Main Island and Naha City]*. Naha: Okinawa Prefecture Archeology Center.

Okinawa Prefecture Archeology Center. 2005. *Okinawaken Sensouiseki Shousai Bunpu Chousa (V) Miyako Shotou Hen [Distribution Survey of Battlefield Sites in Okinawa Prefecture (V): Miyako Islands]*. Naha: Okinawa Prefecture Archeology Center.

Okinawa Prefecture Archeology Center. 2006. *Okinawaken Sensouiseki Shousai Bunpu Chousa (VI) Yaeyama Shotou Hen [Distribution Survey of Battlefield Sites in Okinawa Prefecture (VI): Yaeyama Islands]*. Naha: Okinawa Prefecture Archeology Center.

Okinawa Prefecture Archeology Center. 2015. *Okinawaken no Sensouiseki: Heisei 22–26 Nendo Sensouiseki Shousai Kakunin Chousa Houkokusho [Battlefield Sites in Okinawa Prefecture: 2010–2014 Report of the Distribution Survey of Battlefield Sites in Okinawa Prefecture]*. Naha: Okinawa Prefecture Archeology Center.

Printing Bureau. 1923. 'Amami Oshima Shireibu Secchi' ['Establishment of Amami Oshima Headquarters'], *Kanpou* 3229, 7.

The 8th Heavy Artillery Regiment. 1946. *Jyuuhousei Dai 8 Rentai [Eighth Heavy Artillery Regiment]*. Unpublished Military Record Stored in Japan Center for Asian Historical Records, National Archives of Japan. JACAR.C11110012100.

The 32nd Army Liquidation Department. 1947. *Jyuuhouhei Dai 7 Rentai [Seventh Heavy Artillery Regiment]*. Unpublished military record stored in Japan Center for Asian Historical Records, National Archives of Japan. JACAR.C11110162100.

Yoshihama, S. 2011a. 'Kindai Okinawa no Gunbi–Gunji Shisetsu wo Chuushin ni' ['Military Equipment in Modern Okinawa: Focusing on Military Facilities']. In: Okinawa Prefecture Board of Education, ed. *Okinawa Kenshi Kakuronhen 5: Kinsei [Okinawa Prefecutural History 5: Modern Pelriod]*. Naha: Okinawa Prefecture Board of Education, 571–91.

Yoshihama, S. 2011b. 'Nakagusukuwan Rinji Yousai' ['Nakagusuku Bay Temporary Fort']. In: Yonabaru Town Board of Education, ed. *Yonabaru Choushi Senjikirokuhen: Yonabaru no Okinawa Sen [War Time Record of Yonabaru Town History: The Battle of Okinawa in Yonabaru]*. Yonabaru: Yonabaru Town Board of Education, 24–31.

# PART 4

# Aftermath

# 12

# THE SEARCH FOR AND IDENTIFICATION OF BURIAL PLACES OF JAPANESE PRISONERS OF WAR IN THE TERRITORY OF RUSSIA. OBSERVATIONS, EXPERIENCES, AND PROBLEMS

*Sergey I. Kuznetsov*

## Introduction

Among the numerous necropolises on the territory of the former USSR, burials of prisoners of war (POWs) dating to the Second World War occupy a special place in historical research. Among them are the graves of soldiers and officers of the armies of Germany and its allies – Italy, Hungary, and Japan. The study of the necropolises represents a means of preserving socio-historical and cultural memories, something which in modern Russia is actively being conducted. It should be noted that prevailing circumstances during the Soviet period did not contribute to their preservation and protection. Historically in Russia, cemeteries were created at monasteries and at both urban and rural churches. The deceased were buried at each parish church, and until the 14th century, church yards served as almost the only place for cemeteries. We can say that the Russian legislation on cemeteries began to operate from the time of Catherine II. It was stated in the 'medical statute' that burials at churches were forbidden. According to the legislation, urban cemeteries were to be established at a distance of at least 100 fathoms (or 213 m) from the last dwelling, and in villages at a distance of half a verst (250 fathoms). But in practice, with the growth of cities, this condition was not always respected. Traditionally, cemeteries were run by the clergy since burial was closely associated with a religious cult. Under Russian law, empty cemeteries could not be used as arable land and no building was allowed on them. Administratively, the cemeteries were subject to the jurisdiction of the spiritual authorities, meaning that communities could not exploit empty cemeteries for economic means. During the 18th and 19th centuries, military, naval, prison, infectious disease, and other cemeteries appeared. Everything changed, however, after the coup of October 1917. Soviet laws separated religion from the state and deprived the Church of its influence over ritual and burial culture.

DOI: 10.4324/9780429270468-16

The Soviet state sought to destroy the old traditions, especially if they were associated with church rituals. Over time, this led to a certain deformation in the consciousness of the population with respect to cemeteries and their preservation. In Soviet times, authorities sought to cultivate the image of surrounding countries as potential enemies. As such, cemeteries for foreign military personnel killed in wars or military conflicts with the USSR were not considered sites of cultural or historical significance; the authorities partly worried only about their sanitary condition. Japan was regarded as one of those 'traditional enemies.' It is for this reason that the cemeteries of Japanese internees were managed only during the 1940s, as this was the time when internment camps within the USSR were active. The Japanese death toll outside of Japan during the Pacific War was c. 2.4 million, and the remains of about 1.12 million people have still not been returned to Japan. In the USSR, about 55,000 personnel – mostly soldiers, died in custody in Siberia during the years 1945–49 after they were taken there by Soviet troops at the end of World War II. To date, teams from the Japanese Ministry of Social Security have returned the remains of 21,900 people from Siberia to Japan. Now, the remains of less than 1,000 people killed in the war are returned to Japan annually. Between the introduction of DNA testing and July 2019, 1,160 remains were identified (Nishimura 2019).

## Japanese Burial Sites and the History of their Preservation

One of the outcomes of the Soviet-Japanese war of 1945 was the capture of a large number of Japanese soldiers and officers in Northern China, on Sakhalin, the Kuril Islands, and in Korea. According to various estimates, between 540,000 and 650,000 POWs were interned in the Soviet Union, where they were held in prisoner of war camps and worked in various industries and agriculture. Poor living conditions, hard physical work, poor nutrition, the harsh climate, and inadequate medical care caused up to 60,000 of them to die and be buried here. Mortality in individual camps could range from 7% to 10% – an extremely high figure within a peacetime environment.

The repatriation of POWs began as early as 1946 but proceeded very slowly until the beginning of the 1950s. The controversial issue of Soviet-Japanese relations during the 1960s–80s meant that there were differences in approaches to assessing the loss of Japanese prisoners in Soviet camps, as well as the number of Japanese cemeteries in the USSR itself. The reason for this was the long-term silence of the Soviet Union on this issue and efforts to downplay the number of Japanese dead. Up until the beginning of Mikhail Gorbachev's rule, all requests from Japan to the USSR regarding the number of deaths received the same answer: only 3,957 Japanese POWs had died in captivity, and the remains of these individuals were buried in 26 cemeteries.

In truth, more than seventy camp administrations were instituted to manage Japanese POWs in the USSR, each of which included between two and thirty-four camp branches. They were located in all regions of Siberia and the

Far East, in the Far North, the Urals, and in the former Soviet republics of Kazakhstan, Uzbekistan, Tajikistan, Ukraine, and Georgia (see Figure 12.1). Prisoner of war camps were controlled by the Directorate General for Prisoners of War and interned by the USSR Ministry of Internal Affairs (GUPVI; the Ministry of Internal Affairs of USSR was named the People's Commissariat of Internal Affairs [NKVD] before 1946). Also under the Ministry of Defense's subordination were fifty-four 'individual workers' battalions' (ORB), comprising between 1,000 and 1,500 prisoners each (Gavrilov & Katasonova 2013: 12–13). The consequence of high prisoner mortality was the construction of a separate cemetery at almost every camp unit and ORB. The number of burials at these sites ranges from a single to several hundred graves. The largest number of cemeteries containing Japanese POWs were concentrated in areas where climatic and working conditions were most difficult, i.e., in Siberia and the Far East. There were, for example, eighty-one cemeteries in Irkutsk region, twenty-five in Buryatia, and fifty in Chita region.

The procedure for the burial of the dead was determined by the special instructions of the General Directorate for Prisoners of War and Internment (GUPVI) of August 24th, 1944 (Zagorul'ko 2000: 462–63). As a rule, a land plot located near the camp or camp office was allocated for burial of the dead. Since most of the camps were located in remote areas of Siberia and the Far East, the burial sites were also located there. In circumstances where prisoners were engaged in large-scale construction projects, the camps often moved along with the construction site itself, for example, during the construction of the Taishet-Bratsk railway in the Irkutsk region. After the construction was completed, the camp was transferred and the place of burial remained in the area without settlements – it was therefore abandoned and subsequently neglected.

The main keeper of information regarding the location of POWs in the USSR from World War II was the Center Storage of Historical and Documentary Collections (formerly 'Special Archive,' and now the State Military Archive of the Russian Federation [RGVA]). Previously, this belonged to the secret archival institutions of the country. The formation of its funds began in March 1946. Following the repatriation of POWs, the dismantling of the camps, and the abolition of the USSR Directorate General for Prisoners of War, a great number of documents collected at camp sites were transferred to this archive. In the 1950s and 1960s, documents from liquidated camps from Siberia and the Far Eastern regions were transferred here. The result was a large archival repository, which was sufficiently well processed by archival workers. All documents relating to Japanese POWs in the USSR were classified as 'top secret,' meaning that researchers could not access these sources until the beginning of the 1990s.

The archive has preserved a large array of documentary materials. Among them should be noted forms documenting POW camps, reports from camp administrations, reports of departmental labor use, departmental documents of the anti-fascist struggle and the antifascist school, and others. The exact information about the places of burial of the Japanese are located in the Archives of the

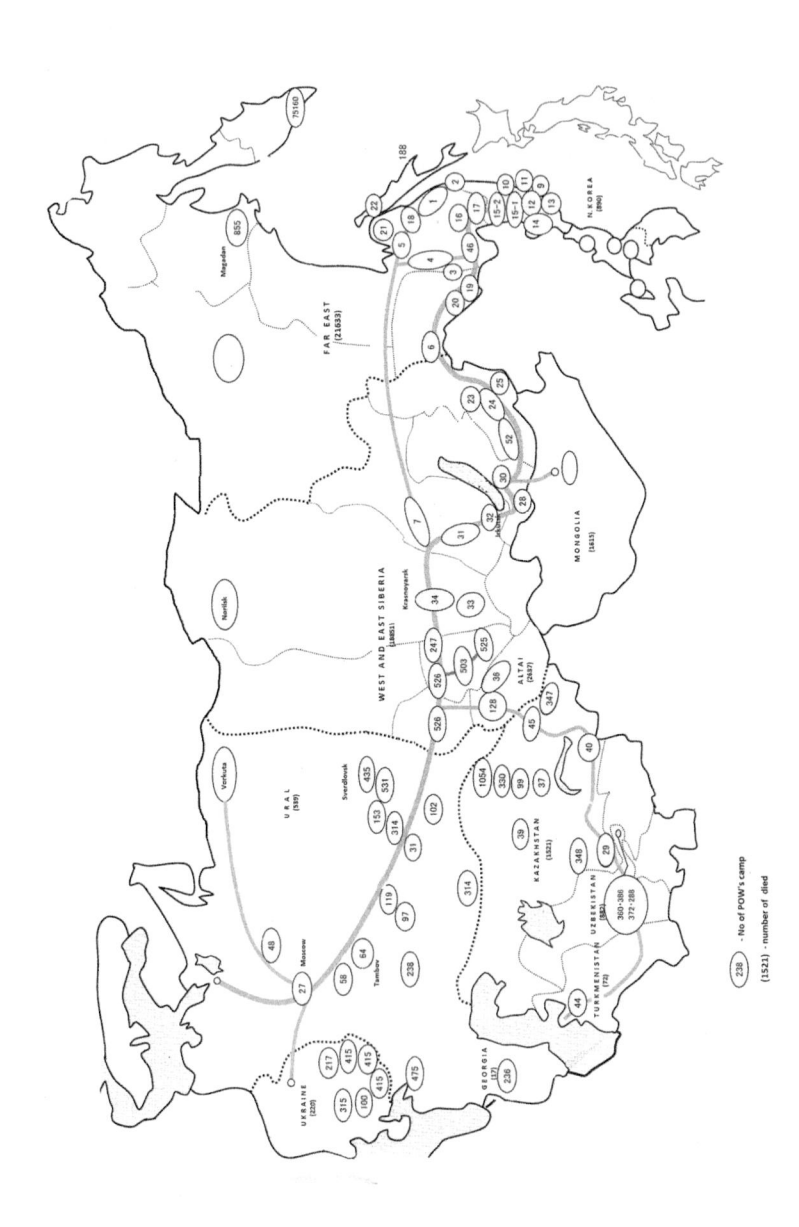

**FIGURE 12.1** Japanese POW camps in the territory of USSR (1945–1949). Image by Sergey Kuznetsov.

Interior Ministry, which were collected in accordance with the instructions of the NKVD (MVD) of the USSR on August 13th, 1943, which were entitled *On the Procedure of Registration of Deceased Prisoners of War*. On the basis of this instruction, the dead were included in ten different lists. Usually, these lists provided information on prisoners' names and surnames, their year of birth, nationality, military rank, account number, and date of death. Details were also provided regarding their place of burial, which included data on the associated cemetery 'square' and number of their grave. According to the August 24th, 1944 instructions of the GUPVI named above, the places of burial of deceased POWs were arranged in the immediate vicinity of the camp or hospital for POWs. The plots should be fenced with barbed wire and divided into squares, each of which should contain twenty-five graves divided into rows of five graves. The numbering began from the upper (northern) row, from left to right. An identification marker was set up on each grave. This comprised a wooden stake with a plate in its upper part indicating the number of the grave and the number of the square, e.g., '2/4,' or 'Grave 2, Square 4.' The name and surname of the prisoner was not indicated. To account for the deceased POWs and their burial places, a special cemetery book was created for each camp, which included the above information about the prisoner of war (name, surname, year of birth, etc.). The cemetery book featured an attached plan of the cemetery, broken down into squares indicating the numbers of squares and numbers of graves (Zagorul'ko 2000: 462–63). In principle, the observance of these conditions and the storage of all documentation would make it possible to later establish the burial place of each particular person with relatively little difficulty. Unfortunately, however, these orders were not always followed carefully. In some cemetery books, the schemes were made very primitively, without observing the elementary rules. As such, they could not be used as a real guide for locating a cemetery at a future date. In 1990, an album of Japanese burial schemes in the USSR was released in Japan (*List of Burial Places*), which was based on the memories of former POWs. Since the compilers of this publication did not have access to archival documents, the accuracy of the plans provided within is poor.

To control the order of burial and registration of cemeteries of POWs, the instruction *On Registration of Deceased Prisoners of War* was issued on December 7th 1945, and checks were carried out. On November 14th 1945, a special directive of the NKVD *On the Order of the Burial of the Bodies of Japanese Prisoners of War* was also issued.

Another circumstance that later hampered the search and identification of Japanese cemeteries was the transfer of their management from the Ministry of Internal Affairs to that of local authorities. The size of funds allocated for the preservation of cemeteries decreased. This meant that within a few years, the cemeteries were destroyed, especially since all grave markers were made of wood and quickly fell into disrepair. Because of this, the cemeteries were subsequently described as having 'self-destructed.' In the mid-1950s, many of the cemeteries were restored in preparation for the reestablishment of diplomatic relations between the USSR and Japan. Despite this, the graves were often found to be displaced from their true location. In some places, such as the Urals, dummies or imitations of cemeteries were even identified. The most promising candidates for exhumation work were the cemeteries of POWs in the Sukholozhsky and Turinsky districts of the Sverdlovsk region. Both of the cemeteries were outside the city limits and had not been converted for use in economic activities, and as such they were anticipated to contain preserved human remains. In the Sukholozhsky district, the location of the Japanese cemetery located near Kunara station had also been established on the basis of numerous eyewitness testimonies. For three days, two excavators dug trenches in the territory of the alleged burial site. However, the search work did not yield the expected result. It turned out that the POW cemetery shown by local residents was in fact a dummy. This conclusion has been confirmed by an explanatory memorandum of the former chief of POW camp no. 153, in which he noted that the cemetery documentation had not been transferred to him by a separate working battalion, and that as a result he did not know where the Japanese burial place was located. The act, dated October 1949, states that there are grave mounds and identifying signs at all Japanese burial sites, and that the cemetery itself should be fenced. Three years later, an imitation of a cemetery, created probably for reporting, was plowed up as directed by the Ministry of Internal Affairs. The search for a Japanese cemetery in the Turin district, near the railway station Porechye, similarly did not meet with success. The cemetery was located in a swampy place, and in 1952 monitoring of its condition was stopped. The scheme of the cemetery, drawn up without clear reference points, made it possible only to approximately locate the place of the desired burials. In connection with these international programs, the exhumation of prisoners buried in the Sverdlovsk was completed.

## The Legal Status of Japanese Graves on the Territory of the Former USSR

During the 1950s–80s, the status of foreign military graves in the USSR was rather uncertain and governed only by the provisions of the 1949 Geneva Convention Act. Under the convention, the signatory countries, which included the USSR, pledged provide security and care for those military burials located in their territory. However, the current situation by no means helped to improve mutual understanding between various states, which became especially apparent at the turn of the 1980s–90s. As a result, the Soviet Union and later the Russian Federation signed, in agreement with other countries that had been adversaries during World War II, a Status Agreement on war graves. In April 1991, the USSR and Japan signed the *Agreement on Persons in Prisoner of War Prisoner Camps*. According to the agreement, Russian authorities were obliged to provide lists of the Japanese prisoners who died in the USSR and information about the location of their burial sites, to maintain these places in proper order, to render assistance in installing memorials and visiting cemeteries, and to facilitate the repatriation of the remains of deceased Japanese prisoners in all cases where this was possible. Japan was in turn obliged, if necessary, to exhume and send home the remains of Japanese soldiers, as well as to keep proper order of Russian burials in the territory of their country. In accordance with Japanese law, the Government of Japan has assumed all costs of the exhumation work and has entrusted the Ministry of Health, Labor and Welfare of Japan to deal with this problem.

With the beginning of 'perestroika' in the USSR and the coming to power of Mikhail Gorbachev, the problem of Japanese burial places, like some others, once again became the focus of attention. In 1991, Gorbachev gave Japan lists concerning the whereabouts of about 40,000 Japanese POWs who were buried in the USSR. Presumably, these are all the lists that were preserved in the archives. In 1993, while on a visit to Japan, President Boris Yeltsin apologized for the historical injustice of 1945 but stated that he could no longer transmit any lists of deceased POWs. The preservation and restoration of Japanese military burials in Russia is determined by several legislative acts: the *Law on Burials* dated June 1st, 1965 (new version 01.01.1993); the *Agreement of Confidence in the Question of Japanese Prisoners of War* (1990); and *Materials of the Joint Russian-American Commission on the Affairs of Prisoners of War and Missing Persons.* In accordance with the Soviet-Japanese agreement of 1991, visits were made to all accessible burial sites, many of which were restored with the active participation of the Japanese associations of former POWs.

## The Japanese POW Cemetery Reburial Program

The reburial program for Japanese cemeteries in the territory of the former Soviet Union was launched by the Japanese Ministry of Health after the signing of the agreement with the Soviet authorities in the early 1990s. By this time, they had vast experience of undertaking similar work across Southeast Asia. There was, however, the problem of locating the cemeteries given that information regarding many of them – especially those located in remote places – had been lost. Several public organizations provided assistance to the Japanese side, and historians later joined in with this work. There were publications of articles and later monographs and collections of documents. To date, Russian historiography has produced more than one hundred works, including those devoted to the search for and location of cemeteries, as well as the reburial program itself. It should be noted that in the 1990s in Japan, there were more than fifty public associations for former POWs. Some of them collaborated with the Ministry of Health and participated in the reburial program. Others, such as the Association of Former Prisoners of War, led by Saito Rokuro, clashed with the Japanese government and even sued it. This organization made independent attempts to search for Japanese cemeteries in Russia using the knowledge of local populations. It also compiled its own database and installed obelisks at cemeteries.

In 1989, the opening of the archives concerning the existence of POWs allowed numerous documents to be extracted. These included lists of POWs, death acts, cemetery books, and correspondence regarding cemeteries, among other things. Another source of information was interviews with local residents and former camp security officers. This allowed WHO to establish the exact location of almost all Japanese cemeteries, for example, in the Irkutsk region and Buryat Republic. The exceptions to this were those cemeteries that had been destroyed as a result of natural disasters. For example, the cemetery of the camp located in the village of Shamanka, in the Irkutsk region, was flooded in an event that destroyed 119 graves. Other cemeteries were flooded due to the construction of hydropower plants as was the case, for example, with a cemetery located in the village of Pashki near Irkutsk, and also several cemeteries near Bratsk. Cemeteries also disappeared as a result of economic activities such as road construction and agricultural work. In 1992, the author published a map of the 'Places of Burial of Japanese POWs in the Irkutsk Region,' where all the Japanese camps and cemeteries in the Irkutsk Region were marked (Kuznetsov 1992). The booklet includes one map of Irkutsk region at a scale of 1:7,500,000 and two enlarged fragments focusing on the Taishet-Bratsk railway at a scale of 1:500,000, and another on the Taishet-Slyudyanka at a scale of 1:1,000,000. Thus, in this publication, the regions where Japanese POWs camps and burial places had been identified were highlighted. On the named fragments of the map of the Irkutsk region, the location of the burial sites identified by the author is shown, which includes both cemeteries and individual burials of Japanese POWs and internees. Additionally, the publication contains a number of photographs found in the archives. The published information on more than eighty Japanese cemeteries in the Irkutsk region was important both for Japanese officials and for relatives of the deceased prisoners. In the early 1990s, official visits to the burial sites by representatives of the Ministry of Health, Labour and Welfare of Japan, public figures, and relatives of deceased prisoners began.

In the summer of 1992, the reburial operation for the Hospital Cemetery of Prisoners no. 3370, which contained 410 graves, began in the Taishet district near the village Toporok, Irkutsk region. The location of the cemetery had been established according to archival documents and information received from local residents. The project was initially supposed to attract Irkutsk archaeologists and historians, but the Japanese side later refused to attend for unknown reasons. The work was performed by local wage workers and members of the Japanese Association of Former Prisoners of War. The work was observed by representatives of the Ministry of Health, Labor and Welfare (Koseisho), and sometimes by local government representatives.

The boundaries of the cemetery were approximately determined by the existing grave mounds and a fire ditch located along the perimeter. The size of the plot is 30 × 100 m. The depth of the burials, dug into a sandy soil, ranges from 60 to 70 cm (reflecting winter conditions) to 120–150 cm (for summer burials). The topsoil, which measured around 50 cm in depth, was removed using an excavator and the plots excavated manually. All bones were recorded by photography before being removed and stored in an individual canvas bag, each of which was assigned a number. Attempts to identify the deceased were not undertaken. In some graves, the remains of planks and nails were found, possibly indicating coffins or decking. Single, small green buttons, pieces of oilcloth, fragments of soles from boots, and a case with pencils were recovered. It was evident that several individuals had been amputees.

After the excavations, a religious ritual and the cremation of the remains was performed. A series of 1.5 × 1.5 m metal sheets was arranged, upon each of which a 'well' of dry wood was built. A bag with bones was placed inside, and the skull was placed on top separately (see Figure 12.2). After cremation, large unburned bone fragments were collected in separate bags and placed in cardboard boxes. The boxes were sealed by a representative of Russian customs. Small fragments and ashes were gathered together and reburied at the cemetery site. A wooden identification marker was installed on top, and later an obelisk of white stone.

Work in the Topoorok village lasted for fifteen days in August 1992 and fifteen days in August 1993. Four-hundred and one burials were exhumed, after which the works were closed. In 1994 and following years, similar work was carried out near Chuksha station, in the area of the Nigne-Udachnoe. This was a place where the cemeteries are available and reliably confirmed as belonging to the camp or hospital of Japanese POWs. In July-August 2003, the reburial was carried out at the cemetery of the Special Hospital no. 1218 in the Irkutsk region, which contained 406 burials. This cemetery was visited by the Japanese back in 1956. It had a fence, a central obelisk, and 406 individual concrete tombstones, each of which was provided with a name plate. The cemetery is located in the outskirts of Marat Irkutsk and borders with the Russian cemetery.

Since the beginning of the new millennium, the same methods have been employed out in Buryatia, Chita region, under our observation. In the Irkutsk region there remained intact cemeteries located in difficult terrain and other boreal areas (for example, the cemetery of the 421st Separate Working Battalion, which contained eighty-nine graves). No work has been carried out at cemeteries that adjoin active Russian cemeteries (e.g., those at Novochunka, Listvyanka, Zima, etc.).

DNA analyses have only been conducted on the remains of repatriated Japanese soldiers since 2003. As a result of this, several individuals who had been returned to Japan were discovered not to be Japanese. In August 2019, the *Asahi* newspaper reported several such scandalous cases. In 2012, for example, an analysis of the DNA of 181 sets of remains found in the Philippines revealed that these did not belong to Japanese soldiers. In 2018, it turned out that the Ministry of Health of Japan had not published the results of the studies, possibly in order to avoid an international scandal. On August 5th, 2019, the Japan Broadcasting Corporation (NHK) reported another case concerning seventy people who had been found in the Trans-Baikal Territory near Chita, Siberia, in the year 2000. According to an examination, carried out in December 2017, the individuals recovered from the site may not have been Japanese (Nishimura 2019). It is unclear how it is possible to solve these problems now.

(a)

(b)

**FIGURE 12.2** Cremations of exhumed POWs being prepared and conducted. Photographs by Sergey Kuznetsov.

In conclusion, we can say that the Ministry of Health, Labour and Welfare of Japan performs tasks that are probably in no way connected with scientific research. These works take a long time and demand considerable material resources. The use of various methods for identifying human remains has increased over the past thirty years, and the work of forensic doctors carried out in the wake of conflicts such as those which occurred in Argentina and the former Yugoslavia has become a kind of milestone in this area. The identification of human remains relating to conflict involves complex scientific, technical, legal, and cultural issues. In recent years, the ability of scientists to identify remains has significantly expanded and improved and also become more complex with the advent of DNA technologies. The DNA from human remains can be obtained, analyzed, compared, and ultimately used determine whether they belong to a living relative, which potentially allows remains to be identified with full scientific accuracy. While the process of identifying human remains can often be fraught with many difficulties, there was a real possibility of identifying remains from several cemeteries where the paperwork was carefully compiled. This was possible even without expensive and lengthy examinations and scientific research. The reluctance to engage in the active identification of deceased prisoners, however, seems to have been a conscious decision. The reason for this perhaps concerns potential difficulties in relation to relatives (for example, the fear of lawsuits), but the only relief for families is reliable information about the death of their loved ones and confidence that the remains of their loved ones were treated with due respect and in accordance with their culture. In this regard, the identification of the remains is an important part of the process of healing wounds, not just for families but also entire communities.

In 1995, the exhumation of the remains of Japanese POWs was carried out in the Urals. Employees of the War Memorials Organization specially created in Russia participated in this work, the results of which have been published in a report compiled by the Ural historian, Professor V.P. Motrevich. It also testifies to the absence of serious research procedures and the immediate destruction of all the extracted material:

> Several thousand Japanese were placed in The Urals. In 1946–1948, they were part of individual working battalions of the USSR Ministry of Defense. Most of the Japanese were stationed in the Orenburg region, the smaller – in the Perm and Chelyabinsk regions, in the Bashkir Autonomous Soviet Socialist Republic. About 500 prisoners were in the Sverdlovsk region, and 54 people died during their stay here. In July 1995, an official Japanese delegation arrived in the region in order to conduct an exhumation at a foreign military cemetery of the Special Hospital No. 2929 of the USSR Ministry of Internal Affairs in the village of Rudnik near Nizhny Tagil. After the talks, the staff of the War Memorials Association, in the presence of an official Japanese delegation and with the help of military personnel of a military unit located near the village, proceeded with the exhumation. The cemetery, where 1,725 prisoners of war and interned foreigners were buried (among them 18 Japanese), was a heavily wooded area measuring 2.4 hectares. Having made all the necessary approvals, the alleged cemetery of Japanese prisoners was established according to the cemetery plan, and the area was cleared. As a result, the rows of graves became clearly visible, which made it possible to determine

the necessary and exhume the remains of 17 people. The terrain on which the exhumation was carried out turned out to be highly marshy, which ensured the preservation at a depth of 1.8–2.0 m not only of wooden coffins, which had to be opened to extract the remains, but often also of soft tissues. The remains were put in special plastic bags, which were marked and transferred to the medical examiner who carried out the identification, comparing the remains with the data from case histories and the cemetery plan [highlighted by us – S.K.]. Upon completion of the exhumation work, the remains were cremated, and then handed over to the Japanese representatives.

*(Motrevich 2013: 275–76).*

Further attempts to identify remains were made during the transfer of the cemetery in Khakassia, in the Krasnoyarsk region, in 2003. According to the report, 164 POWs were buried here, but some of the graves had been washed away by mudslides. A total of eighty-four remains were exhumed and no personal items were found. The cremation of the remains was carried out on the spot. Non-cremated fragments (teeth) were collected from each of the remains for DNA analyses. All the remains are packed in boxes and checked by Khakassky customs.

In the 1990s, efforts were initiated to create a database on foreign military cemeteries in Russia. The authorities created the Association on War Memorials in order to search for POWs cemeteries located on the territory of Russia. Financing of the survey program was carried out by the countries concerned – primarily Germany but also Hungary and Italy. After the discovery and inspection of a foreign military cemetery, a survey report was compiled that included detailed information on the place of burial, its region and the city, area and village name, and details regarding the cemetery's immediate environment (e.g., if the cemetery is located in the countryside). The report also indicates the size of the cemetery, the number of graves and the number of those buried, and details concerning the armed forces to which they belonged. Other useful information is also included: it is indicated, for example, whether memorials and burial mounds are preserved at the cemetery site; whether the site is under threat of destruction and whether it is protected; and the addresses and surnames of eyewitnesses. It is also possible to familiarize yourself with the schemes of cemeteries indicating the nearest landmarks, distances to these, and topography. Where burial mounds remain, a detailed burial plan has been made. The date of the latest inspection of the cemetery, the last name, first name, and patronymic of the inspector, and their address are also indicated. This source therefore provides a high level of detail and facilitates the monitoring of foreign military cemeteries in the territory of the Russian Federation. It is important that the presence of 'war memorials' contributes to the official registration and registration of the cemeteries as a historical monument, which helps to preserve for in the future. At present, obelisks are installed on most of the surviving Japanese cemeteries. Some continue to be visited by groups of relatives and tourists (as in the case of a memorial located in

**FIGURE 12.3**  Listviyanka Japanese cemetery as seen today. Photograph by Sergey Kuznetsov.

the village of Listvyanka near Baikal) and these are officially recorded as historical objects (see Figure 12.3).

## Bibliography

Gavrilov, V.A. & Katasonova, E.L. 2013. *Japanese Prisoners of War in the USSR: 1945–1956. Collection of Documents [Yaponskiye voyennoplennyye v SSSR: 1945–1956. Sbornik dokumentov]*, Moscow: MDF.

Kuznetsov, S. 1992. *Graveyards of War. Prisoners in Irkutsk Region.* Irkutsk: Arkom Publishers.

*List of Burial Places of Japanese Prisoners of War who Died in the Territory of the USSR after the Second World War (Sketches of Circles of Burial Places). (Spisok mest zakhoroneniy voyennoplennykh yapontsev, umershikh v territorii SSSR posle Vtoroy mirovoy voyny (Eskizy okruzhnostey mest zakhoroneniy)).* 1990. Tokyo: Victim Assistance Office of the Ministry of Health and Welfare of Japan. Archive manuscript.

Motrevich, V.P. 2013. 'Exhumation of the Remains of Japanese Prisoners of War in the Urals in 1995–1999', *Tenth Tatishevsky Reading: Reports of Scientific Conference (Ekaterinburg, November 20–21, 2013)* ['Eksgumatsiya ostankov yaponskikh voyenno-plennykh na Urale v 1995–1999 gg.', *Desyatyye Tatishchevskiye chteniya : materialyly nauchnoy konferentsii. (Ekaterinburg. 20–21 noyabrya 2013 goda)*], Yekaterinburg: UMT UPI, 275–76.

Nishimura, K. 2019. 'Questions Raised over Nationality of 70 More Siberian Remains', *Asahi shinbun*, 2019, August 15. http://www.asahi.com/ajw/articles/AJ201908150066.ht.

Zagorul'ko, M.M. 2000. *Prisoners of War in the USSR. 1939–1956. Documents and Materials [Voyennoplennyye v SSSR. 1939–1956. Dokumenty i materialy]*, Moscow: Logos.

# 13

# HIMEYURI PEACE MUSEUM

## The Personal Experience of War

*Noriko Koga*

## Introduction

Himeyuri Peace Museum, located in the southern part of Okinawa's main island, is a well-known museum in Japan with more than 500,000 annual visitors (Figure 13.1). Half of this number consists of junior-high- and high-school students who visit Okinawa for school trips (Himeyuri Peace Foundation 2019: 7–8). The museum celebrated its 30th anniversary in June 2019.

'Himeyuri' is a nickname which indicates 'Okinawa Female Normal School,' and 'Okinawa First Girls' High School.' Prior to the Battle of Okinawa, 240 students and teachers from both schools were mobilized to serve in the Okinawa Army Hospital in Haebaru. 136 died in the fighting (Himeyuri Peace Museum 2010). Since the war, the 240 students and teachers have come to be known as the Himeyuri Student Corps.

Many of visitors describe the museum exhibit as 'an exhibit where we can see everyone's face' (Himeyuri Peace Museum 2019). The visitors see that the students who died in the war were ordinary girls just like them, and they can imagine what the girls thought when they visit the exhibit. They start to see the girls as individuals who actually lived, not just as dead people. In this chapter, the author introduces the exhibit to the reader through a discussion of the history of the museum and the specialized features of the exhibition rooms.

## Before the Establishment of the Museum

As World War II drew to a close, Japanese and US forces fought for control of the island of Okinawa. The battle lasted for three months, from March to June 1945. The battle involved not only military forces but also local residents. The Japanese army mobilized both male and female high-school students in order to make up

DOI: 10.4324/9780429270468-17

**FIGURE 13.1**  Himeyuri Peace Memorial Museum (left) and the Himeyuri Cenotaph (right). Photograph by the author (2021).

for its shortage in military manpower. Total deaths from the Battle of Okinawa would reach beyond 200,000 people.

In April 1946, the Himeyuri Cenotaph was established in the south of Okinawa Island. It is located on top of the cave where more than eighty people, including forty-two Himeyuri students and teachers, died during a US attack. Immediately after the war, the monument became known nationally as tragic symbol of the Battle of Okinawa. A story of the patriotic girls written by a former soldier in a concentration camp became a subject of theater and movie narratives, which portrayed an account of the battle that differed to the experiences of the actual Himeyuri student survivors (Nakada 2016). The survivors themselves did not tell of their experiences for a long time. They felt that they must apologize to their friends who died and their bereaved families, guilty for leaving a wounded friend on the battlefield, and ashamed to have survived (Himeyuri Peace Museum 2012). On June 23rd 1989, forty-three years after the war, the Himeyuri Alumni established the Himeyuri Peace Museum right next to the Himeyuri Cenotaph. Survivors of the Himeyuri Student Corps, who put tremendous effort into the collection of materials, transcription of their interviews, and creation of exhibits, started to tell their war time experiences for the first time.

## Exhibits Made by the Survivors

The main theme of the Himeyuri Peace Museum is 'War and Education.' Himeyuri student survivors tell us that

Forty some odd years later, we still cannot forget the indescribable tragedy we witnessed and experienced, nor can we forget the horror of the militaristic education of that time that blinded us to truth, deprived us of our right to think and judge as individuals, and denied us even the right to live as decent human beings, finally herding us like animals onto a battlefield of certain death.

In 2004, fifteen years after the opening of the museum, the exhibit was renovated to create new space that will continue to convey the survivors' war experiences to future generations. A selection of the collections and all texts and captions in the display panels were created by the survivors (Himeyuri Peace Museum 2010). In April 2021, the museum underwent a second exhibition renewal led by staff members born after the war. Visual information such as illustrations, photos, and videos were increased, and the text was rewritten to be easier to understand, but the method of depicting the Battle of Okinawa from the survivors' perspective has not changed.

### The First Exhibit Room: 'School Life at Himeyuri'

The 'School Life at Himeyuri' exhibit describes the process of school militarization and the conscription of the students into the army (Figure 13.2). The exhibit begins with a photograph of students looking up at the sky from a boarding house window.

The Okinawa Female Normal School and Okinawa First Girls' High School shared their land and facilities. The school had sufficiently good facilities, including buildings and dormitories with red roof tiles, a library, gym, tennis court, and swimming pool, and excellent teachers who graduated from universities on the 'mainland.' The school was a place of fun, filled with the songs and laughter of students who were aged thirteen to nineteen years old. The poses and smiles of students in a photograph tell us of that story. Since elementary school, however, these students had also been taught to work with joy for the Emperor, and to sacrifice their life during wartime. A school was a place to teach loyalty to the Emperor. This is illustrated by the photo of the "Imperial Palace Prayer Service," in which all students and faculty members pay their most respectful salute to the Imperial Palace in Tokyo. Therefore, they thought to be patient until the time when they would win the war. They additionally believed in 'the Greater East Asia Co-Prosperity Sphere,' a slogan created to present an image of co-prosperity in an Asia led by Japan, which would protect Asia from Western countries. This was the goal of the war. The students therefore readily accepted mobilization into the army in order to construct defensive positions and the hospital; they were eager to put themselves to some use for their country.

Before the Battle of Okinawa started, the defeat of Japan had become clear as a result of lost battles on the Pacific frontlines. Military leaders, however, sought to

**FIGURE 13.2**  School Life at Himeyuri exhibit. Photograph by the author (2021).

gain time to prepare for what they perceived to be the coming decisive battle for the Japanese home islands by slowing US forces on Okinawa. The students, who did not know of this, went readily to the battlefield without any single doubt in their minds.

On March 23rd 1945, US forces began the pre-landing bombardment of Okinawa Island. In middle of the night, 222 students with eighteen teachers left the school to go to the Okinawa Army Hospital. The students were aged fifteen to nineteen years old.

## The Second Exhibit Room: 'Himeyuri Students at the Front'

This exhibit room speaks to the realities of the battlefield. The exhibit includes a model of Okinawa Army Hospital ward and medical equipment that was excavated within the cave by the survivors, forty years after the war (Figure 13.3). An exhibit entitled 'Students' Personal Items' highlights the differences between the actual conditions within the Army Hospital and what the students thought they would be like when they were mobilized.

> 'Students brought their belongings with them. They brought school supplies, such as pen cases and writing boards, believing they could get back to school as soon as Japan quickly triumphed. Expecting the battlefield to be

only an extension of their classrooms, they had thought they could keep a diary or read books when they were off duty. Such daily utensils as combs, toothbrushes, and hand mirrors, which all students had with them, were never used once they reached the battlefield, where they had no time to even clean themselves.

*(quote from the second exhibit room 'Himeyuri Students at the Front')*

The students thought that working in a ward with a Red Cross flag would protect them from gunfire, but in reality the battlefield was a place where bullets and artillery shells flew day and night. The wards in the cave were filled up with the smell of blood, pus, and feces, the patients' moans, and roars that never stopped. The students helped care for and treat the wounded soldiers, drew water, delivered food, cleaned feces, carried messages, and buried the dead.

In late May, US forces moved against the Japanese army headquarters at Shuri. Although the Japanese army had lost 80% of its manpower, they retreated to the south without surrendering in order to continue hindering the US advance. A retreat order was issued to the Army Hospital, and the students went to the south with their friends on stretchers. Forests and houses still remained in the south because fewer air raids had taken place. Although students and hospital staff were divided between six caves, the hospital did not function anymore. Before the

FIGURE 13.3  A full-scale model of the ward inside of the Okinawa Army Hospital Cave in the 'Himeyuri Students at the Front' exhibit room. Photograph by the author (2021).

final 'deactivation order' came, three caves were attacked by US forces, generating many casualties.

### The Third Exhibit Room: 'Himeyuri Survivor Testimony Videos'

On the night of June 18th, students were ordered to demobilize and leave the cave without their wounded friends. The expelled students were forced to try and escape under fire and more than 100 died over the next few days. The exhibit room 'Deactivation Order and Wandering Towards Death' plays a movie of survivors' interviews. It consists of twenty stories lasting for fifty-five minutes, but it is edited so that visitors can start and finish watching at any time. The survivors decided to record their testimony so that their stories would be remembered when they are no longer able to tell them. The shooting of the movie took place on location at the hospital caves and shores; the places where the battle actually took place. The survivors, who are projected life-size on the screen, seem as if they are talking in front of the visitors. Many visitors who might not have not read panels or seen the materials often halt without thinking and are drawn into the stories.

### The Fourth Exhibit Room: 'Requiem'

'Requiem' is a room for survivors' testimonies and also features portraits of deceased students and teachers who perished in the Battle of Okinawa (Figure 13.4). A surviving teacher collected the portraits from bereaved families and surviving classmates, and these portraits were donated to the museum. Portraits of eight people are still missing. There are short sentences describing the victim's personalities, which include their names, age, home village, how they died, nicknames, hobbies, and memories. These were written by their surviving classmates. At the back of the exhibit, there is a life-size model of the cave underneath the Himeyuri Cenotaph. When the visitors look up the cave entrance, they can see the same landscape that the students would have seen. The students feared to be captured by US forces because they were repeatedly told that US soldiers were insanely 'brutal' and that they would rape and kill captured women.

The exhibition room features 108 testimonies of seventy survivors, which lie on bookrests. Personal war experiences are conveyed through the eyes of Himeyuri students. Scenes of the battlefield, the last moments of a dying friend, and terrifying days spent inside of the caves are described in graphic detail:

> 'A patient with no legs crawling in the mud.'
> 'Kill me! I'm also the Emperor's subject.'
> 'Dragging classmates' bodies.'

School students who visit the museum with their classmates as part of a large group must face these testimonies alone.

**FIGURE 13.4** Portraits of deceased students and large testimony books in the 'Requiem' exhibit room. Photograph by the author (2021).

### The Fifth Exhibit Room: 'Himeyuri Survivors after the War'

Through the windows, colorful blooming flowers can be seen in the courtyard. This is a room for visitors to reflect on what they have seen in the museum and write down their thoughts and impressions. The exhibit ends with a message:

'I want to walk again in the sun with no fear'
'I'm thirsty… give me water, water…'
'Mom, I want to see my Mom…'

The voices of our friends speaking to us. We went on the battlefield without knowing the truth:

War kills everything–
the life of every single being
therefore our story continues
we will speak of the truth of war, brutality, pain,
engraved in our bodies
and memories.

This message reflects the determination of the survivors to continue to tell the reality of the war through their own individual experiences. After the opening of the museum in 1989, the survivors stood in the exhibition rooms and started to

**FIGURE 13.5**  'Himeyuri Survivors after the War' exhibit room. Photograph by the author (2021).

tell of their experiences. At that time, they could not keep talking because of the tears that came when their friends' faces came to their minds. However, the serious attitude of audiences encouraged them, and they started to understand the importance of their storytelling. Survivors who were initially 'sorry to survive' after the war began to feel that 'this is the reason why I survived' – to tell their story at the museum (Futenma 2015; see Figure 13.5). The exhibit, which was renewed in April 2021, introduces the survivors' postwar history, the construction of the museum, and their testimonial activities.

### The Sixth Exhibit Room: 'The Passage to Peace'

'The Passage to Peace' was newly established during the 2004 renovations as a plaza where the new generation can gather, consider, and discuss peace. Since then, various special exhibits such as 'After War of the Survivors' and 'Activities at the Museum' have been held here.

## The Inheritance from War Survivors to the Next Generation

The Himeyuri student survivors who established Himeyuri Peace Museum thirty-two years ago remind us both of the tragedy of war and the importance of peace. They consider it their mission to do this in order to honor their dead classmates.

The last two decades have witnessed a generational shift, and as such the survivors now continue to relate their wartime experiences to museum curators and guides. Museum staff learn not only historical facts and chronologies but also about the survivors' feelings. In 2018, after the former museum director retired at age of ninety, the first curator to be born after the war became the new director. This was a big moment, marking a shift in the management of the museum from those who bore witness to the war to those who have no experience of conflict themselves. While the original number of survivors working at the museum was twenty-seven, it is now only four people. In March 2020, testimonial activities at the museum were suspended to prevent the transmission of COVID-19. The day is coming when we will no longer be able to hear the survivors speak of their experiences themselves. Although they are indeed survivors, it was never easy for them to do this. We, the museum staff, have watched them work as they talk about their lives to the visitors before them. After many long years, the war is becoming almost a historical past for the young people of Japan. Himeyuri Peace Museum will continue to convey the individual war experiences of the survivors and to promote their legacy: wishes of peace for the future.

## Bibliography

Futenma, A. 2015. 'Himeyuri No Kokoro: Himeyuri Ga Tsutaetekita Mono, Tsutae-teiku Mono ['A Heart of Himeyuri: What Himeyuri Told and will Tell']', *Shiso* 1096, 92–97.

Himeyuri Peace Foundation. 2019. *Nenpou Dai 30 Gou [Annual Report* vol. 30]. Itoman, Okinawa, Japan: Himeyuri Peace Museum. (In Japanese).

Himeyuri Peace Museum. 2010. *Miraie Tsunagu Himeyuri No Kokoro: Himeyuri Heiwa Kinen Shiryoukan 20 Shuunen Kinenshi [Heart Succeeded to the Future: 20th Anniversary Bulletin of Himeyuri Peace Museum]*. Itoman, Okinawa, Japan: Okinawa Prefecture Female Normal School, First Girls' High School Alumni, and Himeyuri Peace Museum. (In Japanese).

Himeyuri Peace Museum. 2012. *Ikinokotta Himeyuri Gakuto Tachi: Shuuyoujyo Kara Kikyoue [Survived Himeyuri Students: From Concentration Camp to Home]*. Itoman, Okinawa, Japan: Himeyuri Peace Museum. (In Japanese).

Himeyuri Peace Museum. 2019. *Kansoubun Shu Himeyuri [Himeyuri: Visitors' Responses 30]*. Itoman, Okinawa, Japan: Himeyuri Peace Museum. (In Japanese).

Nakata, A. 2016. '"Himeyuri" Wo Meguru Katarino Sengoshi ['Oral Post-War History about Himeyuri']. In: Okinawa Prefecture Education Bureau Cultural Property Section Historical Document Editorial Team, ed. *Okinawa Kenshi Kakuronhen Dai 8 Kan Joseishi [Okinawa Prefectural History, Various Discussions Edition, Vol. 8: Women's History]*. Naha: Okinawa Prefecture Board of Education, 344–60. (In Japanese).

# 14

# NEGOTIATING PELELIU

## Agency, Politics, and Place on the Battlefields of the Pacific War

*Neil Price*

## Introduction: The Pacific Margin and the War of the Worlds

The Asia-Pacific Theatre of the Second World War is often marginalized in the public memory of the former Allied nations, relegated to the sidelines in favour of a greater focus on the European and Russian fronts. To take just two recent British histories of the global struggle – Max Hastings' *All Hell Let Loose* (2011) and Antony Beevor's *The Second World War* (2012) – the campaigns take up respectively only 19% and 17% of the narrative. This is a curious phenomenon, in that the fighting in Burma, southeast Asia, and the Pacific was far from overlooked by civilians at home in the combatant nations at the time.

Beyond this imbalance of literary and historical attention, another issue quickly arises in determining the dates of the conflict itself, which in turn affects its context and interpretation. This is perceived very much along national and geopolitical lines. For American historians, whose work has tended to dominate in serving the largest international readership, the war began on the 7th of December 1941 with the attack on Pearl Harbor and concluded with the signing of the Japanese surrender in Tokyo Bay on the 2nd of September 1945. For British and Commonwealth writers, the Pacific Theatre tends to be subsumed into the larger arena of the world war, beginning in 1939. In China, the origins of the fighting are traced to the invasions of 1931 and 1937, both part of the Second Sino-Japanese War. Imperial aggression against Korea has an even longer timeline, extending back into a broader trajectory of colonialism in the peninsula, which was annexed in 1910. Japanese scholars tend to discuss the war in more piecemeal, regional fashion, linked to wider histories of the Shōwa period (1926–89), in the context of what at the time was framed as the pursuit of the 'Greater East Asia Co-Prosperity Sphere' and the supposed liberation of the region from the European powers.

DOI: 10.4324/9780429270468-18

Sometimes these contested chronologies and emphases play out even within national historical traditions. While most US histories of the war focus on the 1941–45 span of American involvement (e.g. Costello 1981; Bergerud 1996; Hornfischer 2016), it is interesting that the two foremost current works in this genre – both multi-volume endeavours, one just concluded and the other just beginning – take opposing views: Ian Toll's *Pacific War Trilogy* of histories (2012, 2015, 2020) maintains the traditional date range, while the new *History of the Asia-Pacific War* by Richard Frank (2020, with more volumes to appear) begins in the 1930s with the conflict in China.

Different though they are, what all these timelines have in common is that they relate to the dates when individual countries commenced active participation in the war, either in aggression or defence. This privilege of perspective among the Allied and Axis nations in fact extends to almost all mediations of the Pacific War, whether in print or on film, focusing upon the Japanese, the Americans, the British and Commonwealth government forces, the small militaries of the Dutch East Indies, the Kuomintang and Communist Chinese, and latterly the Soviets. This is a far from complete picture, and the neglected or wholly ignored communities of the Asia-Pacific embrace many constituencies. Those governed *in* the Commonwealth – Indians, Burmese, and Malayans, to name but a few – are represented to a degree but tend to be subsumed in the armies of the British Empire (the same could be said of the Indonesians in what was then a Dutch possession). For ethnic minorities within the US forces, something similar can be observed with respect to American troops of African, Hispanic, and Chinese descent, in addition of course to Native Americans. On the opposing side, a similar bias overlooks the colonized peoples of the Japanese Empire, in particular the Koreans – many of whom were either conscripted into military service as distinctly second-class personnel, or else compelled to work as forced labour. The Okinawans occupy a special position still today, as a historically independent people long-since politically incorporated into the state of Japan, but with radically different attitudes and legislation to the legacies of the war – as demonstrated by several chapters in this volume.

Adding even to this, and encompassing it all, is the fact that the narratives of the Pacific War tend to be deeply androcentric, as if no women were involved either in the theatre of combat or at home. It does not help that the overwhelming majority of the literature is written by men.

However, serious though these biases are, in the Pacific they are arguably overshadowed by the almost complete erasure of the very people for whom many of the battlefields were and are 'home' – the islanders themselves. At least in public perception, it is as if the entire ocean was uninhabited before the war arrived. For the indigenous peoples of the islands and of the Asia-Pacific region more generally, the chronological frame of the conflict is also subtly different. From these perspectives, the later campaigns of the Second World War either blend into the subsequent struggles to throw off European (e.g. Bayly & Harper 2004, 2007) or Asian (e.g. Peattie 1988) imperial rule, or mark a shift in a centuries-long heritage of colonial dominance (for example from Japan to the United States). This remaking of the political order stretched far into the 1960s and indeed continues in the geopolitical tensions of today. Put simply, for most of the Pacific nations, including the islands, in a sense the war did not fully end in 1945.

The Second World War in the Asia-Pacific was thus a conflict between armies and empires, but also a clash of cultures, mentalities, world views, spiritualities, and identities. It embodied a diversity of experience that extended far beyond the combatant nations, stretching outside the 'traditional' timeframe of the conflict. The *War of the Worlds* project, within which this present volume has been produced, was named advisedly. Its focus on marginalized voices within the main armies, and particularly on the indigenous peoples over whose lands they fought, has arisen as a collaboration that began in the context of work commissioned *by* and *for* islanders. We do not see this as an exercise in postcolonial research, because (while, of course, complex) there is a sense in which this approach can permanently situate formerly colonized peoples in relation to a past that they might in fact prefer to just leave behind. The Pacific peoples of the project, and this book, are firmly decolonialized, always central agents, and it is up to them alone to determine their opinions of the war and its legacies, whether or not to express them publicly or privately, and if so, how to do so. Outsider researchers such as myself can offer our own contributions, but from the periphery.

This distance applies in another context too. In the course of the project, we have naturally encountered veterans in some numbers, mostly American but occasionally Japanese, in addition to civilians who experienced the war. While some members of the project team are ex-military and have served in recent conflicts, none of the archaeological core staff have done so, and we are also conscious of the intellectual pretension and abstraction that tends to creep into so much academic prose. Put simply, in all our work on *War of the Worlds*, we have tried never to write anything that we would be ashamed for a veteran or survivor to read (for expanded thoughts in this vein, see the introduction to one of the finest memoirs of the Burma campaign, George MacDonald Fraser's *Quartered Safe Out Here*, 1993).

In the course of a decade, the project has grown to encompass much of the Pacific region, as the chapters in this book have demonstrated. However, it began in 2010 with work on a single island, taken up in an earlier chapter in this volume, and it is appropriate that we return there at the close of the book.

## The Custodians: *Chad ra Beliliou* – The People of Peleliu

From 2010 to 2015, archaeologists from the universities of Aberdeen and Uppsala – accompanied by international volunteers – undertook a series of field surveys on the island of Peleliu in the Republic of Palau, Micronesia, exploring material remains of the prolonged and vicious battle that took place there in late 1944 (Knecht et al. 2012; Price & Knecht 2012, 2013; Lindsay et al. 2015; Price et al. 2015). The successive phases of work were largely funded through the Micronesian office of the National Park Service of the United States within their American Battlefield Protection Program, together with a variety of private sponsors, and were undertaken in collaboration with the non-profit Peleliu War Historical Society. However, at all times the project was entirely under the management of the Palauan government Bureau of Arts and Culture (now renamed the Bureau of Cultural and Historical Preservation), with connections to Peleliu State and with the traditional chiefs of the island. Palauan archaeologists, anthropologists, guides, rangers, bomb-disposal technicians, and volunteers were full collaborators, sharing in the project from the beginning and throughout. The importance of this indigenous-led approach, and the fact that the foreign teams were working explicitly for the Palauan government and people, cannot be overstated. Indeed, it formed the central pillar of the project itself, reflected in the chapter cited above and elsewhere in this volume.

Ours were not the first outsider efforts to engage with the indigenous story of the Pacific War. Anthropological recording of wartime memories started early, and at least two works on the war have also been produced in regional languages – in Pijin for the Solomons (Bennett et al. 1988), and Bislama for Vanuatu (Lindstrom & Gwero 1998). Several major collections appeared (e.g. White & Lindstrom 1989; White 1991; Fujitani et al. 2001, the latter also incorporating Chinese and Okinawan perspectives), as well as a collation of the unique photographic record of islanders in their wartime interactions with military incomers (Lindstrom & White 1990). Post-war heritage tourism has also received attention, as in de Burlo's 1989 study of Melanesia, and the long-term associations of Pearl Harbor in its very specific Hawaiian setting (White 2016, and references therein to his many related publications).

Several key regions emerge here, though in very different contexts ranging from battlefields to bases. These include the Solomons, Papua New Guinea, the Marianas, and the Marshall Islands for the former, and Vanuatu and Samoa for the latter; Hawaii in a sense spans both categories. The literature cited above gathered almost all of the anthropologists working on the indigenous legacies of the wartime Pacific, many of them with decades of contact and presence in the region, building on personal relationships and also service with organizations such as the US Peace Corps. It is also significant that several of these anthropological studies are authored by women (a total contrast to the military histories) and are based on interactions with female Pacific Islanders.

One area in particular, Micronesia, has been the scene of intensive study in the present century (e.g. Poyer et al. 2001; Falgout et al. 2008). Palau of course lies on its western rim and indeed had featured in a number of the earlier Pacific anthropological surveys. Amongst others, Dirk Ballendorf and colleagues (1986) recorded oral histories of the Japanese administration; Karen Nero (1989) focused on the overwhelming presence of hunger in Palauans' wartime memories; Ubal Tellai (1991) explored Palauans' interactions with the Japanese; and particularly comprehensive programs of work have been undertaken by Wakako Higuchi (e.g. 1986a, 1986b, 1987, 1991) and Karen Walter (1993). Alongside this research, one can also note the ongoing documentation of Palauan oral histories being undertaken island by island with the anthropological section of the Bureau of Cultural and Historical Preservation. These works have been discussed in a previous paper (Price & Knecht 2013), and they combine to provide Palau with perhaps the most comprehensive body of insular wartime memory studies in the entire Pacific – among the few comparable recent works are those by Keith Camacho (2011) on the Marianas, and Anna Annie Kwai (2017) with her insider perspective on the Solomons.

This unusual focus on Palau is particularly evident for the island most affected by the war, namely Peleliu, reflected in the literature through the monumental work of Stephen Murray, first in his 2006 PhD and later in its expanded formal publication from 2016. Tracing the impacts of successive colonial powers, Murray's studies incorporate decades of participant interactions with the *chad ra Beliliou* – the people of Peleliu – and explore the intersections of wartime experience with the island's complex social and political structures. His 2016 volume has been rightly described as having no equal in Pacific Island ethnography, bringing together intellectual, practical, and personal observation in a unique

FIGURE 14.1  Palauan history in wood: gable paintings on a *bai* (men's house) on Babeldoab island. Images such as these were the inspiration for modern storyboards, a major craft product in today's Palau. Photograph by Neil Price.

account of the literal and metaphorical 'battle over Peleliu' (the book also contains perhaps the most comprehensive bibliography for the island – excluding a few works of purely military history – with a focus on the experiences of the *chad ra Beliliou*). Murray's work must be consulted entire and needs no summary here. Of primary importance for this present chapter, however, is his insistence that Peleliu's wartime history can only be understood in the light of its deep-time past, the contrast between Palauan and colonial perceptions of place, and also the webs of connections that tie the islanders to the island.

For the *chad ra Beliliou*, what outsiders perceive as the battlefield is only one component of a much larger social entity, intimately bound up with the land itself, and its spiritual and political resonance. These meshed identities encompass the household and kin, with complex lines of descent; structures of chiefly power, and respect for elders and leaders; labour, production, subsistence, and economy; and broader patterns of belief, morality, values, and behaviour (cf. Petersen 2009: 66–211). In particular, the battlefield is not understood as a pristine military landscape that has lain untouched since the fighting ceased, but rather as a curated burden of care shouldered by the islanders over many decades (including a major struggle against the looting of wartime relics by outsiders). Indeed, it is not primarily seen as a conflict landscape at all, in that the 'battlefield' is merely an overlay above something older, sacred, and numinous that is of much greater importance. These links between people and place, between family identities and the former village sites that were nominally obliterated by the war, are at the centre of Murray's work, where they are eloquently explored at length.

In the final publication of his doctorate, we were very happy to see that he has also picked up our project on Peleliu in this light. A key aspect of our work on the island was the discovery that many of the former village sites in fact still preserve considerable above-ground remains, making possible a physical reconnection with place alongside the mental and spiritual continuity that has never ceased (Price & Knecht 2013; Lindsay et al. 2015). In addition, several cave sites also proved to contain human remains that had been deposited there long before the battle, along with caches of pottery and other artefacts; in other words, many of them were traditional burial sites of the *chad ra Beliliou*.

This has left traces in contemporary attitudes to the caves, associated with the potentially dangerous spirits of the war dead who are believed to inhabit them. The narratives attaching to parts of the battlefield have been obliquely addressed in our second paper on the Peleliu fieldwork (Price & Knecht 2013). However, beyond these anecdotal encounters with an unseen landscape, there of course lies a larger, deeper worldview. In particular, the relationship of the *chad ra Beliliou* with the Peleliu battlefield is linked to island's role in Palauan mortuary beliefs.

The primary sources for Palauan religion and spirituality include early texts from explorers, missionaries, and ethnographers (e.g. Kubary 1888; Krämer 1926, 1929a, 1929b) and more modern texts (e.g. Parmentier 1987; Hijikata 1995; Dobbin 2011: ch.8). However, Palauan spiritual knowledge bearers are the primary custodians of history, custom, and lore throughout the islands. Some of this

**FIGURE 14.2**  The landscape beneath the battle: the extant remains of a bai platform at Ngerdelolk village site, Peleliu, during the 2010 survey. Photograph by Rick Knecht.

is published (e.g. PCAA 1976-78; Palau Society of Historians 1997; Rechebei & McPhetres 1997) but much of this is closed to outsiders – a situation that must of course be respected. For the purposes of this chapter, in connection with mortuary beliefs, it is sufficient to note that the spirit was believed to separate from the body at death, and to then embark on a journey. This involved the passage of the soul along the line of the island chain, from northeast to southwest, stopping to bathe in sacred pools, before finally arriving at the southernmost tip of the archipelago within the encircling reef. This was the south point of Peleliu, from which on the fifth day after death the spirit would swim to Angaur (the smaller island to the southwest, outside the reef), before arriving at Ngedelog beach, where it would at last depart. There was no sense that the spirit ought to return to earth, and the leaving of it was important.

It is in this context that one of the more immediate, and urgent, aspects of the battle's aftermath becomes apparent. Peleliu was not only the scene of carnage and death in 1944, on an unimaginable scale given the island's small size, it was also the place where the souls of *all* the Palauan dead gathered for the passage to Angaur and the next world. The island was therefore seen as thronged with the confused – and visible, embodied – ghosts of the foreign dead, whose inability to move on could potentially disturb the regular passage of Palauan souls (it should be noted that at this time, and to a degree still today, Palauan religion was still a syncretic mix of traditional beliefs and Christianity, especially within the Modekngei movement; Aoyagi 2002).

The south point of Peleliu was the site of some of the fiercest fighting in the battle, a desperate last stand by the Japanese (none survived), with terrible American casualties. Today, the area presents as an expanse of sand with stands of shady palms, bounded by rocks at the edge of the ocean, and by a great wall of jungle on the inland side. It is also the site of the Peace Park Memorial, the Japanese government's monument on the island (Murray 2016: 163). The south point, the beach of the souls, is a beautiful but eerie and disturbing place, especially at night. The sun sets over the water, with the low silhouette of Angaur on the horizon, the sky blazing in bands of dark colour as the light fades; the jungle is of a green so dark as to appear black, and impenetrable. While on the island, we were told many stories of the spirits at this place, including by people who had seen them. Some of these informed the account we gave in our earlier paper (Price & Knecht 2013), but we deliberately omitted a great deal of the experience, and I do so again here. In every sense, these are matters for the *chad ra Beliliou*, not for us.

For the Peleliu islanders, the 'battlefield' is thus not only a highly charged landscape of wartime death, a place where thousands of outsiders died, but also a locus of interaction with their ancestors going back centuries (or millennia) before the war. We have elsewhere already addressed the hoped-for healing functions of our fieldwork, alongside its more conventional dimensions of archaeological recording, in assisting in the peaceful passage of all the Peleliu dead (Price & Knecht 2013). Taking this as a foundation, the second half of this chapter is instead concerned with other resonances of the work, with the social, cultural, and political developments surrounding the legacies of the battle, as they have played out among *non*-Palauan actors before and after 2010 when our survey project began. It is thus a decade retrospective of negotiation, of the stakes involved, and the outcomes that can be achieved.

## Outside Interests: The Battle for Peleliu as Post-War Political History

The general marginalization of the Pacific War in larger wartime histories, mentioned above, also extends to the specifics of its battles. However, as with other theatres of the Second World War, the individual Pacific engagements have also generated an extensive, more tightly focussed literature of tactical analysis and combatant memoir. Several Peleliu books of this type were published from the 1950s through the 1980s, arguably culminating in Sledge's landmark autobiography (1981; see Price & Knecht 2012, 2013 for other works), but from the late 1990s into the 21st century the tone of American military histories changed. As war veterans found themselves at the threshold of extreme old age, their reminiscences were being sought anew, and as time grew short they perhaps also felt more inclined to finally share the experience. The mood was fuelled by TV series such as the D-Day epic *Band of Brothers* (2001), and books began to appear in what Murray (2016: 201–02) has called the 'Greatest Generation' genre. Peleliu was no exception (e.g. Wright 2002; Sloan 2005; Camp 2008), and these works generally conform to type in that while they do not actively glorify the fighting, the narratives are nonetheless conveyed in the language of stoic masculine courage from the perspective of American triumph over infernal adversity.

The trend reached a height with the 2010 HBO miniseries *The Pacific*, a ten-episode drama made as a deliberate companion piece to *Band of Brothers*, charting the American island-hopping campaigns from Guadalcanal to Okinawa. It was built around the stories of three Marines, of whom two – Robert Leckie and Eugene Sledge – had fought on Peleliu and written vivid accounts of their time there. Dramatizing their experiences, the fight for the island occupied three entire episodes and brought the battle to a new audience (Ambrose 2010). This in turn generated a fresh round of American memoirs, written by the last of the veterans (Burgin 2010; Mace & Allen 2012; McEnery & Sloan 2012) including at least one Navajo code-talker (Nez 2011), and further battle analyses (Blair & DeCioccio 2011; Wheelan 2022).

The HBO series was one of the primary catalysts for our original Peleliu project in 2010, raising interest in the battle and bringing visitors to the island for reasons other than the diving that had previously dominated Palau's tourism economy (see Price & Knecht 2012). However, *The Pacific* reached an almost entirely English-speaking or European audience, and a corresponding impact was not felt in Japan or elsewhere in Asia.

Much has of course been written on Japan's complex relationship with its wartime past (e.g. Igarashi 2000; Seraphim 2006; Seaton 2007; Margolin 2014). For Palau and the western Pacific, earlier accounts tended to focus on the loss of the South Seas mandate, and formal military records including official reports of the campaign (e.g. BBKS 1968). Descriptions of the fighting grew more personal over time, as in the controversial but influential work of the Angaur survivor Hiroshi Funasaka (1966–68; Murray 2016: ch.7). The word *gyokusai* ('shattered jewels') appears frequently in these relations of Peleliu and other island battles. Stemming from a 7th-century Chinese text, by the 1940s it was used to denote the concept of 'honourable death,' embracing a range of terminal strategies that included doomed *banzai* charges and literal suicide both individual and collective.

The Pacific War also attracted its modest share of Japanese fiction, including a handful of novels that focus on the karst warfare of the islands. Alongside modern classics such as Hikaru Okuizumi's *Ishi no raireki* (1993; translated as *The Stones Cry Out*, 1999), one novel has been devoted to the battle for Peleliu itself, Makoto Oda's *Gyokusai* (1998; translated as *The Breaking Jewel*, 2003), which we discuss in our 2013 paper. This formed something of a corrective to what had long been the predominant Japanese public memory of the Peleliu defence, in the form of conservative messages from veteran writers such as Funasaka. There were few works of general military history with a more balanced outlook until the present century.

The politicized memorialization of the Peleliu battle is a particular concern of Murray's, not only in his main works (2006, 2016: pt.III), but also in a subsequent paper dedicated to the post-war Japanese relationship to the fighting, and the media through which it has been constructed (2017). In analysing the commemorative installations set up on the island by a variety of Japanese groups, mostly on the political right, he shows how Peleliu has for decades been a surrogate arena for the expression of views on the war that are not acceptable in Japanese public discourse at home. On some memorials extolling the courage of the defenders, the Japanese text includes specific phrasing, sentiments, or symbols that indicate coded (and sometimes outright) approval of imperial aggression; these sections are omitted from the English 'translations' on the same monuments. In the past, there has also been limited pushback from other organizations, as on a dedicatory stone from a peace group in Hiroshima, which has an English-language text explicitly admitting guilt for wartime acts, that is absent from the main Japanese inscription – in this case, a left-wing message concealed from those who do not read English (Murray 2016: 158–65).

There are also further dynamics present in the memorials. Other than as opponents responsible for the annihilation of the defending garrison, the Japanese monuments do not tend to mention the Americans at all. Most of the US markers are dedicated to military units, actions, and individuals and also overlook their former enemies – with one exception. In 1994, during a US naval visit to Peleliu, an official stone was erected bearing a quote from Chester Nimitz (1885–1966), who was Commander in Chief of the Pacific Fleet during the war: 'Tourists from every country who visit this island should be told how courageous and patriotic were the Japanese soldiers who all died defending this island.'

However, these monuments *all* ignore the *chad ra Beliliou* (and also, on the Japanese side, the Korean and Okinawan casualties). The only exception is the Peace Park Memorial at the south point, mentioned above, which is the largest Japanese government monument. A stylized trilithon resembling a torii gate, its inscription is simple ('In memory of all those who sacrificed their lives in the islands and seas of the West Pacific during World War II and in dedication to world peace'), geographically inclusive, and rendered in Japanese, English, and Palauan. As Murray observes (2016: 163), the memorial 'recognises that islanders suffered too and should be able to read its message in their own language.'

## The Imperial Touch: Peleliu in Contemporary Geopolitics

In the decade since 2010, this pattern of outside involvement in the memory of the Peleliu battle has begun to change, at times quite rapidly, with direct links to the broader situation in the Asia-Pacific sphere, and with resonances in the archaeological surveys. Just as it did during the war, so still today Palau finds itself occupying a strategic position within the geopolitics of the region. The Palauan people are proud of their independence, their cultural traditions, and of their island home. At the same time – echoing the long colonial history that began in the late 1700s – this tiny nation of less than 20,000 people is clearly vulnerable to economic pressure not only from the United States and Japan, the two countries that fought over it more than half a century ago, but also from China. The picture is further complicated by the fact that Palau is one of the world's few states to have formally recognized Taiwan and has received considerable aid from that quarter. The maintenance of Palau's international relations requires tact, subtlety in communications, and a political balancing act of rare skill.

The modern geopolitics of the war are tangled, complex, and cannot be easily summarised. As in other theatres, the long-term personal impact is still felt strongly throughout the Pacific as a legacy of family bereavement and communal loss. However, a sharp difference between this and the European and Russian fronts is the controversy that still attaches to the aggressor's current position on its activities of those years. These unhealed wounds take several forms, but centre on the relationship of two countries with their former wartime foe. In China, there is still deep resentment over the Japanese invasion of Manchuria and other parts of the mainland, and the colossal cost in human suffering. Special grievances persist around a long history of Japanese ambivalence concerning atrocities such as the massacres of Chinese nationals in Nanjing and elsewhere. A similar sense of unfinished business is felt in Korea, occupied even before the war as 'Peninsular Japan'; here, there is a particular focus on the sexual enslavement of so-called 'comfort women' in military brothels (a fate that also befell female captives from other Asian territories conquered by Japan).

Never fully resolved despite the passage of decades, disagreement over these issues steadily worsened following the 2012 election of the late Shinzō Abe's conservative Liberal Democratic Party as the governing majority in Japan. The sense of a resurgence on the Japanese right, and an increasing belligerence about war-related memory, was clear. Tensions with China and Korea were exacerbated by historical revisionist rhetoric, deliberately provocative political visits to the Yasakuni war shrine in Tokyo, and similar acts.

Against this background, and in the context of China's expansionist agenda in the region, it was no coincidence that the major Pacific powers began to look to Palau as an area of strategic interest. Amidst constant rumours of American military investment and the reactivation of Peleliu as a base to counter possible Chinese aggression, a number of senior US politicians and presidential hopefuls visited the island and made PR capital of honouring their nation's dead. Arizona senator John McCain came to Peleliu with his son in 2013, and the following year Texas governor Rick Perry posed for photo opportunities with American veterans and the President of Palau.

Late in 2014, the situation reached a curious pitch in the official announcement of the plans made by the Japanese imperial court for events to commemorate the 70th anniversary of the end of the war. The constitutional role of the emperor requires that distance be maintained from party politics. However, throughout his reign Akihito – who was eleven years old when the atomic bombs fell on the nation ruled by his then-divine father – had made it emphatically clear that he harboured no nostalgia for Japan's bellicose past, and instead deplored the suffering inflicted on other nations, specifically naming China and Korea. The emperor's implied rejection of the Abe government's revisionist agenda, and its geopolitical ramifications, thus made the choice of site visit for the commemoration ceremonies all the more acute: in April 2015, in their only overseas memorial event, the imperial couple would travel to Peleliu. For the course of a critical few days in modern Pacific history, this tiny island of less than 700 people – and the Republic of which it was a part – would once more find itself in the global spotlight.

Palau handled the logistical challenges with aplomb, and rightly received great credit for the smooth and respectful reception given to the imperial delegation. American diplomats and military were also represented. Together with project co-director Rick Knecht, I was present during the imperial visit, and in a modest capacity we assisted with some of the preparations at the south point Peace Park Memorial, where the emperor and empress paid their respects to all the dead (an action which had rather wider dimensions at that specific place, for reasons discussed above). For the most part, however, we mingled with the crowds of Peleliu citizens who gathered to see the visitors as they travelled around the island. A sense of deep honour was palpable, mingled with curiosity and a degree of optimistic scepticism as to what this might really mean for Palau.

The emperor's visit to Peleliu was widely reported by the world's press, but the solidly positive coverage also concealed underlying issues. Right-wing activists flew in from Japan to dole out propaganda materials along the route taken by the imperial vehicles, and there were also awkward sub-texts connected to the requested opening of sealed caves to retrieve human remains (Murray 2017). Despite these shadows, however, the court largely maintained its integrity and political distance without compromising Akihito's personal principles. Upon the emperor's abdication in 2019, media summaries of his Heisei era consistently noted the trip as one of only four imperial visits to wartime battlefields – the others being Okinawa, Saipan, and the Philippines – and claimed the Peleliu ceremony as an important milestone in his reign (e.g. McCurry 2019). In January 2016 at the annual New Year Poetry Reading Ceremony held at the imperial palace, the emperor chose for his own verse the moment of mourning at the Peleliu south point, and the sight of Angaur on the horizon (Kyodo 2016). Composed on the theme of *hito*, 'the person,' it has an official English translation:

> In fierce battles there
> Countless persons lost their lives
> I now see the isle
> Across and beyond the sea
> Lying so green and serene.

Although some tensions were defused, the occasion did not influence the Abe administration's policies (e.g. Baird 2015; Renouard 2017). The Palauan

**FIGURE 14.3**  Heisei Emperor Akihito and Empress Michiko paying their respects to the fallen at the Peace Park Memorial on the south point of Peleliu, April 2015; Angaur can be seen on the horizon. Photograph by David McQuillen, used by kind permission.

government maintains a difficult position between the regional powers, but always with primary respect for the islanders' traditions. Assistance is provided to the Japanese bone retrieval teams, while the Bureau of Cultural and Historical Preservation does its best to enforce adherence to the proper protocols for archaeological recording and documentation. At a larger level of political influence, the United States too is flexing its muscle across the region, clearly exploring options for the re-militarization of Palau with a focus on the airfields of Peleliu and Angaur (Tuzel 2019). Here again, Palau is playing a difficult hand well, as in President Remengesau's 2019 opinion piece in *The Hill*, speaking directly to American politicians and setting possible military basing in the context of investment in civil infrastructure and better terms for the renegotiated Compact of Free Association with the US. The situation remains volatile and continues to develop; as this chapter went to press, there is again an American military presence in Palau, with the construction of radio and radar towers, and the refurbishment of airfields and port facilities (Ligaiula 2022).

## Peleliu and its Publics from Heisei to Reiwa

The imperial visit to Peleliu in 2015 also had other impacts, perhaps less easy to foresee, but nonetheless palpable and maybe of even greater lasting consequence for a younger constituency that had not previously engaged with the battle and its legacies.

The first signs of this shift came with the appearance of Japanese military histories of the Peleliu campaign that more resembled the American works of the previous decade. Carefully researched, they did not seek to glorify the imperial cause but nonetheless credited the endurance of the individual combatants – in effect, a 'Greatest Generation' of Japan, but one based upon fatal endurance rather than victory. Several such works have been produced by the Pacific War Research Group, focussing on the soldiers' experiences as recorded in the 1970s by Masao Hiratsuka and newly published (e.g. 2015, 2018). The combination of these books and the massive domestic coverage given in Japan to the emperor's remembrance activities on Peleliu sparked a new engagement with the battle in a medium that had never been used for this purpose before – the popular culture of uniquely Japanese *manga* comic books.

*Peleliu – Rakuen no Guernica* (*Peleliu – Guernica of Paradise*) has been written and drawn by Kazuyoshi Takeda and is solely dedicated to the fight for the island. After an initial one-shot commissioned to coincide with the emperor's visit, the first Japanese instalments of the series were published in 2016, and a French edition began two years later (it has also been translated into other Asian languages); nine volumes have appeared in Japan as of early 2020 and the series is still ongoing. The story follows a group of Japanese soldiers stationed on Peleliu, from the weeks prior to the American landings through to the end of the main fighting and beyond. The narrative is told only from their perspective, especially that of the central character Tamaru, who is an aspiring *mangaka* (manga artist) and clearly an avatar of the author.

The books are eye-opening partly for their unflinching depiction of subjects unfamiliar to Japanese and foreign audiences alike, and also for their humanitarian stance that honours the suffering of the imperial forces while rejecting its ideological cause. Some of the scenes are of a brutality shocking even to those with a thorough knowledge of the published narratives, such as when Tamaru's squad attempts a rescue of their missing comrades whom they suddenly realize have been entombed for weeks in a cave sealed by the Americans. What they discover inside is one of several passages that prompt the reader to lay the book down for some time before continuing.

Takeda also takes up other themes absent from other histories of the battle, again relying on candid interviews from Hiratsuka's work. For example, in a series of flashbacks prompted by the unexpected discovery of lipstick in an American supply cache appropriated by the Japanese, one soldier, Izumi, is revealed to be concealing an identity sharply at odds with the conservative norms of the army. We see his teenage love of women's clothing and make-up, the mockery he receives in basic training for his perceived effeminacy, and his suppressed feelings for the only officer who is kind to him. He later dies horribly, a Marine extracting his gold teeth while he is still alive. The gentle Izumi is unrecognizable in a pool of blood, his face and jaw a slashed wreck; a simple panel text reproduces the telegram that his mother will receive: *Koichi Izumi, 21 years, deceased.*

In Takeda's eyes, Peleliu is a paradise to which both Japanese and Americans have brought a polluting ugliness that consumes youth, laughter, and promise. The Japanese soldiers are not actively rebellious, but despairing and confused, while a small minority are ruthlessly suicidal fanatics who frighten even their superior officers. 'Heroic sacrifice' for the emperor is clearly revealed as sordid and pointless death. As Peleliu finally falls to the Americans (the narrative continues past the formal end of the battle) the island's jungles echo to a vast scream of powerless rage. It is also interesting that, like Oda's novel, Takeda's manga includes Palauan characters – in this case children, who have lost their parents in the chaos of the fighting. In reality, the *chad ra Beliliou* had been forcibly evacuated to Koror and Babeldoab by the imperial forces, though it is not impossible that some became separated in the process.

In general, Takeda's narrative contains few historical errors (he wrongly shows the American forces to be racially integrated, for example, a topic addressed in our 2013 paper) and the care taken with the books is evident throughout. Takeda visited the island himself in the course of writing the series, and his work is thoroughly informed by the material culture and archaeology of the battlefield. The later books include a comprehensive bibliography of primarily Japanese works, supplements featuring photos of places that appear in the story, and additional background information is available online. Takeda was assisted throughout by Hiratsuka, who is credited as supervizing the manga. Illustrated vignettes are included as part of the story, almost in the manner of visual footnotes, referencing interviews with informants. In a curious link to our own project, these included Steve Ballinger who leads Cleared Ground Demining, the UXO team that accompanied us in the field, as well as Palauans and Japanese veterans. Among the latter were Yōji Kurata, a survivor of Angaur with a very different political perspective to his former comrade Funasaka (see Hoshi 2008), and Kiyokazu Tsuchida, one of the handful of holdouts who hid in a cave until 1947. He was an annual visitor to Peleliu so long as his health permitted (see Hisayama 2015; his experiences are also referenced in our earlier papers, Price & Knecht 2012, 2013).

Takeda did not always meet with a welcoming reception from veterans. Keiji Nagai had been a sergeant among the same group of holdouts but had almost never spoken of the war and had declined interview requests for decades. According to Hiratsuka, Nagai was one of the very last to accept the fact of surrender (Kano 2019). Again, this changed with the imperial visit, when the emperor himself requested a meeting with Nagai and Tsuchida. Having confessed that 'I never would have guessed that I would talk with the emperor in my lifetime,' Nagai began giving media interviews and doing school visits to warn of the dangers of war. However, he refused to cooperate with the manga project, due to what he saw as its triviality in relation to the subject matter. 'I think about the people who died in Peleliu, and a cartoon is too shallow [...] I don't agree with the format,' he said when a journalist approached him to discuss the comic, and even avoided touching a copy (Takeuchi 2018).

**FIGURE 14.4** Peleliu and the Pacific War in manga: volume 3 of Mizuki's *Showa* (left) and volume 4 of Takeda's *Peleliu – Guernica of Paradise* (right), in their English and French editions. Photographs by Neil Price.

There have been other mangas written on the theme of the Pacific War (Chua 2014), but these tend either to lay a thin pacifist message over 'cheap thrills and [...] a festishistic fascination with war machinery' (Schodt 2014) or promote a right-wing 'historically corrective' perspective. The exceptions have mostly been semi-autobiographical accounts produced by older mangaka, including two fundamental works both written by civilians who experienced the allied bombing: *Hadashi no Gen* (1973-87; in English as *Barefoot Gen*, 2004-10) by the Hiroshima survivor Keiji Nakazawa, and *Kami no Toride* (1974, *The Paper Fortress*), by Osamu Tezuka who was present during the 1945 firestorm in Osaka. The best-known in Japan are those produced by one of the most influential mangaka of all, Shigeru Mizuki (1922-2015). A veteran of the New Guinea campaign where he lost an arm, prior to which he was in fact briefly stationed at Ngatpang on the Palauan island of Babeldoab, Mizuki documented his experiences first as direct memoir (1973) and then in the extraordinary four-volume epic work originally published 1988-89 and later translated as *Shōwa 1926-1989: a History of Japan*. These books explicitly rejected both the Japanese and American militarism of the war and had major social impact due to Mizuki's already widespread fame.

Takeda has acknowledged making extensive use of Mizuki's work, and drawing inspiration from his anti-war message (interview by Fasulo 2019, here and below). The Peleliu manga series has clearly struck a chord in popular culture and was designed to do so. Takeda, who was born in 1975, admits that he had never heard of the battle or the place before the imperial visit, and it was clear to him from the start that this was a typical response: 'you know, the title *Peleliu* says absolutely nothing to the Japanese public.' To provide a point of reference that would function for a younger demographic, Takeda added the apparently incongruous subtitle alluding to the notorious bombing incident of the Spanish Civil War as immortalized by Picasso. Reader reaction has borne out Takeda's hopes, as exemplified by an interview with Hiromi Suzuki, whose grandfather was another Peleliu survivor who never spoke of the war (he died in 2015). His granddaughter now feels closer to his experience through the work and passes it on to her own teenage daughter: 'I want you to read this manga because grandpa was on this island,' Hiromi tells her (NHK World 2017). The multi-volume work won the Japan Cartoonists Association Award for 2017, one of the country's highest in the field.

The same comic-book medium has also been adopted in neighbouring cultural contexts, also to present critical views of the war – for example Keum Suk Gendry-Kim's 2017 graphic novel *Pool* (translated as *Grass*), a biography of a Korean so-called 'comfort woman' based on the author's interviews. A different perspective again is seen in actor George Takei's 2019 memoir *They Called Us Enemy*, about his family's experience of internment in wartime America. It is clear that graphic novels and manga will continue to be an important vector of memory in the new Reiwa era of Emperor Naruhito, especially among the young, and can provide crucial correctives to the misinformation of denialists. As Kiyokazu Tsuchida, the most active of the Peleliu veterans, observed 'we were told that we would die honourably, and be remembered forever, but in the end, this manga [Takeda's *Peleliu* series] is what will remain in people's consciousness' (NHK World 2017).

## Peleliu Passing: The Last Veterans, the Living, and the Dead

Kiyokazu Tsuchida died in 2018, and in November the following year Keiji Nagai, the very last of the Japanese defenders of Peleliu, also passed away; they both lived to be ninety-eight. Yōji Kurata, who fought on Angaur, died the same month at the age of ninety-one. The American veterans, though many more in number, are rapidly fading too. Arthur Jackson, who won the Medal of Honor for killing fifty Japanese at the south point on Peleliu – the beach of the souls – died a few months before Nagai, at ninety-two years of age (Bernstein 2019). Soon after this book's publication, nobody who fought in the battle will be left. As Nagai himself observed in his final days, having at last begun to share his memories, 'once the people who have wartime experience are gone [we] will lose the knowledge of the soldier's world' (Kano 2019.

Both former combatant nations continue to search for their dead. The Americans combine the official recovery missions of the Defense POW/MIA Accounting Agency (formerly JPAC), with the private initiatives of organizations such as BentProp (Hylton 2013). Other communities, such as the Navajo, remember in

**FIGURE 14.5** Palauan memory and the Peleliu caves: a local UXO technician on the Cleared Ground Demining team during the 2014 survey. Photograph by Rick Knecht.

their own ways. In Japan, regardless of the diverging political agendas involved, the desire to repatriate the cremated bones of the fallen soothes a deep national wound and a need to formally console the souls of the dead – a notion encoded into the name of the government department responsible for war graves.

For the people of Palau, and the *chad ra Beliliou*, the battlefield and its dead may be inescapable, but they are far from the forefront of their concerns. As islander Kent Giramur expresses it (quoted in Murray 2016: 223):

> The war in Peleliu is a small thing as far as we're concerned; it's tiny compared to what Peleliu has to offer. It's a big thing for the US and the Japanese. I want people to know Peleliu as a happy place, not come to Peleliu and be reminded of bad things that have happened. I want people to come to enjoy themselves, to see Peleliu as Peleliu, not be reminded of the ugliness national governments get into. I want them to remember Peleliu as paradise, not a place of massacres, of wars that didn't have to happen.

Perhaps the best, highest ambition for the legacies of the Pacific War should be that this island – and others like it – can be a place of memory but also of reconciliation; a place where visitors naturally acknowledge *everyone* involved in that conflict; and above all, a place that ultimately moves into the future, its wounds healed, as its people get on with their lives and the war of the worlds ends at last.

## Acknowledgements on Behalf of the Aberdeen-Uppsala Peleliu Archaeological Survey

After a decade of intermittent fieldwork and general engagement with an island community, no acknowledgements can ever capture the extent of the debts owed, the hospitality generously given and gratefully received, the conversations great and small. Above all, our work on Peleliu and in Palau has only been possible by the invitation of the Palauan people and government at national and state level, through their daily collaboration, and by the ongoing relationships thereby forged. Anything we have achieved has come about together with, and for, our Palauan friends.

Our fieldwork on the wartime heritage of Palau is not only related to the underlying cognitive landscape, but also of course to its more conventional archaeological record. In this context we would like to acknowledge the decades of work by the Bureau of Arts and Culture (now the Bureau of Cultural and Historical Preservation), Belau National Museum, the Micronesian Historic Preservation Offices of the US National Park Service, the American Battlefield Protection Programme, and many others. We especially wish to recognize and honour the work of the late Rita Olsudong, Calvin Emesiochel, and Errolflynn Kloulechad, to name but a few. The Bureau is currently led by Sunny Ochob Ngirmang, to whom we pay particular respect here. An excellent bibliography and overview of Palauan archaeology can be found in Liston and Miko (2011).

At the most practical level of all – staying alive – none of our work on Peleliu would have been possible without Cleared Ground Demining, responsible for all the UXO clearance on the project. We thank all the staff and crew for years of collaboration: you kept us safe, the bottom line. Our particular thanks to Steve Ballinger, co-owner and operations manager; we were delighted to see Steve's work on Palau recognized in the British New Year Honours List for 2020 with the well-deserved award of an MBE. Medical field support on Peleliu was provided by David McQuillen, who also worked alongside us in the archaeological survey; David, we are in your debt.

Lastly, my own best regards to everyone who participated in the Peleliu surveys, in particular Gavin Lindsay, Ben Raffield, and above all, Rick Knecht.

## References

Ambrose, H. 2010. *The Pacific*. Edinburgh: Canongate.

Aoyagi, M. 2002. *Modekngei: A New Religion in Belau, Micronesia*. Tokyo: Shinsensha.

Ballendorf, D., Shuster, D.M. & Higuchi, W. 1986. *An Oral Historiography of the Japanese Administration in Palau*. Agana: Micronesian Area Research Center, University of Guam.

Bayly, C. & Harper, T. 2004. *Forgotten Armies: The Fall of British Asia, 1941–45*. London: Penguin.

Bayly, C. & Harper, T. 2007. *Forgotten Wars: The End of Britain's Asian Empire*. London: Penguin.

BBKS/Bōeicho Bōei Kenshūjō Sensishitsu [Self-Defence Agency, Self-Defence Research Institute, War History Office] 1968. *Chūbu Taiheiyō rikugun sakusen 2: Periryū, Angauru, Iōtō [Army Operations in the Central Pacific 2: Peleliu, Angaur, Iwo Jima]*. Tokyo: Asagumo Shimbun Sha.

Beevor, A. 2012. *The Second World War*. London: Weidenfeld & Nicolson.

Bennett, W. et al. 1988. *Bikfala Faet. Olketa Solomon Aelanda Rimembarem Wol Wo Tu*. Suva: University of the South Pacific.

Bergerud, E. 1996. *Touched with Fire: The Land War in the South Pacific*. New York: Penguin.

Blair, B.C. & DeCioccio, J.P. 2011. *Victory at Peleliu: The 81st Infantry Division's Pacific Campaign*. Norman: University of Oklahoma Press.

Burgin, R.V. 2010. *Islands of the Damned: A Marine at War in the Pacific*. New York: New American Library.

Camacho, K.L. 2011. *Cultures of Commemoration: The Politics of War, Memory, and History in the Mariana Islands*. Honolulu: University of Hawai'i Press.

Camp, D. 2008. *Last Man Standing: The 1st Marine Regiment on Peleliu*. Minneapolis: Zenith.

Costello, J. 1981. *The Pacific War 1941–1945*. New York: Rawson, Wade.

De Burlo, C. 1989. 'Islanders, Soldiers, and Tourists: The War and the Shaping of Tourism in Melanesia.' In: White, G. and Lindstrom, L., eds. *The Pacific Theater: Island Representations of World War II*. Honolulu: University of Hawai'i Press, 299–325.

Dobbin, J. 2011. *Summoning the Powers Beyond: Traditional Religions in Micronesia*. Honolulu: University of Hawai'i Press.

Falgout, S., Poyer, L. & Carucci, L.M. 2008. *Memories of War: Micronesians in the Pacific War*. Honolulu: University of Hawai'i Press.

Frank, R.B. 2020. *Tower of Skulls: A History of the Asia-Pacific War, Vol. 1: July 1937–May 1942*. New York: Norton.

Fraser, G.M. 1993. *Quartered Safe out Here: A Recollection of the War in Burma*. London: Harvill.

Fujitani, T., White, G.M. & Yoneyama, L., eds. 2001. *Perilous Memories: The Asia-Pacific War(s)*. Durham, NC: Duke University Press.

Funasaka, H. 1966. *Eirei no Zekkyō: gyokusaitō Angauru [Scream of the Eirei: The Honourable Suicide of Angaur]*. Tokyo: Bungei Shunjū [English translation 1986, *Falling Blossoms*. Singapore: Times Books].

Funasaka, H. 1967. *Sakura sakura: Periryū tō dōkutsu sen [Cherry Blossoms, Cherry Blossoms: the Battle for the Peleliu Caves]*. Tokyo: Mainichi News Press.

Funasaka, H. 1968. *Gyokusai: Angō denbun detsuzuru Parao no shitō [Broken Jewels: Deadly Battle for Palau Written in Coded Radio Transmissions]*. Tokyo: Yomiuri News Press.

Hastings, M. 2011. *All Hell Let Loose: The World at War 1939–1945*. London: Harper.

Higuchi, W. 1986a. *Micronesians and the Pacific War: The Palauans*. Micronesian Area Research Center. Agana: University of Guam.

Higuchi, W. 1986b. *Palauan Interviews. Unpublished ms. Pacific Collection, Hamilton Library*. Honolulu: University of Hawai'i.

Higuchi, W. 1987. *Micronesia under the Japanese Administration: Interviews with Former South Sea Bureau and Military Officials*. Micronesian Area Research Center. Agana: University of Guam.

Higuchi, W. 1991. 'War in Palau: Morikawa and the Palauans.' In: G.M. White, ed. *Remembering the Pacific War*. Honolulu: University of Hawai'i Press, 145–56.

Hijikata, H. 1995. *Gods and Religion of Palau*. Tokyo: Sasakawa Peace Foundation.

Hiratsuka, M. 2015. *Gyokusai no shimajima. [Islands of Honourable Suicide: Saipan, Guam, Peleliu, Iwo]*. Tokyo: Yosensha.

Hiratsuka, M. 2018. *Gyokusai no shima Periryū [Peleliu: Island of Honourable Suicide]*. Tokyo: PHP Editors Group.

Hisayama, S. 2015. *Periryū takatai imada owarazu [Peleliu: the Trauma Continues]*. Tokyo: Ushio Shobu Kojin Shinsha.

Hornfischer, J.D. 2016. *The Fleet at Flood Tide: America at Total War in the Pacific, 1944–1945*. New York: Ballantine.

Hoshi, R. 2008. *Angauru, Periryū: senki gyokusai o ikinobite [Angaur, Peleliu: A Record of the War Surviving Honourable Suicide]*. Tokyo: Kawade Shobu Shinsha.

Hylton, W.S. 2013. *Vanished: The Sixty-Year Search for the Missing Men of World War II*. New York: Riverhead.

Igarashi, Y. 2000. *Bodies of Memory: Narratives of War in Postwar Japanese Culture, 1945–1970*. Princeton, NJ: Princeton University Press.

Knecht, R., Price, N. & Lindsay, G. 2012. *WWII Battlefield Survey of Peleliu Island, Peleliu State, Republic of Palau*. Archive report lodged with the Bureau of Arts and Culture, Koror, Palau, and the US National Park Service, Guam.

Krämer, A. 1926, 1929a&b. *Palau*. Vols. 3–5 II.B.3 of Thilenius, G., ed. *Ergebnisse der Südsee Expedition 1908–1910*. Hamburg: DeGruyter.

Kubary, J. 1888. 'Die Religion der Palauer', *Allerlei aus Volks- und Menschenkunde*, 1, 1–69.

Kwai, A.A. 2017. *Solomon Islanders in World War II: an Indigenous Perspective*. Canberra: Australian National University Press.

Lindsay, G., Knecht, R., Price, N., Raffield, B. & Ashlock, P.T. 2015. *Peleliu Archaeological Survey 2014. World War II battlefield survey of Peleliu Island, Peleliu State, Republic of Palau*. Archive report lodged with the Bureau of Arts and Culture, Koror, Palau, and the US National Park Service, American Battlefield Protection Program.

Lindstrom, L. & Gwero, J., eds. 1998. *Big Wok. Storian blong Wol Wo Tu long Vanuatu*. Suva: University of the South Pacific.

Lindstrom, L. & White, G. 1990. *Island Encounters: Black and White Memories of the Pacific War*. Washington, DC: Smithsonian Institution.

Liston, J. & Miko, M. 2011. 'Oral Tradition and Archaeology: Palau's Earth Architecture.' In: J. Liston, G. Clarke and D. Alexander, eds. *Pacific Island Archaeology in the 21st Century: Relevance and Engagement*. Canberra: ANU Press, 181–203.

Mace, S. & Allen, N. 2012. *Battleground Pacific: A Marine Rifleman's Combat Odyssey in K/3/5*. New York: St. Martin's Press.

Margolin, J-L. 2014. 'Japanese History Text-Books and the Asia-Pacific War: Apportioning Blame.' In M. Baildon, L.K. Seng, I.M. Lim, G. İnanç and J. Jaffar, eds. *Controversial History in Asian Contexts*. London: Routledge, 109–22.

McEnery, J. & Sloan, B. 2012. *Hell in the Pacific: A Marine Rifleman's Journey from Guadalcanal to Peleliu*. New York: Simon & Schuster.

Murray, S.C. 2006. *War and Remembrance on Peleliu: Islander, Japanese, and American Memories of a Battle in the Pacific War*. PhD thesis in Anthropology, University of California, Santa Barbara.

Murray, S.C. 2016. *The Battle over Peleliu: Islander, Japanese, and American Memories of War*. Tuscaloosa: University of Alabama Press.

Murray, S.C. 2017. 'Emperors, Bones, and Dissonant Memories: Japanese Commemoration of the Battle for Peleliu Island.' In: D.R. Mallett, ed. *Monumental Conflicts: Twentieth-Century Wars and the Evolution of Public Memory*. London: Routledge, 91–110.

Nero, K.L. 1989. 'Time of Famine, Time of Transformation: Hell in the Pacific, Palau.' In: G. White and L. Lindstrom, eds. *The Pacific Theater: Island Representations of World War II*. Honolulu: University of Hawai'i Press, 117–47.

Nez, C. 2011. *Code Talker*. New York: Berkeley Caliber.

Palau Society of Historians. 1997. *Rechuodel: Traditional Culture and Lifeways Long Ago in Palau*. San Francisco: US National Park Service.

Parmentier, R. 1987. *The Sacred Remains: Myth, History, and Polity in Belau*. Chicago: University of Chicago Press.

PCAA/Palau Community Action Agency. 1976–78. *A History of Palau*. 3 vols. Koror: PCAA.

Peattie, M.R. 1988. *Nan'yō: the Rise and Fall of the Japanese in Micronesia, 1885–1945*. Honolulu: University of Hawai'i Press.

Petersen, G. 2009. *Traditional Micronesian Societies: Adaptation, Integration, and Political Organization*. Honolulu: University of Hawai'i Press.

Poyer, L., Falgout, S. & Carucci, L.M. 2001. *The Typhoon of War: Micronesian Experiences of the Pacific War*. Honolulu: University of Hawai'i Press.

Price, N. & Knecht, R. 2012. 'Peleliu 1944: The Archaeology of a South Pacific D-Day', *Journal of Conflict Archaeology*, 7 (1), 5–48.

Price, N. & Knecht, R. 2013. 'After the Typhoon: Multicultural Archaeologies of World War II on Peleliu, Palau, Micronesia', *Journal of Conflict Archaeology*, 8 (3), 193–248.

Price, N., Knecht, R. & Lindsay, G. 2015. 'The Sacred and the Profane: Souvenir and Collecting Behaviours on the WWII Battlefields of Peleliu, Palau, Micronesia.' In: G. Carr and K. Reeves, eds. *Heritage and Memory of War: Responses from Small Islands*. London: Routledge, 219–33.

Rechebei, E.D. & McPhetres, S.M. 1997. *History of Palau: Heritage of an Emerging Nation*. Koror: Ministry of Education.

Seaton, P.A. 2007. *Japan's Contested War Memories: The 'Memory Rifts' in Historical Consciousness of World War II*. London: Routledge.

Seraphim, F. 2006. *War Memory and Social Politics in Japan, 1945–2005*. Cambridge, MA: Harvard University.

Sledge, E.B. 1981. *With the Old Breed: At Peleliu and Okinawa*. Novato: Presidio Press.

Sloan, B. 2005. *Brotherhood of Heroes: The Marines at Peleliu, 1944*. New York: Simon & Schuster.

Tellai, U. 1991. 'Palauans and the Japanese Military Experience.' In: G.M. White, ed. *Remembering the Pacific War*. Honolulu: University of Hawai'i Press, 157–60.

Toll, I.W. 2012. *Pacific Crucible: War at Sea in the Pacific, 1941–1942*. New York: Norton.

Toll, I.W. 2015. *The Conquering Tide: War in the Pacific Islands, 1942–1944*. New York: Norton.

Toll, I.W. 2020. *Twilight of the Gods: War in the Western Pacific, 1944–1945*. New York: Norton.

Walter, K.R. 1993. *Through the Looking Glass: Palauan Experiences of War and Reconstruction, 1944–1951*. 2 vols. PhD thesis in History. University of Adelaide, Adelaide.

Wheelan, J. 2022. *Bitter Peleliu: The Forgotten Struggle on the Pacific War's Worst Battlefield*. Oxford: Osprey.

White, G.M., ed. 1991. *Remembering the Pacific War*. Honolulu: University of Hawai'i Press.

White, G.M. 2016. *Memorializing Pearl Harbor: Unfinished Histories and the Work of Remembrance*. Durham, NC: Duke University Press.

White, G.M. & Lindstrom, L., eds. 1989. *The Pacific Theater: Island Representations of World War II*. Honolulu: University of Hawai'i Press.

Wright, D. 2002. *To the Far Side of Hell: The Battle for Peleliu, 1944*. Ramsbury: Crowood Press.

### Graphic Novels, Prose Fiction, and Related Critique

Chua, K.I.C. 2014. 'Representing the War in Manga.' In: M. Baildon, L.K. Seng, I.M. Lim, G. İnanç and J. Jaffar, eds. *Controversial History in Asian Contexts*. London: Routledge, 123–39.

Fasulo, F. 2019. 'Interview with Kazuyoshi Takeda.' In Takeda, K. *Peleliu – Guernica of Paradise*, vol. 4. Paris: Éditions Vega.

Gendry-Kim, K.S. 2017. *Pool*. Seoul: Bori Publishing [English translation 2019, *Grass*. Montréal: Drawn and Quarterly].

Misuki, S. 1973. *Sōin Gyokusai seyo!* Tokyo: Kodansha [English translation 2011, *Onward Towards our Noble Deaths*. Montréal: Drawn and Quarterly].

Misuki, S. 1988–89. *Komikku Shōwa-shi*. 8 vols. Tokyo: Kodansha [English translation 2013–15 in 4 vols, *Showa 1926–1989: A History of Japan*. Montréal: Drawn and Quarterly].

Nakazawa, K. 1973–87. *Hadashi no Gen*. 10 vols. Serialised in *Weekly shōnen jump*, Tokyo [English translation 2004–10 in 10 vols, *Barefoot Gen*. San Francisco: Last Gasp].

Oda, M. 1998. *Gyokusai*. Tokyo: Shinchōsa [English translation 2003, *The Breaking Jewel*. New York: Columbia University Press].

Okuizumi, H. 1993 *Ishi no reireki*. Tokyo: Bungeishunju [English translation 1999, *The Stones Cry Out*. Orlando Harcourt].

Schodt, F. 2014. 'Introduction.' In: S. Misuki, ed. *Showa 1939–1944: A History of Japan*. Montréal: Drawn and Quarterly, 11–13.

Takeda, K. 2016. *Peleliu - Rakuen no Guernica*. 9 vols and ongoing. Tokyo: Young Animal Comics [French translations 2018-, *Peleliu – Guernica of Paradise*. Paris: Éditions Vega].

Takei, G. 2019. *They Called Us Enemy*. Marietta: Top Shelf Comics.

Tezuka, O. 1974. *Kami no Toride [The Paper Fortress]*. Serialised in *Weekly shōnen king*, Tokyo.

### Newspapers and Online Media Reportage [All Sources Accessed November 2022]

Baird, J.K. 2015. 'Abe's Japan Cannot Apologise for the Pacific War,' *The Diplomat* 2015-05-13. [WWW] https://thediplomat.com/2015/05/abes-japan-cannot-apologize-for-the-pacific-war/ (accessed 29/11/2022).

Bernstein, A. 2019. 'Arthur Jackson, Medal of Honor Recipient for WWII 'One-Man Assault' at Peleliu, Dies at 92,' *The Washington Post* 2019-06-17. [WWW] https://www.washingtonpost.com/local/obituaries/arthur-jackson-medal-of-honor-recipient-for-wwii-one-man-assault-at-peleliu-dies-at-92/2017/06/16/a7a134d4-52a4-11e7-be25-3a519335381c_story.html (accessed 29/11/2022).

Kano, M. 2019. 'Last Survivor from Battle of Peleliu Leaves Anti-War Message,' *Asahi Shimbun* 2019-12-09. [WWW] https://www.asahi.com/ajw/articles/13055603 (accessed 29/11/2022).

Kyodo 2016. 'In Annual Poem, Emperor Recalls Trip to Palau to Mourn War Dead,' *The Japan Times* 2016-01-14. [WWW] https://www.japantimes.co.jp/news/2016/01/14/national/annual-poem-emperor-recalls-trip-palau-mourn-war-dead/#.XpdO1y-9h1js (accessed 29/11/2022).

Ligaiula, P. 2022. 'Ambassador Kyota: 'U.S. Military Presence in Palau Is a Good Sign,' *Pacific News Service* 06/06/2022 [WWW] https://pina.com.fj/2022/06/06/ambassador-kyota-u-s-military-presence-in-palau-is-a-good-sign/ (accessed 29/11/2022).

McCurry, J. 2019. 'End of an Era in Japan as Emperor Prepares to Abdicate,' *The Guardian* 2019-04-21. [WWW] https://www.theguardian.com/world/2019/apr/21/end-of-an-era-in-japan-as-emperor-akihito-abdicates (accessed 29/11/2022).

NHK World. 2017. 'Drawing Truth about War,' *NHK* 2017-08-10. [Archive only – online pages expired] (checked 29/11/2022).

Remengesau, T. 2019. 'Pacific Defense Pact Renewal Vital to the US Amid Rising Tension with China,' *The Hill* 2019-05-17. [WWW] https://thehill.com/blogs/congress-blog/foreign-policy/444291-pacific-defense-pact-renewal-vital-to-the-us-amid-rising (accessed 29/11/2022).

Renouard, J. 2017. 'Japan, China, and the Strains of Historical Memory,' *The Diplomat* 2016-12-26. [WWW] https://thediplomat.com/2017/12/japan-china-and-the-strains-of-historical-memory/ (accessed 29/11/2022).

Takeuchi, A. 2018. 'Cartoon on Battle of Peleliu Tries to Show Misery of War Despite Claims of Shallow Style,' *The Mainichi* 2018-08-14. [WWW] https://mainichi.jp/english/articles/20180814/p2a/00m/0na/005000c (accessed 29/11/2022).

Tuzel, M. 2019. 'Making the Case for Increased US Basing in the Pacific,' *The Diplomat* 2019-11-28. [WWW] https://thediplomat.com/2019/11/making-the-case-for-increased-us-basing-in-the-pacific/ (accessed 29/11/2022).

# INDEX